Theodore Dreiser's Uncollected Magazine Articles, 1897–1902

Edited by

Yoshinobu Hakutani

DELAWARE
Newark: University of Delaware Press
London: Associated University Presses

Associated University Presses
2010 Eastpark Boulevard
Cranbury, NJ 08512

Associated University Presses
Unit 304, The Chandlery
50 Westminster Bridge Road
London SE1 7QY, England

Associated University Presses
P.O. Box 338, Port Credit
Mississauga, Ontario
Canada L5G 4L8

The paper used in this publication meets the requirements of the American National Standard for Permanence of Paper for Printed Library Materials Z38.48-1984.

Library of Congress Cataloging-in-Publication Data

Dreiser, Theodore, 1871–1945.
    [Essays. Selections]
    Theodore Dreiser's uncollected magazine articles, 1897–1902 / edited by Yoshinobu Hakutani.
        p. cm.
    Includes bibliographical references and index.
    ISBN 0-87413-818-3 (alk. paper)
    I. Title: Uncollected magazine articles, 1897–1902. II. Hakutani, Yoshinobu, 1935–   III. Title.
PS3507.R55 A6 2003
813'.52—dc21

                                                             2003002453

PRINTED IN THE UNITED STATES OF AMERICA

For Philip Gerber

Contents

7

Acknowledgments

I WOULD LIKE TO THANK THE FOLLOWING LIBRARIES FOR THEIR COUR-
tesy: the Library of Congress; the public libraries of New York, Boston,
Chicago, and Cleveland; and the academic libraries at Kent State University, Oberlin College, the University of Illinois, and the University of
Pennsylvania. I also wish to thank Cindy Kristof of the Interlibrary Services at Kent State University for her assistance in borrowing many magazines and Michiko Hakutani for photographic reproduction of the
illustrations.

I am particularly grateful to Robert Elias, the anonymous readers for the
University of Delaware Press, and Michiko Hakutani, who read part or all
of the manuscript and offered useful comments and suggestions.

Editorial Note

BETWEEN 1897 AND 1902 DREISER PUBLISHED 111 FREE-LANCE MAGA-
zine articles on various topics. 77 of them have been collected in my earlier
editions: *Selected Magazine Articles of Theodore Dreiser: Life and Art in
the American 1890s,* 2 vols. (Rutherford, NJ: Fairleigh Dickinson University Press, 1985, 1987); and *Art, Music, and Literature, 1897–1902* by
Theodore Dreiser (Urbana: University of Illinois Press, 2001). The rest, 34
articles, collected in this volume, have not been republished before, except
for the three articles included in other collections. "A Talk with America's
Leading Lawyers: Joseph H. Choate" was reprinted in *Little Visits with
Great Americans,* ed. Orison Swett Marden (New York: The Success Com-
pany, 1903), as well as in part in Edward S. Martin, *The Life of Joseph
Hodges Choate* (New York: Scribner's Sons, 1921). "A Leader of Young
Manhood: Frank W. Gunsaulus" was reprinted as "The Power of Oratory;
And Counsel by a Leader of Young Men" in *Talks with Great Workers,* ed.
Orison Swell Marden (New York: Thomas Y. Crowell, 1901), and as "An
Inspiring Personality Wins a Noted Preacher Fame—Frank W. Gun-
saulus" in *Little Visits with Great Americans.* "A Doer of the Word" was
reprinted in Dreiser's *Twelve Men* (New York: Boni and Liveright, 1919),
and also reprinted as a short story in *The Best Short Stories of Theodore
Dreiser,* ed. with an introduction by Howard Fast (Cleveland: World,
1947).

Bibliographical information for each of the articles in this edition is
given in its footnote. I have provided an appendix for Dreiser's magazine
articles in this period at the end of this volume. The most comprehensive
bibliography of Dreiser's writings is Donald Pizer, Richard W. Dowell,
and Frederick E. Rusch, *Theodore Dreiser: A Primary and Secondary
Bibliography* (Boston: G. K. Hall, 1991).

The text of this edition is that of the original publication of each magazine article. All articles are signed by Dreiser unless otherwise indicated
in the footnotes. In editing the text for this volume, I have emended ob-
vious spelling errors, but retained the original typography concern-

ing spelling, capitalization, hyphenation, and punctuation as much as possible.

For the illustrations included in this edition, I tried to reproduce a few essential photographs and drawings in each article. Several articles had no illustrations in the original publication.

Theodore Dreiser's
Uncollected Magazine Articles,
1897–1902

Introduction

BEFORE THEODORE DREISER TRIED HIS HAND AT WRITING A NOVEL, THE famous *Sister Carrie,* published late in 1900 but suppressed for seven years, he was a successful magazine writer. He did not accomplish this writing overnight. As an apprentice the twenty-year-old college dropout wrote his first newspaper article for the Chicago *Globe* in 1892. For three years the young Dreiser earned his living as a newspaper reporter in Chicago, St. Louis, Toledo, Pittsburgh, and finally in New York. In 1895 he was working for the New York *World* but the owner Joseph Pulitzer's dictatorial personality and the ferocious working conditions for cub reporters did not suit his temperament. The young journalist was appalled at the discrepancy between the appearance of such a moralizing paper as the *World* and the merciless reality of its internal struggle. Only after a few months of frustrating, underpaid work did Dreiser leave the profession for good.

In 1895, the young journalist was ambitious and had a great deal of confidence in his writing ability but he scarcely knew what was in store for him. During the next few years Dreiser nevertheless made up his mind to become a novelist, and whatever move he made he was anxiously awaiting an opportunity to write as uninhibitedly as possible. In May 1895 his brother Paul Dresser, fortunately, was a partner in the newly established music firm of Howley, Haviland & Company in New York. They were thinking of starting a magazine to promote their music sales. Frederick B. Haviland—still a shareholder of another firm, the Ditson Company, which published a popular magazine called *Musical Record*—argued that another magazine in the field would sell. Although Dreiser knew practically nothing about music then, he agreed with Haviland and proposed that they let him edit the magazine. Dreiser got the job, which paid as poorly as did the newspaper, but it rescued him from stress and overwork. He named the magazine *Ev'ry Month,* and its first issue appeared on 1 October 1895 with a description on the cover, "Edited and Arranged by Theodore Dreiser."[1] Not only was he proud, he thrived on the work at the office in the midst of a vaudevillian trying out a new song with piano, as vividly described in "Whence the Song," which appeared in the December 1900 issue of *Harper's Weekly.*

15

As his editing proceeded, however, he felt restricted by the publishers. When Arthur Henry, to whom *Sister Carrie* was dedicated, asked him in the fall of 1897 whether he was succeeding as editor, he complained: "I am drawing a good salary. The things I am able to get the boss to publish that I believe in are very few. The rest must tickle the vanity or cater to the foibles and prejudices of readers. From my standpoint, I am not succeeding."[2] Evidently he had a disagreement with the publishers on the magazine's editorial policy, and he was forced to resign.[3] During the two short years as the producer of a new professional magazine, Dreiser nonetheless learned the writing and editing skills required of the trade and seized numerous opportunities to visit studios and various editorial offices in the city.

Between his resignation from the editorship of *Ev'ry Month* in September 1897 and the publication of his essay "Christmas in the Tenements" in *Harper's Weekly* in December 1902, he wrote well over 125 pieces, mostly articles, that appeared in various popular magazines. Besides the numerous essays he wrote on art, music, and literature, he also wrote equally numerous essays on other aspects of American culture and society. Dreiser's interest was remarkably diverse, his vision quite wide, and he was truly successful in capturing the key sites and scenes of American life at the dawn of the twentieth century.

This massive body of writing, unparalleled by that of any other writer, casts significant light not only upon Dreiser the novelist, but more importantly upon the turn of the century, an exciting era in the development of American civilization. As a cultural historian, and more interestingly as a young individual who was to become a major American writer of the new century, Dreiser freely expressed his views on contemporary Americans and their endeavors. At the end of the old century, shortly after the worst depression the United States had experienced, the nation had a booming economy inspired by the advancement of technology and industry, and the dissemination of new ideas in science, philosophy, and law. In response to the ever-changing lives of the American people, he wrote many of his magazine articles on the spectacle of contemporary society. He often was a dispassionate chronicler of science, technology, and industry, but at the same time he dramatized the delights and struggles of the common people as he celebrated the efforts and successes of eminent professionals in various fields.

❧

The period following the Civil War is notable for numerous writings about the ideal of success in American life. It looks as though the rise of industry and business in the pioneering nation single-handedly promoted such writings. Because of their mundane and materialistic connotations, the contemporary reader may abhor their import or else dismiss such stories as representative of an unseemly aspect of national character. But those who expressed the ideal—be they storytellers, evangelists, or journalists—were indeed serious and took pride in their beliefs. Whether one emulates it or not, the story of success has been so finely ingrained in American life that it has become an essential part of the American psyche. In fact, few American novelists have remained indifferent to this prevailing order of thought and dream in their portrayals of characters, including young women like Dreiser's Sister Carrie.

What makes the American story of success interesting to read is its composite nature. Historically it goes back to the nation's incipient religious precepts—the puritan ethic. A major poet of the period, E. A. Robinson, attacked the doctrine, saying: "My philosophy does not swallow this teaching of our good old grand fathers who worked sixteen hours and sang psalms and praised heaven that a life is what we make it."[4] But the revolt against the story of success did not occur until the dawn of the twentieth century; even so, the general public has since ignored such criticism of the sacred American doctrine. The success story is, indeed, related to the nation's immigration history. Children and grand children of the immigrants have been indoctrinated with the ideal, not because of their religious convictions, but because of their natural survival tactics. This ideal is guaranteed by the Declaration of Independence with its apotheosis on "the pursuit of Happiness." The success doctrine also received blessing from the two of the most influential thinkers at the crucial points in its development: Benjamin Franklin for his eloquent expression of individualism at the time of the nation's independence, and the English philosopher Herbert Spencer for his social Darwinist theory of inevitable and immutable progress at the time of industrialism toward the end of the nineteenth century.

At the popular level, Horatio Alger made the success story into a literary genre in the post Civil War years through the Gilded Age by writing volume after volume on the same theme. With his Ragged Dicks and Tattered Toms with slight variations, he glorified the poor but honest boy who, through pluck and hard work, fought his way against formidable obstacles to fame and fortune. The popularity of the story is clearly demonstrable not only by its sheer bulk but its influences on other literary genres. The most successful author of the dime novel, Harlan Halsey, could thus weave the same motif into his *Old Sleuth* series with patterned sensational incidents and old messages of immaculate morality—in which vice is duly punished and virtue rewarded. Young readers swallowed such a story without much resistance since they had earlier gone through, with delight, *The Swiss Family Robinson, Hans Brinker,* and Mrs. Alcott's *Little Men*

and *Little Women*. Older readers were more fascinated by a Baptist minister, Russell H. Conwell, who wrote his *Acres of Diamonds* originally as a
sermon, repeated thousands of times and brought out by a religiously
oriented business organization.[5] Romancers of the day, too, like Mary J.
Holmes, Bertha M. Clay, and Laura Jean Libbey—the last being Dreiser's
boyhood favorite in the early 1880s—interpolated the ideal into their
stories. All these stories are united by their avowed emphasis on the ideals
of *thrift, industry,* and *enterprise*—the exact words Dreiser elicited from
the great public figures interviewed for his magazine articles.

In an ever-changing and complex society a reaction against such sim-
plistic and idealistic code of ethics was inevitable. Mark Twain, to be sure,
snared at the idealism just as other eminent writers, too, despite the prevalent Darwinian and Spencerian theories of social progress, came to reject
this naive, self-serving dream of success. Henry James's *The American*
and, later, Dreiser's Cowperwood trilogy were the monumental works
expressing the revolt against commercial success. In *The Rise of Silas
Lapham,* William Dean Howells explicitly defined success as a necessarily
pecuniary loss and called it one's moral rise. By the end of the nineteenth
century the concept of material success had transformed into that per-
verse side of human nature, as shown, for example, by Frank Norris's
McTeague—in which winning a large sum of money in a lottery and
marrying a greedy husband turns the heroine to thrift, parsimony, and
finally a murder victim. The danger inherent in the success ideal, as perhaps all the critics of the doctrine agreed, would eventually destroy true
human ethics.

At the close of the nineteenth century, journalists like Jacob Riis and B.
O. Flower, social historians like Richard T. Ely and J. P. Altgeld, and
young writers like Stephen Crane and Dreiser all shared visions of society
founded on human brotherhood. Even Orison Swett Marden—who commissioned Dreiser to write success stories based on the earlier ethics of
puritanism and individualism—understood the human heart and the al-
truistic motive to be the noblest qualities of national character. By the time
Dreiser wrote his success stories for the popular magazines in the late
1890s, he was well acquainted with both the traditional success story often
associated with Horatio Alger and the newly awaken social consciousness
in the manner of Riis's *How the Other Half Lives* (1890).

Dreiser's success stories are grouped into two categories: one based on
the traditional success story and the other modified, or perhaps reversed,
by the principle of humanitarianism. As Dreiser told Robert Elias, his
biographer, years later, Dreiser had contributed most of the first group to
Marden's *Success Magazine* only to make money.[6] But this does not mean
that Dreiser despised the ideal of material success implied in these interviews. On the contrary, Dreiser believed that the type of material success

advocated by the celebrated public figures in the 1890s gave rise to beauty, which money and leisure could buy and enjoy in America. For him this ideal can not and should not be sneered at, much less denied, because material success is only a resilient spring board to the composite goal of an individual's happiness on earth, and in American life in particular.

Even though Dreiser suspected in reporting America's industrial development that some individuals had built their fortunes in the name of progress for all people, he tried to find noble, genuinely admirable qualities in these successful figures. Earlier, when he was a newspaperman, he observed successful men like Andrew Carnegie and Joseph Pulitzer, but he chose to remain reticent about their private conduct, which he could not admire. Now as a freelance writer he was able to comment on these wealthy men as he pleased. Through his initial magazine work in New York, he became acquainted with Dr. Orison Swett Marden, the founder and editor of *Success,* the first issue of which appeared in December 1897. Impressed by Dreiser's abilities to brighten up the contemporary scene, Marden wanted Dreiser to interview successful men in business, industry, science, art, music, and literature, including such legendary figures as Thomas Edison, Andrew Carnegie, and Marshall Field.

Dreiser swiftly wrote down these interviews, for such an article appeared almost every month in the first two years of *Success.*[7] The monotonous similarity of these articles came from several identical questions he put to the men he interviewed: "What quality in you was most essential to your success?" "Were you rich or poor before starting a career?" "Were reading and schooling necessary for your success?" "What is your philosophy of happiness?" To stock questions there were stock answers. All the men, of course, said that hard work led to their success. To this they added such traits as "perseverance" and "consistency" in their work; they all stressed "honesty" and "integrity" as the moral principles rewarded by success. Except for Edison, they did not believe in "overwork." All were convinced that the fewer advantages one had in one's youth, the greater chances for success one could hope for. Even a man coming from a relatively distinguished family such as Joseph H. Choate, a leading lawyer and later an ambassador, whose interview is reprinted in this volume, said: "I never met a great man who was born rich."[8] They all advocated thrift, saving, and investment as necessary means to accumulate wealth. They also stated that education and book learning had little influence on their careers: given his own experience, Dreiser dared not dispute their point.

Despite the prestige and glory accorded to successful men, Dreiser learned that only constant labor, not luxury and wealth, constituted their happiness. "When it is all done and is a success," Edison confessed, "I can't bear the sight of it. I haven't used a telephone in ten years, and I would go out of my way any day to miss an incandescent light."[9] Once these men achieved their success and fame, most of them looked for satisfaction in their humanitarian cause, but to them labor itself preempted their happiness. Philip D. Armour, a businessman and philanthropist, explained: "If you give the world better material, better measure, better opportunities for living respectably, there is happiness in that. You cannot give the world anything without labor, and there is no satisfaction in anything but labor that looks toward doing this, and does it."[10] Even though Dreiser had earlier expressed some reservations about Andrew Carnegie, Dreiser, in *Success* magazine, somewhat inflated Carnegie's motive for a large-hearted liberality.

Not only did his success stories concern American cultural heroes, but Dreiser was fascinated by many unsung, nameless heroes, as well as by some less famous men and women professionals. Among Dreiser's thirty *Success* articles, exactly half were later republished in three separate volumes edited by Marden: *How They Succeeded* (1901), *Talks with Great Workers* (1901), and *Little Visits with Great Americans* (1903). Apparently Marden selected each of those articles to dramatize the life story of a single figure; seven of the articles that were not selected, such as "American Women as Successful Playwrights" and "America's Greatest Portrait Painters," dealt with more than one individual. Whether or not Marden disagreed with Dreiser's point of view on the subject of the unselected articles is unknown, but most of the eliminated articles from the volumes of reprints lacked a sense of glamour associated with the American Dream of Success. Marden's intention was to inspire young men and women who wanted to be somebody but felt that they had no chance in life. However, the list of Dreiser's *Success* stories that were omitted—for example, interviews with H. Barrington Cox (an inventor), Edward Atkinson (a food scientist), and Thomas Brackett Reed (a one-time Speaker of the House), all reprinted in this volume, and Clara S. Folts (a leading woman lawyer), reprinted in *Selected Magazine Articles*—showed, contrary to common belief, that success was necessarily derived from one's advantages over others at the start of life, including a solid educational background.

What is most significant about Marden's selection is that he was not interested in Dreiser's enthusiasm for humanistically oriented portrayals of successful individuals. Two articles of this nature were carefully omitted from Marden's reprints: "A Cripple Whose Energy Gives Inspiration" and "A Touch of Human Brotherhood."[11] In the first essay Dreiser, as if writing a short story, describes how bleak a small fishing town on the coast of Connecticut had become through a decline in the whaling business and shipbuilding industry. Focusing on a handicapped youth and a trivial incident, Dreiser turned his argument about human existence to the necessity of doing something to promote human organization and intelligence. Dreiser's ensuing narration intimates an idea which would later clarify the meaning of struggle in his novels: while other young boys, complaining about their unfortunate social and economic conditions, cursed the world and idled away their time and energy, a physically handicapped youth, persisting in his labor and winning public trust and love, achieved happiness and success in life.

The other story "A Touch of Human Brotherhood," included in this volume under "The City," concerns the philosophy of success and happiness according to a least glamorous and singularly strange figure, whom Dreiser had found on Broadway and Fifth Avenue in New York. This man's story was so striking that Dreiser used it toward the end of *Sister Carrie*, where a lone, poverty-stricken man known only by his title of Captain created a job for himself.[12] The Captain solicits passersby to contribute money to shelter homeless men during nights when the cold was like that pictured in Alfred Stieglitz's photograph. In the eyes of this self-styled philanthropist, people think that life is beautiful outside like "hotels and theaters, the carriages and fine homes,—they're all in the eye . . . it's only for a season." Dreiser, thinking of his own work and of the Captain's for a noble, selfless cause, said: "Yes, I know . . . but mine is self-remembrance, while yours is self-forgetfulness." The man at once responded: "Don't you believe it. . . . I get as much fun out of my life as you get out of yours. . . . I don't have to worry over who is going to hire or discharge me. I have a job, and no one ever tries to take it away from me."[13] What this individual taught Dreiser was a simple representation of national character and idealism: independence, individualism, and freedom. Not surprisingly, the interview also revealed that the Captain, keeping a small room in the slums, lived quite happily among black men and poor white men.

∞

Darwinism, so momentous in its influence on the natural sciences, precipitated in America a fierce battle between science and religion. By the end of the nineteenth century, evolution had gradually won the battle, not only because it offered a better explanation for the origin and development of the species, but because the corollaries of science—technology and industry—became the indispensable facts of modern life. Herbert Spencer, the chief spokesman in America for evolution, extended the theory of natural selection to other fields and applied it to diverse phenomena. Men of different persuasions and crafts in the period—John Fiske, William James, Stephen Crane, and Frank Norris to mention a few—came under his influence. Dreiser's public worship of this philosopher in *Ev'ry Month* suggests the widespread acceptance of doctrine in the American 1890s. The popularity of Spencer's theory was significant not so much for his refutation of traditional faith as for his famous "First Principles" of a universal change from homogeneity to heterogeneity. For the optimistic Americans, Spencer's ideas suggested an inevitable political and social progress for the nation.

Under this climate the last decade of the nineteenth century continued to produce numerous studies in the fields as various as medicine, geology, agronomy, and food and health sciences. In such inquiries the evolutionary concept was reflected in the researcher's emphasis on continuity and growth as the key to understanding human development. Even a generalist like Dreiser developed an eye for enumeration and verification in dealing with subjects other than arts and literature, as shown in many of Dreiser's magazine articles republished in this volume. John Burroughs, a famous philosopher of the generation, whom Dreiser interviewed for his magazine articles, described living beings around his hut for their own sake—without any of the confidence and authority characteristic of the earlier thinkers like Emerson and Thoreau.[14]

In the scientific writings of the age there was as before an unmistakable emphasis on the umbilical cord connecting humanity and nature. But writers like Burroughs and Dreiser went beyond: they now looked at plants and animals around them with as much sympathy and respect as they would view their fellow human beings. The introduction of automobiles into American life must have given such a compassionate man as Dreiser a sense of relief, because watching clattering horses in the street was "itself too often an object of real and piteous interest."[15] As a naturalist in the vein of Thoreau and Burroughs, Dreiser could scarcely promote the cause of human happiness on earth without due consideration for the welfare of other living beings. In his article "Carrier Pigeons in War Time," re-published in this volume under "Other Sites and Scenes," Dreiser was curious about the intelligence and efficiency of pigeons as they were used for secret communications. But at the same time he expressed his charac-teristic concern for pigeons as he concluded his essay with a quotation from his favorite poem by William Bryant, "To a Waterfowl."[16] As his articles like "The New Knowledge of Weeds," republished in this volume, and "Plant Life Underground" show, Dreiser was fascinated with the thriv-ing world of nature. Discussing the importance of studying plant roots scientifically, he illustrated how a microscope could trace down their "infinitesimal . . . threads as light as gossamer, almost—they did not naturally end." "In that unseen part," he wrote, "there was a friendly union between the life of the plant and the life of the earth, and the latter had given some of itself to course up the hair-like root and become a part of the plant."[17] On the basis of new research on the relationship of weeds to the soil, Dreiser even pleaded for preservation of some weeds: "There are weeds that are soil renewers, weeds that are food for man and beast, and weeds without which thousands of acres of our most fertile lands would be wastes to-day."[18]

As new discoveries in nature increased there came inventions. The closing decades of the nineteenth century regarded inventors and industrial promoters as heroes, as Dreiser's many success stories well attest. By the turn of the century the fears of technology and industry had subsided. Some journalists went so far as to declare the invention of automobiles as beneficial to human health, as did Dreiser, a flawed observation of which they scarcely were aware and an idea unthinkable today. Dreiser contributed several well-researched articles on transportation such as "The Town of Pullman," "New York's Underground Railroad," both of which are republished in this volume. The Pullman car, with "sofas and arm-chairs bulging with soft and velvet-bound cushions," not only overcame one's apprehension but created a sense of luxury and excitement.[19] Half a century earlier Thoreau had questioned the value of the telegraph; even Thomas Edison, as mentioned earlier, told Dreiser that he had avoided the use of a telephone for a decade and that he had literally gone out of his way "any day to miss an incandescent light."[20]

But such symbolic protests notwithstanding, invention in the period multiplied and compelled, rather than fulfilled, need. The thought of menace often accompanied technological advancements, as Dreiser contemplated on the pollution that marred the Chicago canals. In such articles as "Where Battleships Are Built," "The Making of Small Arms," and "Scenes in a Cartridge Factory," all republished in this volume, Dreiser discussed the sinister purpose for which the production of arms and weapons was carried out. These articles, providing well-detailed technical information, also express Dreiser's feelings about the time-honored issue of war and peace. He considered weapon production a necessary evil "because men slay and will not be at peace, and so the mind carries the thought as a burden. And yet this is sometimes modified by the higher thought that it is the enemy of war, in that the motive is to make implements wherewith to compel peace." A sense of relief and wishful thinking can be detected in Dreiser's account: "In such a light the endless procession of guns is not so bad, nay, it is even satisfying in that war by them is made so swift and decisive, that after a while there may be no longer need of war."[21]

In this period of writing, Dreiser was unmistakably a champion of technology and industry for the sake of the common people. When one-eighth of the families in the United States in 1895 controlled seven-eighths of its property, despite the advancements made in science and technology, poverty continued to exist as Dreiser's articles on the city demonstrate.[22] But the common people at the turn of the century owed to the multifold mechanical inventions and to the efforts of public and private agencies in establishing better living standards. By the turn of the century many Americans, particularly urban residents, enjoyed improved methods of plumbing, better lighting systems, new modes of transportation in cities and suburbs—a scene that made a striking contrast with that of another country described in Dreiser's article "Japanese Home Life," republished in this volume under "Other Sites and Scenes." The common people in the United States also benefited from their local governments, which provided them with water purification, sewerage, roads, parks, and public hygiene. Although the nation experienced an economic depression in the mid-1890s, the general condition of the masses was not materially affected for the worse.

The greatest impact of technology, however, was not on the public but on the giant railroads that crisscrossed the country. The rapid railroad construction supplied markets for other industries. During the 1890s the production of various agricultural goods doubled while that of mechanical and electrical apparatus increased more than four times. Industry was not only growing but becoming more diverse.[23] During the 1890s, technology and industry developed hand in hand, but it is more true that technological innovations enhanced industrial productivity, as Dreiser's articles on this subject bear out. The most serious development in the eyes of society was that industry was moving toward monopoly, or what the age called "trusts," a central issue of the decade as discussed in Dreiser's magazine article "The Railroad and the People."[24] His argument was to correct the term "soulless corporation" that was often used to assail the nation's railroads, the largest commercial organization then existing in the United States. The railroads were usually described as "dark, sinister, dishonest associations which robbed the people 'right and left,' . . . and gave nothing in return." But like Shelgrim, the railroad president in Frank Norris's *The Octopus,* Dreiser argued in favor of the industry's "cordial and sympathetic relationship with [the] public" and, with meticulous details, illustrated how both would benefit under such an enterprise. Dreiser's view of capitalism in this instance is evenhanded. "For if the public has had nothing save greed and rapacity to expect of its railroads," he went on, "the sight of the latter adopting a reasonable business policy, whereby they seek to educate and make prosperous the public in order that they in turn may be prosperous, is one which, if not inspiring, is at least optimistic" ("The Railroad and the People," 479).

Reflecting the jubilant cultural climate in the period, Dreiser's articles on technology and industry celebrated the spirit of democracy. He contrasted the enterprise of road construction to that of Imperial Rome, which thrived on slavery. As if to evoke Lincoln, he emphasized that American roads came into being "with awakening reason and sympathy in all the hearts of men" and that true greatness lay in the fact the roads were built by the people and for the people. "Unlike the magnificent public structure of the empires long since departed," he asserted, "they will neither conceal squalor nor want, nor yet a race of whip-driven Helots, but rather bespeak a nation of freemen and beauty lovers—men strong in the devotion and enjoyment of good."[25] Whether Dreiser was describing how trains were manufactured in the Midwest, how pilot boats were operated in New York Harbor, how trolleys ran between New York and Boston, how the subway was laid in New York, his vision of progress dramatized the involvement and excitement of the common people.

∞

Students of the American landscape can look to Frank Lloyd Wright, who not only shaped modern architecture but epitomized all the varied and conflicting aspirations in American life. The significance of Wright's designing was his ability to accept the values of the machine and industrialism without sacrificing emotional values. An American writer like Dreiser looked at native landscapes in much the same spirit as did Wright. This attitude was not limited to the artists and writers of the turn of the century; it was evident in many of the historians and philosophers of the generation. Henry Adams, for example, attempted a unification and continuation of the Virgin with the dynamo. Even Henry Ford—the inventor and capitalist of modern America—decorated his Greenfield Village with reconstructed preindustrial relics.

The synthesis and dialectics these individuals had prophesied were, in fact, reflected by the very changes caused by industrialization and urbanization in the United States. Today people may abhor the age of rampant computer technology and cold, lifeless machines and plastics, but a century ago many Americans took a less horrified view of the new civilization. To Lester Kane, the protagonist of Dreiser's *Jennie Gerhardt,* technology constituted "[the] tremendous and complicated development of our material civilization, the multiplicity and variety of our social forms, the depth, subtlety and sophistry of our mental cogitations, gathered, remultiplied and phantasmagorically disseminated as they are by these other agencies—the railroad, the express and post-office, the telegraph, telephone, the newspaper and, in short, the whole art of printing and distributing—have so combined as to produce what may be termed a kaleidoscopic glitter, a dazzling and confusing showpiece. . . . "[26] The uneasiness with an unknown order of life Lester, let alone many Americans, must have felt was understandable, yet they tried to find in it the humane comforts and delights totally denied them in the past.

Had the Southerners before the Civil War relished such advantages on the plantation, the Northerners after the war would have been able to find similar comfort and pleasure in the city. Richard Harding Davis told his readers in 1892 with humor and sarcasm that "any man who will live in a log house at the foot of a mountain, and drink melted snow any longer than he had to do so . . . when he could live in the Knickerbocker Flats, and drive forth in a hansom with rubber tires, is no longer an object of interest"[27] If the Western frontier had disappeared by the 1890s as Frederick Jackson Turner declared, the city in America would indeed have replaced it.

Turner was right in saying that the influence of the frontier experience would remain in American life. Such American virtues as individualism, freedom, and simplicity—with which the Western frontier is associated—buttressed the character of early Americans. Frontier or no frontier, as history has shown, these qualities were to remain. A decade earlier Mark Twain noted that the freedom and innocence of the old times on the Mississippi were being supplanted by the marching of technocracy. But even Twain, realizing that the age offered no other havens for Americans to enter, managed a temporary affirmation of the values of both the old and the new. Rather than resist the inevitable change, Americans of that generation sought a reconciliation of the machine and the garden.

By the end of the century, when Dreiser came to view the commerce on the River, described in "The Trade of the Mississippi," not only did he see a harmony of the new with the old, but he even suggested a modification of the old to suit the new. "The overseers," Dreiser saw, "threaten the idle, curse the active, bluff the bystanders, and add prodigiously to the tumult of the scene without otherwise affecting it. . . . The character of the negro in this situation is no doubt picturesque, but the fact that the business is more or less dependent upon such labor, and the impossibility of securing active, systematic, skilled service forms one of the serious problems in the commerce of the river."[28] Though aware of the river's scenic charms and cultural and literary memories, Dreiser thought its traditions to be an anachronism in the light of the new century.

The influence of the machine on the American landscapes in this period also extended to the hinterland. Industrialization, at first, affected city life but soon became the business of the entire nation, penetrating every corner of the land by the powerful railroads and ever-expanding markets. A conflict between the rural and the urban communities seemed inevitable, but it failed to materialize for the simple reason that both needed each other. Soon the farmer became an adjunct to the city, while the city dweller missed in his or her daily living the peace and comfort of the rural landscape—the American pastoral. Each was not completely satisfied with the scene of the other, but both sought substitute consolations found in the American past.

Beginning with the centennial celebration of Independence, America became the land of memorials. Much of Dreiser's commentary on the landscape contains references to the historical events and episodes that occurred around the Revolutionary War. In such an article he discusses the retreat into the past by focusing on the cultural and aesthetic life of a particular locale, as he does in his portrayal of Washington Irving's Sleepy Hollow.[29] Dreiser is describing, besides the celebrated romancer and that era in American history, the long train of knowledge in science, technology, and commerce that has so subtly marked the face of the land since. "On the Field of Brandywine," republished in this volume, Dreiser also reflects on the Revolutionary War, fought over the picturesque landscape, and contrasts the violence caused by the war with the tranquillity of nature. For Dreiser, the valley of Brandywine is "consecrated by nature, by history and art. On its hillsides, so lovely at morning, have sounded the drums and guns of war. Where its limpid waters flow slow and still over gleaming pebbles men fought for liberty; and ducks now float through the idle hours where soldiers crossed."[30]

By the 1890s, the appreciation of nature had been so finely ingrained in American life that the World's Columbian Exposition in Chicago in 1893 was able to render this experience even more conscious to the public. Creation of the White City in the busiest metropolis of the Midwest has been praised as well as disparaged not because of its location but because of its white classical architecture. European culture and American technology were both abundantly evident at the Fair, but anyone coming from the East Coast or abroad was overwhelmed by the beauty of an inland city on the shores of Lake Michigan. Dreiser, who had visited the Fair as a feature correspondent for the St. Louis *Republic,* was commissioned to write a long magazine article, "The Story of the States No. III—Illinois," for *Pearson's,* republished in this volume. While he celebrated the state's history for launching the antislavery movement, he also traced the history of Chicago: "The parks contain monuments, the public institutions paintings, the walls of several theatres reliefs of the most delicate modeling, detailing in a feeling way the story of these adventures, which will yet form the basis for a world of American romance."[31] "Illinois," Dreiser observed, "is essentially a State of new ideas and great enterprises"; in terms of the cityscape, Chicago represents "the generation and evolution of the idea that it is cheaper to build high than to build wide, and so on" (543). Those who wished the native landscape to rival the Alps or Mount Fuji wished to see a new blend of nature and art. Louis Sullivan might not have fully realized this unique beauty in designing the first skyscrapers in Chicago in the early 1890s, but soon his follower Frank Lloyd Wright sharpened Americans' awareness of a sense of place by planning his houses to hug the contours of the land.[32]

The concept of nature in America has also implied space. In the late nineteenth century the vast expanse of land from coast to coast was covered with railways, roads, and cities. Bigness necessarily patterned na-

tional aspirations, and technological developments whetted the taste for it. Openness in modern architecture was enhanced by the mass production of plate-glass windows, while the multistoried building was a direct result of the low-cost manufacturing of steel and iron as well as the invention of the elevator. The Brooklyn Bridge, completed in 1883, became a symbol of this new conquest of space made possible by technology. To Dreiser, the northern end of Manhattan Island at the turn of the century was a single most beautiful landscape in America, not for the Harlem River Speedway as the title of his article suggests, but for the spacious scenery accented by various bridges, tunnels, terraces, forts, and mansions.[33]

The harmony of architecture with nature was also exemplified by the types of row houses, apartments, and suburban villas built around the turn of the century. This blending was a salient feature of the modern architectural feasts like the Brooklyn Bridge and the George Washington Bridge, each of which commanded a strange beauty of space for the age. All these new structures embodied the dictum that in an increasingly urbanized community living, form followed function. The idea of "organic architecture" in the twentieth century that form not simply follows function but form and function are the same was to derive from this consideration of art as the product of its essential backgrounds: nature and technology. Dreiser's vision of the landscape at the turn of the century thus reflects a new passage in American cultural history.

No other social phenomena in America had so radically changed the face of the nation than the rise of the city toward the end of nineteenth century. With the development of transportation, the growth of industry and commerce was draining the countryside of its young people allured by the excitements and adventures of urban life. Chicago, as Dreiser wrote in *Sister Carrie,* possessed the power of "the magnet attracting" for Caroline Meeber, an eighteen-year-old country girl from Wisconsin who timidly looked out the window aboard a train in the summer of 1889.[34] For most young men and women of the generation, the bright attractions of the city were irresistible, much as the city's ease and luxuries the young Hamlin Garland himself longed for in his home on the Middle Border. Farmers were likely to compare the worst features of their existence with the best aspects of city life. For the young at least, the city offered greater business opportunities and physically easier work.

The transformation of a rural and agricultural society to an urban and industrial one might not have been typically American, but its cause and manner were unique in world history. The change took place at an extremely rapid pace. In the 1880s the population of New York City grew from two to almost three and half a million, that of Chicago from half a million to a million and a half. Cities like Cleveland, Detroit, and Milwaukee doubled in size.[35] While cities in the West and the South, some of them populous and prosperous, were isolated in the widespread rural regions, the Midwest was fast becoming a collection of closely knit urban communities. In 1880 one out of every five Midwesterners lived in a city of four thousand or more, a decade later one out of every three. In 1890 Illinois and Ohio boasted over one hundred cities, while 30 percent of the population even in Minnesota and Missouri was urban.[36] It looked as though the closing of the West gave rise to the birth of cities within. By the end of the century, as noted earlier, the American frontier had changed into an industrial frontier.

Another feature of urban growth in the United States was a massive European immigration to the northern cities. In 1890 a third of the population in Boston and a fourth in Philadelphia were foreign-born. No other cities in the world at that time had more immigrants than New York, where virtually everyone, except for African Americans, was said to be of foreign birth or parentage. In Greater New York City including Brooklyn there were half as many Italians as in Naples, as many Germans as in Hamburg, twice as many Irish as in Dublin, and two and a half times as many Jewish people as in Warsaw[37] Noting a strange occurrence of cosmopolitanism in the mid-1880s, Andrew Carnegie counted almost a thousand foreign-language newspapers in the United States.[38] Those who were born in America and proud of their older stock viewed such concentration of foreign population in urban industrial centers with great apprehension. The ways in which the immigrants were forced to adjust to their lot in a city like New York were hard, if not inhumane, as reported in *How the Other Half Lives* (1890) by Jacob Riis, himself an immigrant. Assimilation took place slowly and unevenly not so much because of their religious backgrounds as because of their social and economic conditions. In Chicago, for instance, the sweatshops in the garment industry were occupied largely by Bohemian and Jewish entrepreneurs, the building trades by Irish and Italians, and the peddler by Jewish.[39] Integration among the immigrants, let alone interracial marriage, went on at as uneven a pace as that between today's African and European Americans. All kinds of racial complexes on the part of the older residents and timidity and ignorance on the part of the younger retarded the process.

For both new arrivals and natives, the wide stretches of wilderness—the very images of the American pastoral to older myth makers like Irving, Cooper, and Twain—created not a sense of nostalgia but a feeling of impersonality and loneliness. On the other hand, to live in a large urban community at the turn of the century was indeed stimulating, for the city was the generating center for intellectual, scientific, and artistic progress as Dreiser's magazine articles have amply shown. One could find there the best schools, the best libraries, the best newspapers, the best theaters, and the best entertainments. The city was a haven not only for intellectuals and literates, but for common working men and women as well. To a harbor pilot, Dreiser wrote in 1899, "[the] little bright-windowed main street in New Brighten was . . . a kind of earthly heaven. To be there of an evening when people were passing, to loaf on the corner and see the bright-eyed girls go by, to be in the village hubbub was to him the epitome of living." For the same pilot, "[the] great, silent, suggestive sea"—another pastoral of which Melville had earlier made a myth of life—meant nothing.[40]

Unlike nineteenth-century American novelists, a host of modern American novelists ranging from Howells and Dreiser to Henry James and Edith Wharton recognized the hazards and miseries of city life but nevertheless suggested humanly satisfying patterns of life. The city is traditionally associated with evil and hell, as in from Shakespeare and Dante down to Baudelaire and Zola. And to many twentieth-century modernist writers it is a wasteland. T. S. Eliot called it an "Unreal City": he showed in the context of *The Waste Land* (1922) that regeneration is not achieved in the city, suggesting that ultimately salvation for him is neither specifically urban nor rural. John Burroughs, the sage of late-nineteenth-century America, mentioned earlier, pleaded for the value of nature and warned against humankind's overindulgence in materialism. But such warnings went unheeded. After the turn of the century, however, as shown by an architect like Frank Lloyd Wright, as noted earlier, Americans began to absorb nature into their consciousness. If nature did not completely vanish from the daily activities of one's living, it became steadily accommodated by them.

The "gay" 1890s derived its term from the flourishing lifestyles of the city, but the spirit of the decade suffered from the country's worst economic depression of the century. Although the problem first started with the dropping of prices in agricultural products and the wayward railroad expansion in the West, the depression dealt city residents the hardest blow. Strikers were everywhere—and became violent as those at the Homestead plants in Pittsburgh in 1892, as Dreiser witnessed as a newspaper reporter. The strikers at the Pullman factory near Chicago in 1894 were also well known, but in his magazine article "The Town of Pullman," republished in this volume, Dreiser was reticent about the strike, perhaps, to stress the contribution and achievement of George Pullman, the late American inventor. The strikers at the Brooklyn streetcar lines in 1896 also hit the newspaper headlines: using this scene, Dreiser describes Hurstwood's ordeal as a scab in *Sister Carrie*. Between 1894 and 1898 the number of unemployed tripled. At the worst stage of the depression in the mid-1890s, 20 percent of labor force in the entire nation was out of work. The wide gulf dividing the rich and the poor became a literary theme—so vividly depicted in Stephen Crane's "An Experiment in Misery" with the soaring commercial buildings and the tattered tramps roaming the Bowery, or in Dreiser's "Curious Shifts of the Poor," in cold winter with the life of gaiety on Broadway and the long bread lines a few blocks away.

The social problems of the 1890s, however, was not solely the making of the decade. Rather it was a direct result of the Industrial Revolution that had steadily developed since the Civil War. The march of industry and commerce often compelled the city government to sacrifice the necessary public service projects such as street pavement, water supply, and sewage treatment. It was a dilemma of the age that, while technology improved the systems of lighting, communication, and transportation, the slums in a city like New York produced the darkest alleys and the most wretched living conditions anywhere in the world. The problem was not merely one of economics; it stemmed from local politics. All forms of corruption—bribery, extortion, larceny, and blackmail—had been facts of life in a large metropolis well before the turn of the century.

The last decade of the nineteenth century produced famous muckrakers. After Jacob Riis came another immigrant journalist, S. S. McClure, who founded the first muckraking magazine. "When I came to this country . . . in 1866," McClure wrote, "I believed that the government of the United States was the flower of all the ages—that nothing could possibly corrupt it."[41] Not surprisingly, all these journalists—even including the less idealistic immigrant Joseph Pulitzer and the sensation-seeking Californian Randolph Hearst—came to realize that the decade's utopian vision was constantly assaulted by their revelation of corruption. This kind of muckraking resulted in the 1894 Lexow Committee's investigation of the New York Police Department, the overthrow of the Tammany government, and the appointment of Theodore Roosevelt as police commissioner. But the effect of the various reform movements that sprang up in the 1890s was not felt until well beyond the turn of the century.

While Dreiser as a journalist of the period made a reference from time to time to such a political site as Tammany Hall, he was more seriously concerned with the stories of human interest than with those of economic, social, and political events. Dreiser's articles on tenement living in New York, such as "The Transmigration of the Sweat Shop" and "The Tenement Toilers," present less ferocity and more hope than those of Riis's a decade earlier.[42] Dreiser's interest in human stories is also shown by his article on a boys' reformatory, "Little Clubmen of the Tenements," in which he proudly reported that there was among the public at the end of the century a wide acceptance of, and appreciation for, such movements.[43]

Such an article as "Little Clubmen of the Tenements" demonstrates Dreiser's acumen and insight, unsurpassed by those of any other journalist of the period, in analyzing human problems. This article served Dreiser for a counter argument to Stephen Crane's "An Experiment in Misery": Dreiser's experiment shows that however poorly such children were brought up in the tenements, they could still acquire good manners and attitudes once they were placed in the club. In the past, some of the boys had lived with alcoholic parents; others had been orphans, motherless, fatherless, and had been turned out to roam the streets at night. Scars of environment on the children were deep, yet Dreiser learned they could be healed.

"Delaware's Blue Laws," republished in this volume under "The City," was also a penetrating study of reform. Interviewing those familiar with the public exhibition of corporal punishment, Dreiser reached a consensus that such punishment failed to deter crime. He asked an African American waiter, "Don't you think it stops these people from doing the same thing over again?" The man replied, "No, suh, not any mo' than jail would. They is men here that has been whipped an' wipped until they is so hard they don't care no more foh it than foh a flea. It juss makes 'em wuss, I think."[44] Even a jailer who does the whipping told Dreiser: "it is all wrong. . . . Because it degrades the man that does the whipping, and if it degrades him, I know it must have much the same effect upon those who see it" (57). Dreiser was appalled that while black offenders had no chance to lessen their punishment, the white offenders who had a high standing in their community and could afford to offer their possessions and leave the state escaped this public punishment. He concluded his study: "It is the man with conscience and feeling upon whom this relic of an older order of civilization weighs unjustly. The hardened criminal whom it is supposed to reach does not suffer at all, and is not corrected thereby" (56).

All in all, Dreiser's early magazine journalism shows a characteristic insight into his material. His attitude resulted from his lifelong conviction, stated in *Ev'ry Month* in 1896, that "the surest guide is a true and respon-sive heart."[45] Many of his magazine articles addressing human problems reveal Dreiser's conviction that a human being was not necessarily a victim of his or her conditions; it should always be possible for the individ-ual as well as for society to ameliorate them. Sympathy and compassion indisputably color his fiction, but his magazine work bears witness to the fact that Dreiser was not a simple commiserator, as Edward D. McDonald portrayed him to be: in tears, devouring a tragic story in the newspaper.[46] His compassionate appreciation of all stories of human interest cannot be doubted, but Dreiser before *Sister Carrie* also acquired a capacity for detachment and objectivity. Rarely do his magazine essays display pas-sionate outbursts. In effect, Dreiser was a literary realist and modernist in the best sense of the words. These magazine pieces suggest that although he was eager to learn from literary and philosophical sources, he trusted his own vision and portrayed life firsthand.

After 1900 Dreiser's writing fluctuated between naturalism and vitalism, but at the turn of the century Dreiser was clearly a vitalist in his freelance work. This vitalist philosophy was so deeply rooted in the most important period of his development that it likely remained with him for the rest of his career. In his novels Dreiser often writes of the apparently indifferent and uncontrollable forces that sweep over human life, but in reality he does not seem to have abandoned a belief in human beings' capacity to determine their own destiny. Although Dreiser has often been labeled as a literary naturalist, his magazine writing suggests that he was, at least in his early years, a naturalist in the vein of Thoreau and Burroughs.

NOTES

1. The complete edition of this magazine has recently been published: Theodore Dreiser, *Ev'ry Month,* ed. Nancy Warner Barrineau (Athens: University of Georgia Press, 1996), 347 pp.

2. Arthur Henry, *Lodgings in Town* (New York: A. S. Barnes, 1905), 83.

3. Dreiser, *Twelve Men* (New York: Liveright, 1919), 101.

4. See letter of 20 December 1893 to George W. Latham in Harvard University Library. Quoted in Lawrence Thompson, introduction to *Tilbury Town: Selected Poems of Edwin Arlington Robinson* (New York: Macmillan, 1953), xv.

5. Russell H. Conwell, *Acres of Diamonds* (Philadelphia: J. Y. Huber, 1890).

6. Letter to Robert H. Elias of 17 April 1937 in Robert H. Elias, ed., *Letters of Theodore Dreiser* (Philadelphia: University of Pennsylvania Press, 1959), 3:784–85.

7. See Dreiser, "A Talk with America's Leading Lawyer: Joseph H. Choate," *Success* 1 (January 1898): 40–41; rpt. in this collection. "A Photographic Talk with Edison," *Success* 1 (February 1898): 8–9; rpt. in *Selected Magazine Articles,* 1:111–19. "Life Stories of Successful Men—No. 10: Philip D. Armour," *Success* 1 (October 1898): 3–4; rpt. in *Selected Magazine Articles,* 1:120–29. "Life Stories of Successful Men—No. 11: Chauncey M. Depew," *Success* 1 (November 1898): 3–4; rpt. in this collection. "Life Stories of Successful Men—No. 12: Marshall Field," *Success* 2 (8 December 1898): 7–8; rpt. in *Selected Magazine Articles,* 1: 130–38. "A Leader of Young Manhood: Frank W. Gunsaulus," *Success* 2 (15 December 1898): 23–24; rpt. in this collection. "A Monarch of Metal Workers: Andrew Carnegie," *Success* 2 (3 June 1899): 453–54; rpt. in *Selected Magazine Articles,* 1:158–69.

8. See "A Talk with America's Leading Lawyer: Joseph H. Choate" in this collection.

9. Dreiser, "A Photographic Talk with Edison," 9.

10. Dreiser, "Life Stories of Successful Men—No. 10: Philip D. Armour," 4.

11. Dreiser, "A Cripple Whose Energy Gives Inspiration," *Success* 5 (February 1902): 72–73; rpt. in *Selected Magazine Articles,* 1:193–201. Dreiser, "A Touch of Human Brotherhood," *Success* 5 (March 1902): 140–41, 176; rpt. in this collection.

12. See Dreiser, *Sister Carrie,* ed. James L. W. West III, (Philadelphia: University of Pennsylvania Press, 1981), 488–93.

13. See "A Touch of Human Brotherhood" in this collection.

14. See Dreiser, "Fame Found in Quiet Nooks," *Success* 1 (September 1898): 5–6; rpt. in *Selected Magazine Articles,* 1:50–56.

15. See Dreiser, "The Horseless Age," *Demorest's* 35 (May 1899): 153–55; rpt. in *Selected Magazine Articles,* 2: 152–60.

16. See Dreiser, "Carrier Pigeons in War Time," *Demorest's* 34 (July 1898): 861–62; rpt. in this collection.

17. See Dreiser, "Plant Life Underground," *Pearson's* 11 (June 1901: 861–62; rpt. in *Selected Magazine Articles,* 2:172–77.

18. See Dreiser, "The New Knowledge of Weeds," *Ainslee's* 8 (January 1902): 533–38; rpt. in this collection.

19. George M. Towle, *American Society* (London: Chapman and Hall, 1870), 2:180.

20. See Dreiser, "A Photographic Talk with Edison."

21. See Dreiser, "The Making of Small Arms," *Ainslee's* 1 (July 1898): 540–49; rpt. in this collection.

22. Charles B. Spahr, "An Essay on the Present Distribution of Wealth in the United States," in *Library of Economics and Politics,* ed. R. Toely (New York/Boston: T. Y. Crowell, 1896), 69.

23. Harold U. Faulkner, *Politics, Reform and Expansion* (New York: Harper, 1959), 73.

24. See Dreiser, "The Railroad and the People," *Harper's Monthly* 100 (February 1900): 479–84; rpt. in *Selected Magazine Articles,* 2:161–71.

25. See Dreiser, "The Harlem River Speedway," *Ainslee's* 2 (August 1898): 49–56; rpt. in *Selected Magazine Articles,* 2:70–76.

26. Dreiser, *Jennie Gerhardt,* ed. James L. W. West III (Philadelphia: University of Pennsylvania Press, 1992), 125.

27. Gerald Langford, *The Richard Harding Davis Years: A Biography of a Mother and Son* (New York: Holt, Rinehart and Winston, 1961), 122.

28. See Dreiser, "The Trade of the Mississippi," *Ainslee's* 4 (January 1900): 742–43; rpt. in *Selected Magazine Articles,* 2:106–16.

29. See Dreiser, "Historic Tarrytown," *Ainslee's* 1 (March 1898): 25–31; rpt. in *Selected Magazine Articles,* 2:65–69.

30. See Dreiser, "On the Field of Brandywine," *Truth* 16 (6 November 1897): 7–10; rpt. in this collection.

31. See Dreiser, "The Story of the States No. III—Illinois," *Pearson's* 11 (April 1901): 513–43; rpt. in this collection.

32. Such an innovation characteristic of Wright's earliest works can be seen in his designing of *Winslow House* (1893) in River Forest, Illinois.

33. See Dreiser, "The Harlem River Speedway."

34. Dreiser, *Sister Carrie* (New York: Doubleday, Page & Co., 1900), 1.

35. Faulkner, *Politics, Reform and Expansion,* 23.

36. Bureau of the Census, *U. S. Twelfth Census* (1900), 1: lxvi, lxxxiv–lxxxv.

37. In 1890 New York had more Irish, English, Germans, and Italians than Chicago, the latter having a larger number of Scandinavians and East Europeans. See Arthur M. Schlesinger, *The Rise of the City, 1878–1898* (New York: Macmillan, 1933), 73.

38. Andrew Carnegie, *Triumphant Democracy* (New York: Scribner's Sons, 1886), 344–45.

39. Schlesinger, *Rise of the City,* 65–66.

40. See Dreiser, "The Log of an Ocean Pilot," *Ainslee's* 3 (July 1899): 683–92; rpt. in *Selected Magazine Articles,* 2:192–204.

41. S. S. McClure, *My Autobiography* (New York: Frederick A. Stokes, 1914), 265.

42. See Dreiser, "The Transmigration of the Sweat Shop," *Puritan* 8 (July 1900): 498–502; rpt. in *Selected Magazine Articles,* 2:214–21; Dreiser, "The Tenement Toilers," *Success* 5 (April 1902): 213–14, 232; rpt. in *Selected Magazine Articles,* 2:222–32.

43. See Dreiser, "Little Clubmen of the Tenements," *Puritan* 7 (February 1900): 665–72; rpt. in *Selected Magazine Articles,* 2:205–13.

44. See Dreiser, "Delaware's Blue Laws," *Ainslee's* 7 (February 1901): 53–57; rpt. in this collection.

45. Dreiser, "Reflections," *Ev'ry Month* 2 (1 September 1896): 2.

46. Edward D. McDonald, "Dreiser before 'Sister Carrie,'" *The Bookman* (U.S.) 67 (June 1928): facing 369.

Part I
Success Stories

1

A Talk with America's Leading Lawyer: Joseph H. Choate

With Photographic Illustrations, Taken Specially for *Success*

"You may say what you will," said a young lawyer in a conversation wherein Joseph H. Choate and his ability were the topics of conversation; "a man cannot hope to distinguish himself without special opportunities."[1]

"Not even in law?" questioned one.

"There least of all," was the answer.

"Well," said another, "the period in which Mr. Choate began his career in New York is commonly referred to as the golden age of the metropolitan bar. James B. Brady was a conspicuous figure in the popular eye.[2] Charles O'Connor had already made a lasting impression.[3] Mr. Evarts was in the front rank in politics as well as in law.[4] Mr. Hoffman was equally prominent on the Democratic side, and Mr. Stanford's brilliancy in cross-examination had given him an enviable reputation.[5] The legal heavens were studded with stars of such lustre as to make any newcomer feel doubtful about his ability to compete. But Choate displayed no anxiety. He hung out his shingle and began to look for clients, and they came."

A Young Lawyer's Chances Then and Now

"That was before the war," resumed the original speaker. "Do you imagine he could have attained his position as the foremost American lawyer under conditions as they exist to-day without special advantages?"

"Possibly," I said, and added that it was probable that Mr. Choate, if approached, would kindly throw light on the subject.

In pursuance of this idea, I called one evening at the residence of Mr. Choate. Previous inquiry at the law office of Evarts, Choate, and Beaman, on Wall Street, elicited the information that Mr. Choate's days were filled to overflowing with legal affairs of great importance. Consequently it was surprising to find him so ready to see a stranger at his home.

It was into a long room on the ground floor that I was introduced, three of its walls lined with tall, dark walnut book-laden cases, lighted by a bright grate fire and by a student's lamp on the table by night, and by two heavily-shaded windows by day. As I entered, the great lawyer was busy prodding the fire, and voiced a resonant "good-evening" without turning. In a moment or two he had evoked a blaze, and assumed a standing attitude before the fire, his hands behind him.

ARE SPECIAL ADVANTAGES NECESSARY?

"Well, sir," he began, "what do you wish?"

"A few minutes of your time," I answered.

"Why?" he questioned succinctly.

"I wish to discover whether you believe special advantages at the beginning of a youth's career are necessary to success?"

"Why my opinion?"

I was rather floored for an instant, but endeavored to make plain the natural interest of the public in the subject and his opinion, but he interrupted me with the query:—

"Why don't you ask a man who never had any advantages," at the same time fixing upon me one of his famous "what's in thy heart?" glances.

"Then you have had them?" I said, grasping wildly at the straw that might keep the interviewer afloat.

"A few, not many," he replied.

"Are advantages necessary to success to-day?"

"Define advantages and success," he said abruptly, evidently questioning whether it was worth while to talk. A distinguished looking figure he made, looking on, as I collected my defining ability. The room seemed full of his atmosphere. He is a tall man, oaken in strength, with broad, intelligent face, high forehead, alert, wide-set eyes, and firm, even lips expressive of great self-control. His fluency, his wit and humor, his sound knowledge, his strength and perfect self-possession, were all suggested by his face and expression, and by the firmness of his squarely set head and massive shoulders.

"Let us," I said, "say money, opportunity, friends, good advice, and personal popularity for early advantages."

"The first isn't necessary," said the jurist, leisurely adjusting his hands in his pockets. "Opportunity comes to everyone, but all have not a mind to

"Opportunity comes to everyone, but all have not a mind to see."

see; friends you can do without for a time; good advice we take too late, and popularity usually comes too early or too tardy to be appreciated. Define success."

What Success Means

"I might mention fame, position, income, as examples of what the world deems success."

"Foolish world!" said Mr. Choate. "The most successful men sometimes have not one of all these. All I can say is that early advantages won't bring a man a knowledge of the law, nor enable him to convince a jury. What he needs is years of close application, the ability to stick until he has mastered the necessary knowledge."

"Where did you obtain your wide knowledge of the law?" I asked.

"Reading at home and fighting in the courts,—principally, fighting in the courts."

"And was there any good luck about obtaining your first case? Was it secured by special effort?"

The Good Luck of Being Prepared

"None, unless it was the good luck of having a sign out, large enough for people to see. The rest of it was hard work, getting the evidence and the law fixed in my mind."

"You believe, of course," I ventured, "that advantageous opportunities do come to all?"

"Yes," said he, drawing up a chair and resignedly seating himself. "I believe that opportunities come to all,—not the same opportunities, nor the same kind of opportunities, nor opportunities half so valuable in some cases as in others, but they do come, and if seen and grasped will work a vast improvement in the life and character of an individual. Every boy cannot be President, but my word for it, if he is industrious, he can improve his position in the world."

Turning Obstacles into Aids

"It has been said, Mr. Choate," I went on, "that you often ascribe both your success in particular cases, and your general success at the bar, to good luck and happy accidents."

"Just so, just so," he answered, smiling in a manner that is at once a question and a mark of approbation. "I hope I have always made the most of good luck and happy accidents. We all should. My friend John E. Parsons once denounced a defendant insurance company as a 'vampire,— one of those bloodless creatures that feed on the blood of the people.' It was a savage address of the old-fashioned style, and convincing, until I asked the judge and jury if they knew what a vampire really is. 'Look at the Quaker gentleman who is president of this company,' I said, pointing him out. 'Also look at that innocent young man, his attorney, who sits next to him with a smile on his face. You thought vampires were something out of the way when Brother Parsons described them, but these are regular, genuine vampires.' That brought a laugh and good feeling, and I suppose you might call the whole thing an opportunity to turn a bad assault into a helpful incident."

The great lawyer was a study as he spoke, his easy, unaffected attitude and bearing itself carrying weight. His manner of accepting the intrusion with mild acquiescence and attention, but with no intention of allowing himself to be bored, was interesting. It has become customary to say that he is a poor politician, and as the term is ordinarily employed and under-stood, he is, because he is ever ready to say what he really thinks. It is precisely this quality, this freedom from cowardice, this detestation of truckling to ignorance and brutality, this independence, that cause him to stand out so boldly in the legal profession.

Does Lack of Opportunity Justify Failure?

"If equally valuable opportunities do not come to all," I went on, "hasn't an individual a right to complain and justify his failure?"

"We have passed the period when we believe that all men are equal," said Mr. Choate. "We know they're free, but some men are born less powerful than others. But if an individual does not admit to himself that he is deficient in strength or reasoning powers, if he claims all the rights and privileges given others because he is 'as good as they,' then his success or failure is upon his own head. He should prove that he is what he thinks he is, and be what he aspires to be."

"You believe, of course, that an individual may overestimate his abilities."

"Believe it," he answered, with a deprecatory wave of the hand, "trust the law to teach that. But if a man does overestimate himself, he still owes it to himself to endeavor to prove that his estimate of himself is correct. We all need to. If he fails, he will be learning his limitations, which is better than never finding them out. No man can justify inaction."

"What do you consider to be the genuine battle of a youth to-day?—the struggle to bear poverty while working to conquer?"

"Not at all," came the quick answer. "Poor clothes and poor food and a poor place to dwell in are disagreeable things and must be made to give place to better, of course, but one can be partially indifferent to them. The real struggle is to hang on to every advantage, and strengthen the mind at every step. There are persons who have learned to endure poverty so well that they don't mind it any longer. The struggle comes in maintaining a purpose through poverty to the end. It is just as difficult to maintain a purpose through riches."

"Money is not an end, then, in your estimation."

"Never, and need is only an incentive. Erskine made his greatest speech with his hungry children tugging at his coat-tails.[6] That intense feeling that something has got to be done is the thing that works the doing. I never met a great man who was born rich."

Mr. Choate's Antecedents

This remark seemed rather striking in a way, because of the fact that Mr. Choate's parents were not poor in the accepted sense. The family is rather distinguished in New England annals. His father was a cousin of the famous Rufus Choate, and the latter, at the date of Joseph's birth, January 24, 1832, was just entering his second term in Congress to distinguish himself by a great speech on the tariff.[7] Mr. Choate was the youngest of four brothers, and, after receiving a fair school education in Salem, was sent to Harvard, where he was graduated in 1852, and later from its law school in 1854. Influence procured him a position in a Boston law office. After a year of practical study, he was admitted to the Bar of Massachusetts. In October of that year he made a tour of observation in the Western states, in company with his brother William, and on his return determined to settle in New York.

"Isn't it possible, Mr. Choate," I ventured, "that your having had little or no worry over poverty in your youth might cause you to underestimate the effect of it on another, and overestimate the importance of sticking with determination to an idea through wealth or deprivation?"

"No," he replied, after a few moments' delay, in which he picked up one of the volumes near by as if to consult it; "no, the end to be attained makes important the need of hanging on. I am sure it is quite often more difficult to rise with money than without."

DOES SUCCESS BRING CONTENT AND HAPPINESS?

"You have had long years of distinction and comfort; do you find that success brings content and happiness?"

"Well," he answered, contracting his brows with legal severity, "constant labor is happiness, and success simply means ability to do more labor,—more deeds far-reaching in their power and effect. Such success brings about as much happiness as the world provides."

"I mean," I explained, "the fruits of that which is conventionally accepted as success; few hours of toil, a luxuriously furnished home, hosts of friends, the applause of the people, sumptuous repasts, and content in idleness, knowing that enough has been done."

"We never know that enough has been done," said the lawyer. "All this sounds pleasant, but the truth is that the men whose great efforts have made such things possible for themselves are the very last to desire them. You have described what appeals to the idler, the energyless dreamer, the fashionable dawdler, and the listless voluptuary. Enjoyment of such things would sap the strength and deaden the ambition of a Lincoln. The man who has attained to the position where these things are possible is the one whose life has been a constant refutation of the need of these things. He is the one who has abstained, who has conserved his mental and physical strength by living a simple and frugal life. He has not taken more than he needed, and never, if possible, less. His enjoyment has been in working, and I guarantee that you will find successful men ever to be plain-mannered persons of simple tastes, to whom sumptuous repasts are a bore, and luxury a thing apart. They may live surrounded by these things, but personally take little interest in them, knowing them to be mere trappings, which neither add to nor detract from character."

THE DELUSION OF LUXURY AND EASE

"Is there no pleasure then in luxury and ease without toil?" I questioned.

"None," said the speaker, emphatically. "There is pleasure in rest after labor. It is gratifying to relax when you really need relaxation, to be weary and be able to rest. But to enjoy anything you must first feel the need of it. But no more," he said, putting up his hand conclusively. "Surely you have enough to make clear what you wish to know."

Mr. Choate had talked for ten minutes. His ease of manner, quickness of reply, smoothness of expression, and incisive diction, were fascinating beyond description. As I was about to leave, I inquired if he would object to my making our conversation the subject of an article, to which he smiled his willingness, waiving objection with a slight movement of the hand.

MR. CHOATE'S SHARE OF NEW YORK'S LAW BUSINESS

In court circles it is common report that Mr. Choate's contemporaries divide half of the business among them, and Mr. Choate has the other half to himself.

This is due to his wonderful simplicity and directness, which never falters for a moment for thought or word. He drives straight for the heart and head of client or officer, witness or counsel, judge or juryman. A distinguished barrister has said of him:

"Where other lawyers are solemn and portentous, or wild or unpleasant, he is humorous and human. He assumes no superior air; often he speaks with his hands in his pockets. He strives to stir up no dark passions. While he is always a little bit keener, a little finer and more witty than the man in the box or on the bench, yet he is always a brother man to him."

NOTES

"A Talk with America's Leading Lawyer: Joseph H. Choate," *Success* 1 (January 1898): 40–41. Reprinted as "Making the Most of His Opportunities Wins a Coveted Embassy— Joseph H. Choate" in *Little Visits with Great Americans,* ed. Orison Swett Marden (New York: The Success Company, 1903), 196–206; also in part in Edward S. Martin, *The Life of Joseph Hodges Choate* (New York: Charles Scribner's Sons, 1921), 2:79–80.

1. Joseph H. Choate (1832–1917).

2. James Buchanan Brady (1856–1917), American financier, was regarded as a bon vivant of the day. He possessed an impressive collection of diamonds and was known as

"Diamond Jim." More noticeable than his solid financial abilities were his display in clothes and jewelry and his reckless generosity.

3. Charles O'Connor (1804–84), American lawyer and politician. In the Tweed suits he acted for the prosecution with William M. Evarts and W. H. Pechan. O'Connor wrote *Peculation Triumphant,* a record of the Tweed ring.

4. William Maxwell Evarts (1818–1901), American lawyer and statesman.

5. Leland Stanford (1824–93), American financier, served as governor of California (1861–63) and as U. S. Senator (1886–90). He founded Stanford University in 1887.

6. John Erskine (1695–1768), Scottish legal expert, was known as Erskine of Carnock.

7. Rufus Choate (1799–1859), American lawyer and political leader, was deeply devoted to the law and phenomenally successful at its practice.

2

A Vision of Fairy Lamps: H. Barrington Cox

Inventor Cox's Wonderful Little Machine for Cheaply Converting Heat into Electricity, to Light Our Dwellings

A corner in the inventor's electrical workshop

To SAY THAT HEAT MAY BE DIRECTLY CHANGED INTO ELECTRICITY, WITH-out the aid of either engine or steam, or the use of dynamos, is to announce something which should arrest the attention of the scientific world. That by heating a few layers of metal, a strong current of electricity may be in-stantly generated, and that telegraph lines, fire-alarm signals, electric bells, annunciators, fan motors, and sewing machines may be operated by the current thus produced, is sufficiently wonderful to awaken the widest interest.

H. Barrington Cox, whose invention is at present a subject of eager discussion among electricians the world over, and who has recently been called to lecture upon his discovery before the Fellows of the British Royal Society, is a nephew of the late United States Senator, S. S. Cox, and a more distant relative of Kenyon Cox, the artist.[1] Concerning his discovery, Mr. Cox makes a statement which will aid the readers of *Success* in comprehending its character and purpose.

"My idea," he said to me, "was to produce a machine which has no moving parts, automatically regulated, wholly metal and without liquid of any kind, which will practically digest coal and produce energy in the form of electricity; this energy to run electric lights, motors, and, more particularly, to furnish a complete electric plant, for use in individual households,—such a plant as can be run by a maid-servant. I have succeeded in producing such a machine."

The machine in question is certainly a simply-arranged affair. It is a round metal case, in which circular layers of metal are super-imposed one upon another, the whole being insulated and duly covered for protection against atmospheric interference and wear and tear. To these layers heat is applied, either by burning coal, oil, or gas, underneath; and the heat generated in the machine is transformed into electrical energy, which is conducted forth on wires and made to do practical service. In this way heat may be made to cool a room, as it can be transformed into a current which will operate an electric fan.

How this metal, when heated, gives off electricity, Mr. Cox explains, is one of the mysteries of nature. Dr. Seebeck, a German scientist, made the discovery, in 1821, that if two dissimilar metals are united and heat applied at or near the point of juncture, an electric current is generated.[2] The patient development of this principle has resulted in the Cox machine.

"We have a working plant in England," he explained, "which supplies the laboratories of the leading colleges, as the machines have quite generally been added to the apparatus used for class instruction. The whole telegraphic system of Queensland is now run by these machines, instead of by primary batteries. They will supplant cell batteries for ringing bells. They will take the place of hot-air and gas engines, which are used for pumping water, and they are sure to be adopted as the best and cheapest means of lighting separate houses with electricity. The lighting of a single room, or the lifting of a pound weight, in a new and saving way, is just as marvelous as, by a greater expenditure of similar energy, the propelling of a ship or the pulling of a train."

"Thus far the securing of electricity direct from coal has only been carried to the point where an ordinary dwelling-house may be illuminated with incandescent lights."

"To do this in the old way," said Mr. Cox, "one would have to set up a small engine, furnace, boiler and dynamo. Some one, of course, would have to tend them. The new machine is merely supplied with a hod of coal, which is set burning. The heat of the coal, affecting the dissimilar metals, is immediately converted into electrical energy and conducted to the bulbs by wires. One hodful of coal will last an entire evening and supply enough electricity to keep twenty lights at a glow all the time. There is no noise, because there is no visible action. There is no machinery of any kind, and the cost of the twenty lights is, practically, the cost of the bucket of coal."

Under the new system of heat conversion, it is estimated that the cost of lighting a dwelling, with 16-candle power lights, would average 1-25th of 1 cent per light per hour.

The inventor was first interested in the subject of heat conversion by a paragraph which appeared in a newspaper in 1882, which stated that there were three great inventions soon to come:—the direct conversion of heat into electricity; a light without heat, and a successful flying-machine.

"That set me to thinking, and I decided to investigate the first of the three. I was then nineteen years old and a railroad clerk, and saw little before me in that field. I spent much time reading, but found nothing on the subject, save the fact already stated concerning Prof. Seebeck's experiment. I began experimenting in a small way, and in the course of my work invented an electric railway signal,—a little apparatus by which a conductor can signal from within the cars to the engine. This helped me in a way, by bringing me $500, which I needed very badly. I sold the signal to a railroad company, and it did service for a time, although it has now been superseded by the Westinghouse whistle. With this money I supplied myself with an electrical apparatus, and, while steadily experimenting in one direction, discovered other practical things. Some small devices I was working upon at the time were seen by an agent of the German government, and I was called to Berlin, where I sold them. I also obtained money from the Russian government for a chemical formula, which they used in connection with their field batteries. With the money I maintained myself in Berlin, studied languages, read German books on electricity, interviewed German scientists and attended their lectures, all the while becoming more convinced of the possibility of accomplishing my purpose. I persevered until 1888, when I returned to New York and opened a small laboratory here, having learned enough to convince me that, with proper facilities, I should yet be successful. I perfected my machine in 1892. I may say that, from the beginning, I had always had in my mind a perfect picture of what I wanted to do, and only needed to work it out in metal. But getting metal harmoniously shaped and operative, is a long way from merely making sketches of it. There is always a hitch somewhere in the reality. I found the kinds of dissimilar metals that would give the greatest current for the least expenditure of heat. Then I spent several years in

Mr. H. Barrington Cox
The young inventor, who proposes to revolutionize present lighting methods

harmonizing the mechanical difficulties. The time from 1892 to 1895 was passed in testing it. I made duplicate machines, and placed them here and there to be watched and to have their defects noted. One machine ran, without stopping, for four years in my laboratory. The heat was never withdrawn and the electric fan never stopped. It was to test the durability of the machine. My experiments during those years took everything I had. No one can really understand the word 'disheartening,' until he sets himself to discover something in electricity. I would prepare a machine and attend supposedly to every detail. My hope would run with every step toward its completion. Then all would be ready, only to find upon the application of heat that all was wrong,—the work of months and the value of time and money all dissipated in a few minutes. At the collapse of the last machine, which preceded the successful one, one of my assistants,—a man who had worked with me for years,—broke down and cried. I remember he turned tearfully to me, and said, 'Why don't you cry?' 'That's what you're hired for,' I answered. He quit then, unable to begin again, but two weeks later I had the machine perfected."

Mr. Cox looks like a man who can endure rebuffs and still maintain an equable temper. He is tall and slim, with a Yankee twist to his physiognomy. His eyes are blue-gray, a kind of eye that seems to gaze unflinchingly into the face of all facts, favorable or destructive.

"Do you believe that it requires special aptitude,—a genius for discovery,—in order to thus take up a problem and solve it?" I asked him, at parting.

"I believe it takes an ordinary perception," he said modestly; "but what I am fully convinced of is that it takes ten times as much perseverance as it does brains. Any man having qualities in such a proportion could take any problem and solve it."

NOTES

"A Vision of Fairy Lamps: H. Barrington Cox," *Success* 1 (March 1898): 23. Signed "Edward Al."

1. Kenyon Cox (1856–1919), American painter, pupil of Carolus Duran and Jean Léon Gérôme in Paris, specialized in portraits, figure pieces, and mural decoration. Dreiser published a magazine article, "Work of Mrs. Kenyon Cox," *Cosmopolitan* 24 (March 1898): 477–80.

2. Thomas Johan Seebeck (1770–1831), German physicist, in 1821 made the first discovery of a thermoelectric effect, now called the Seebeck effect in his honor. He studied at Berlin and Göttingen and became a friend of Goethe, with whom he worked on a theory of color and the effect of colored light.

3

Life Stories of Successful Men—No. 11: Chauncey M. Depew

Chauncey Mitchell Depew, Orator, Humorist, Lawyer, Diplomat, and Controller of Thirty Railroad Companies—The Sturdy, Self-Reliant Country Boy Who Achieved Wealth and International Fame

OF THE BUSY MEN OF THE WORLD, THERE ARE NONE MORE SO THAN Chauncey M. Depew, until recently president of the New York Central and Hudson River Railroad, and now president of the Board which looks after all the Vanderbilt interests.[1] One must have something worthy his attention to gain admittance to the busy man, and I need say no more for the present interview than that the distinguished orator and statesman saw fit to discuss the possibilities of young men and their future, and gave readily of his time and opinions. I stated to him the object of my interview,—that it was intended to obtain his views as to what qualities in young men best make for success, and to ask him, if possible, to point out the way, by the aid of example, to better work and greater success for them. He smiled approvingly, and, to my question, whether, in his opinion, the opportunities awaiting ambitions young men are less or more than they have been in the past, replied:—

"More, decidedly more. Our needs in every field were never greater. The country is larger, and, while the population is greater, the means to supply its increased wants require more and more talent, so that any young man may gain a foothold who makes his effort with industry and intelligence."

"Do you mean to say that there is an excellent position awaiting everyone?"

"I mean to say that, while positions are not so numerous that any kind of a young man will do, yet they are so plentiful that you can scarcely find a

Mr. Depew in his private office in New York City

young man of real energy and intelligence who does not hold a responsible position of some kind. The chief affairs are in the hands of young men."

"Was it different in your day, when you were beginning?"

"Energy and industry told heavily in the balance then, as now, but the high places were not available for young men because the positions were not in existence. We had to make the places, in those days; and not only that, but we were obliged to call ourselves to the tasks. To-day, a man fits himself and is called. There are more things to do."

"How was it with boys, in your day, who wanted to get an education?"

"With most of them, it was a thing to earn. Why, the thing that I knew more about than anything else, as I grew from year to year, was the fact that I had nothing to expect, and must look out for myself. I can't tell you how clear my parents made this point to me. It absolutely glittered, so plain was it."

"Your parents were Americans?"

"Yes. I was born at Peekskill, in 1834."

Although Mr. Depew modestly refrains from discussing his ancestry, he comes from the best New England stock. He descends, through remote paternal ancestors, from French Huguenots, who were among those who came to America in the early days of the country, and who founded the village of New Rochelle, in Westchester county.[2] His mother, Martha Mitchell, was of illustrious and patriotic New England descent, being a member of the family to which belonged Roger Sherman, a signer of the Declaration of Independence; and he is a lineal descendant of the Rev. Josiah Sherman, chaplain of the Seventh Connecticut Continental infantry, and of Gabriel Ogden, of the New Jersey militia, both of whom served in the American Revolution.[3]

"Had you any superior advantages in the way of money, books, or training?" I continued.

"If you want to call excellent training a superior advantage, I had it. Training was a great point with us. We trained with the plow, the ax, and almost any other implement we could lay our hands on. I might even call the switch used at our house an early advantage, and, I might say, superior to any other in our vicinity. I had some books, but our family was not rich, even for those times. We were comfortably situated, nothing more."

"Do you owe more to your general reading than you do to your early school training?"

"Yes, I think so. I attended the school in our village regularly, until I went to college; but I was not distinguished for scholarship, except on the ballground."

"Do you attribute much of your success in life to physical strength?"

"It is almost indispensable. I was always strong. The conditions tended to make strong men, in those days. I went to college in my eighteenth year. I think I acquired a broader view there, and sound ideals which have been great helps. It was not a period of toil, however, as some would have made it."

His time at Yale was in no respect wasted. The vigorous, athletic, fun-loving boy was developing into a man with a strength and independence of character, very imperfectly understood at first by the already long list of men who liked him.

"What profession did you fix upon as the field for your life work?" I asked.

"That of the law. I always looked forward to that; and, after my graduation, in 1856, I went into a law office (that of Hon. William Nelson,) at Peekskill, and prepared for practice. That was a time of intense political excitement. There were factions in the Democratic party, and the Whig party seemed to be passing away. The Republican party, or People's party, as it had first been called, was organized in 1856, and men were changing from side to side. Naturally, I was mixed in the argument, and joined the Republican party.

"When I was graduated at Yale College, in 1856," he continued, "I came home to the village of Peekskill to meet my father, my grandfather, my uncles and my brothers, all old Hunker, state-rights, pro-slavery Democrats. But I had been through the fiery furnace of the Kansas-Nebraska excitement at New Haven, and had come out of it a free-soil Republican.

Two days after my return, I stood, a trembling boy, upon a platform to give voice in the campaign which was then in progress, to that conversion which nearly broke my father's heart, and almost severed me from all family ties. It seemed then as if the end of the world had come for me in the necessity for this declaration of convictions and principles, but I expressed my full belief. In this sense, I believe a young man should be strong, and that such difficult action is good for him."

"Is that where you began your career as an orator?" I asked.

"You mean as a stump-speaker? Yes. I talked for Fremont and Dayton, our candidates, but they were defeated. We really did not expect success, though, and yet we carried eleven states. After that, I went back to my law books, and was admitted to the bar in 1858. That was another campaign year, and I spoke for the party then, as I did two years later, when I was a candidate for the State Assembly, and won."

The real glory hidden by this modest statement is that Mr. Depew's oratory in the campaign of 1858 gained him such distinction that he was too prominent to be passed over in 1860. During that campaign, he stumped the entire State, winning rare oratorical triumphs, and aiding the party almost more than anyone else. How deep an impression the young member from Peekskill really made in the state legislature by his admirable mastery of the complex public business brought before him, may be gathered from the fact that when, two years later, he was reelected, he was speedily made chairman of the committee on ways and means. He was also elected speaker, *pro tem.,* and at the next election, when his party was practically defeated all along the line, he was returned.

After briefly referring to the active part he took in the Lincoln campaign, I asked:—

"When did you decide upon your career as a railroad official?"

"In 1866. I was retained by Commodore Vanderbilt as attorney for the New York and Harlem Road."

"To what do you attribute your rise as an official in that field?"

"Hard work. That was a period of railroad growth. There were many small roads and plenty of warring elements. Out of these many small roads, when once united, came the great systems which now make it possible to reach California in a few days. Anyone who entered upon the work at that time had to encounter those conditions, and if he continued at it, to change them. I was merely a counselor at first."

In 1869, Mr. Depew was made attorney for the New York Central and Hudson River Railroad, and afterwards a director. This was the period of the development of the Vanderbilt system. Mr. Depew was a constant adviser of the Vanderbilts, and, by his good judgment and sagacious counsel, maintained their constant respect and friendship. In 1875, he was made general counsel for the entire system and a director in each one of the roads.

It has often been urged by the sinister-minded, that it was something against him to have gained so much at the hands of the Vanderbilts. The truth is that this is his chief badge of honor. Many times he has won influence and votes for the Vanderbilt interests, but always by the use of wit, oratorical persuasion and legitimate, honorable argument,—never by the methods of the lobbyist. Commodore Vanderbilt engaged him as counsel for the New York Central Railroad, at a salary of $25,000 a year,— then equal to the salary of the President of the United States,—and he always acknowledged that Mr. Depew earned the money.

He is now the head of the entire Vanderbilt system, or the controlling spirit of thirty distinct railroads, besides being a director in the Wagner Palace Car Company, the Union Trust Company, the Western Union Telegraph Company, the Equitable Life Insurance Society, the Western Transit Company, the West Shore and International Bridge Company, the Morris Run Coal Mining Company, the Clearfield Bituminous Coal Corporation, the Hudson River Bridge Company, the Canada Southern Bridge Company, the Niagara River Bridge Company, the Niagara Grand Island Bridge Company, the Tonawanda Island Bridge Company, the American Safe Deposit Company, the Mutual Gas Light Company, and the Brooklyn Storage and Warehouse Company.

"How much of your time each day," I asked, "have you given, upon an average, to your professional duties?"

"Only a moderate number of hours. I do not believe in overwork. The affairs of life are not important enough to require it, and the body cannot endure it. Just an ordinary day's labor of eight or ten hours has been my standard."

"Your official duties never drew you wholly from the political field, I believe?"

"Entirely, except special needs of the party, when I have been urged to accept one task after another. I believe that every man's energies should be at the disposal of his country."

"On the political side, what do you think is the essential thing for success?"

"The very things that are essential anywhere else—honesty, consistency and hard work."

"It requires no strain of character, no vacillation?"

"For twenty-five years," answered Mr. Depew, "I was on all occasions in the front of political battles, and I never found that political opinions or activity made it necessary to break friendships or make them."

Mr. Depew's political career is already so well known that it need not be reviewed here.

After three years of service as vice-president of the New York Central Railroad, he was elevated, in 1885, to the presidency. While thus given a position of great influence in the business world, his growing reputation made him eligible for greater political honors than any for which he had yet been named. In 1888 he was the Presidential candidate of the republicans of New York State, at the national convention of the party, and received the solid vote of his State delegation, but withdrew his name. President Harrison offered him the position of secretary of state, to succeed Mr. Blaine, but he again declined.[4]

"What do you think of the opportunities to-day? Has the recent war aided us?"

"It is the best thing for the young man of to-day that could have happened! The new possessions mean everything to young men, who are going to be old men by and by. We, as a nation, are going to find, by the wise utilization of the conditions forced upon us, how to add incalculably to American enterprise and opportunity by becoming masters of the sea, and entering, with the surplus of our manufactures, the markets of the world. The solid merchants are to undertake the extension of American trade, but the young men will be called in to do the work under their guidance. The young man who is ready is naturally the one chosen."

"You think a tide of prosperity waits for every young American?"

"It may not exactly wait, but he can catch it easily."

"It is said," I went on, "that any field or profession carefully followed, will bring material success. Is that the thing to be aimed at?"

"Material success does not constitute an honorable aim. If that were true, a grasping miser would be the most honorable creature on earth, while a man like Gladstone, great without money, would have been an impossibility.[5] The truth is that material success is usually the result of a great aim, which looks to some great public improvement. Some man plans to be an intelligent servant of some great public need, and the result of great energy in serving the public intelligently is wealth. It never has been possible to become notable in this respect in any other way."

"It is often said that the excellent opportunities for young men are gone."

"If you listen to ordinary comment," said Mr. Depew, "you can come to believe that almost anything is dead—patriotism, honor, possibilities, trade—in fact, anything, and it's all according with whom you talk. There was a belief, not long ago, that the great orators were dead, and had left no successors. Papers and magazines were said to supply this excellent tonic. Yet orators have appeared, great ones, and in the face of the beauty and grace and fire which animate some of them, you read the speeches of the older celebrities, and wonder what it was in them that stirred men."

"And this field is also open to young men?"

"Not as a profession, of course, but as a means to real distinction, certainly. The field was never before so open. I have listened to Stephen A.

Douglas, with his vigorous argument, slow enunciation and lack of magnetism, to Abraham Lincoln, with his resistless logic and quaint humor; to Tom Corwin, Salmon P. Chase, William H. Seward, Charles Sumner, and Wendell Phillips; and, as I look back and recall what they said, and the effect which they produced, and then estimate what they might do with the highly cultivated and critical audiences of to-day, I see the opportunity that awaits the young man here.[6] Only Wendell Phillips strikes me as possessing qualities which are not yet duplicated or surpassed."

"You recognize more that one kind of success in this world, then?"

"Yes; we can't all be Presidents of the United States. Any man is successful who does well what comes to his hand, and who works to improve himself so that he may do it better. The man with the ideal, struggling to carry it out, is the successful man. Of course, there are all grades of ideals, and the man with the highest, given the proportionate energy, is the most successful. The world makes way for that kind of young man. I know we would do it in the railroad world."

"Do you consider that happiness in the successful man consists in reflecting over what he has done or what he may do?"

"I should say that it consists in both. No man who has accomplished a great deal could sit down and fold his hands. The enjoyment of life would be instantly gone if you removed the possibility of doing something. When through with his individual affairs, a man wants a wider field, and of course that can only be in public affairs. Whether the beginner believes it or not, he will find that he cannot drop interest in life at the end, whatever he may think about it in the beginning."

"The aim of the young man of to-day should be, then—?"

"To do something worth doing, honestly. Get wealth, if it is gotten in the course of an honorable public service. I think, however, the best thing to get is the means of doing good, and then doing it. It is the most satisfactory aim I know of."

NOTES

"Life Stories of Successful Men—No. 11: Chauncey M. Depew," *Success* 1 (November 1898): 3–4. Reprinted as "A Life of Aspiration—The Career of Senator Depew" in *Talks with Great Workers,* 1–11; also as "A Village Boy's Gift of Oratory Earns Him Wealth and Fame—Chauncey M. Depew" in *Little Visits with Great Americans,* 207–18.

1. Cornelius Vanderbilt (1794–1877), American financier.

2. Huguenots were members of the Protestant political faction in France that first took shape in 1560. They constituted one of the parties in the French religious wars during most of the rest of the sixteenth century and became less important through much of the seventeenth century.

3. Roger Sherman (1721–93), American jurist and statesman, was a signer of the Declaration of Independence.

4. Benjamin Harrison (1833–1901), 23rd President of the United States (1889–93). James Gillespie Blaine (1830–93), American statesman, was Secretary of State.

5. William Ewart Gladstone (1809–98), British statesman, was Prime Minister (1868–74, 1880–85, 1886, 1892–94).

6. Stephen Arnold Douglas (1813–61), American politician. Thomas Corwin (1794–1865), American political leader, opposed the Mexican War, contending it was being waged for gaining territory. He was in the U.S. Senate (1845–50). Salmon Portland Chase (1808–73), American statesman, was Chief Justice of U.S. Supreme Court (1864–73). William Henry Seward (1801–72), American statesman, was Secretary of State (1861–69). Charles Sumner (1811–74), American statesman and orator. Wendell Phillips (1811–84), American orator and reformer.

4

A Leader of Young Manhood:
Frank W. Gunsaulus

Frank W. Gunsaulus, Orator, Educator, Practical Reformer, and Founder of the Armour Institute— Millions Raised by a Single Sermon

ONE OF THE BRIGHTEST EXAMPLES OF EARLY SUCCESS IN LIFE IS FRANK W. Gunsaulus, D.D., one of the sincerest friends of young men striving to climb upward, that America has produced.[1] Chicago has helped him, and he has helped Chicago, to do great things. During his six years of ministry in that city, before he left the pulpit and became president of Armour Institute, he founded two notable institutions and raised over $7,000,000 in money for charitable purposes. On the stormiest of Sunday evenings, after a newspaper announcement that he will speak, an audience two thousand five hundred strong will gather to hear him. It was not an uncommon sight, during his last series of winter sermons, for men anxious to hear the splendid orator, to be lifted through windows of Central Music Hall, when no more could get in at the doors. His most conspicuous labor has been the founding of the famous Armour Institute of Technology, which now has twelve hundred students, and of which he is the president.[2]

CAN A PREACHER BE A POWER?

I found him in the president's office of Armour Institute.

"Do you think," I said, "that it is more difficult for a preacher to become a power in a nation than it is for a merchant, a lawyer, or a politician?"

"Rather hard to say," he answered. "There are prejudices against and sympathies in favor of every class and profession. I think, however, that a preacher is more like a doctor in his career. He is likely to make a strong local impression, but not apt to become a national figure. Given powerful convictions, an undertaking of things as they are to-day, and steady work in the direction of setting things right, and you may be sure a man is at least heading in the direction of public favor, whether he ever attains it or not."

"How did you manage to do the work you have done, in so short a time?"

"In the first place, I don't think I have done so very much; and, in the second place, the time seems rather long for what I have done. I have worked hard, however.

"I thought to be a lawyer in my youth, and did study law and oratory. My father was a country lawyer at Chesterfield, Ohio, where I was born, and was a member of the Ohio Legislature during the war. He was a very effective public speaker himself and thought that I ought to be an orator. So he did everything to give me a bent in that direction, and often took me as many as twenty miles to hear a good oration.

Men Who Influence Him

"I admired Fisher Ames, to begin with, and, of course, Webster.[3] I think Wendell Phillips and Bishop Matthew Simpson, whom I heard a few times, had the greatest influence on me.[4] I considered them wonderful, moving speakers, and I do yet. Later on, Henry Ward Beecher and Phillips Brooks attracted my admiration."[5]

"Did you have leisure for study and time to hear orations when you were beginning life?"

"In early years, I attended the district school. From twelfth to my eighteenth year, I worked on the farm and studied nights. For all my father's urgings toward the bar, I always felt an inward drawing toward the ministry, because I felt that I could do more there. My father was not a member of any church, though my mother was an earnest Presbyterian. Without any prompting from my parents, I leaned toward the ministry, and finally entered it of my own accord. I was fortunate enough to find a young companion who was also studying for the ministry. We were the best of friends and helped each other a great deal. It was our custom to prepare sermons and preach them in each others' presence. Our audience in that case, unlike that of the church, never hesitated to point out errors. The result was that some sermons ended in arguments between the audience and the preacher, as to facts involved.

He Did Not Pretend to Piety

"I was graduated from the Ohio Wesleyan Seminary in debt. I had no reputation for piety, and I don't remember that I pretended to any. I had convictions, however, and a burning desire to do something, to achieve something for the benefit of my fellowmen, and I was ready for the first opportunity."

"Was it long in coming?"

"No, but you would not have considered it much of an opportunity. I took charge of a small church at Harrisburg, Ohio, at a salary of three hundred and twenty dollars a year. In preaching regularly I soon found it necessary to formulate some kind of a theory of life,—to strike for some definite object. I began to feel the weight of the social problem."

ARE THE DICE OF LIFE LOADED?

"One important fact began to make itself plain, and that was that the modern young man is more or less discouraged by the growing belief that all things are falling into the hands of great corporations and trusts, and that the individual no longer has much chance. My father had been more or less of a fatalist in his view of life, and often quoted Emerson to me, to the effect that the dice of life are loaded, and fall according to a plan. My mother leaned to the doctrine of Calvin,—to predestination. I inherited a streak of the same feeling, and the conditions I observed made me feel that there was probably something in the theory. I had to battle this down and convince myself that we are what we choose to make ourselves. Then I had to get to work to counteract the discouraging view taken by the young people about me."

"You were a Methodist, then?"

"Yes, I was admitted to preach in that body, but it was not long before I had an attack of transcendentalism, and fell out with the Methodist elder of my district. The elder was wholly justified. He was a dry old gentleman, with a fund of common sense. After one of my flights, in which I advocated perfection far above the range of humankind, he came to me and said: 'My dear young man, don't you know that people have to live on this planet?' The rebuke struck me as earthly then, but it has grown in humor and common sense since.

"I left voluntarily. I knew I was not satisfactory, and so I went away. I married when I was twenty. I preached in several places, and obtained a charge at Columbus, Ohio."

A MINISTER'S TRUE IDEAL

"When did you begin to have a visible influence on affairs, such as you have since exercised?"

"Just as soon as I began to formulate and follow what I considered to be the true ideal of the minister."

"And that ideal was?"

"That the question to be handled by a preacher must not be theological, but sociological."

"How did this conviction work out at Columbus?"

"The church became too small for the congregation, and so we had to move to the opera house.

"My work there showed me that any place may be a pulpit,—editorial chair, managerial chair, almost anything. I began to realize that a whole and proper work would be to get hold of the Christian forces outside the ecclesiastical machine and get them organized into activity. I was not sure about my plan yet, however, and so I left Columbus for Newtonville, Massachusetts, and took time to review my studies. There I came under the influence of Phillips Brooks. When I began once more to get a clear idea of what I wanted to do, I went to Baltimore, on a call, and preached two years at Brown Memorial Presbyterian Church.

"I came to Chicago in 1872. Plymouth Church offered an absolutely free pulpit, and an opportunity to work out some plans that I thought desirable."

His Work in Chicago

"How did you go about your work in this city?"

"The first thing that seemed necessary for me to do was to find a place where homeless boys of the city who had drifted into error and troubles of various kinds could be taken into the country and educated. I preached a sermon on this subject, and one member gave a fine farm of two hundred and forty acres for the purpose. Plymouth Church built Plymouth Cottage there, and the Illinois Training School was moved there, and other additions were made, gradually adding to its usefulness."

"The church grew under your ministration there, did it not?"

"You can leave off that about me. It grew, yes, and we established a mission."

"Was there not a sum raised for this?"

"Yes; Mr. Joseph Armour gave a hundred thousand dollars to house this mission, and the church has since aided it in various ways."

"This Armour Institute is an idea of yours, is it not?"

"Well, it is in line with my ideas in what it accomplishes. It is the outcome of Mr. Armour's great philanthropy."

"Do you find, now that you have experimented so much, that your ideals concerning what ought to be done for the world were too high?" I asked.

"On the contrary," answered Dr. Gunsaulus, "I have sometimes felt that they were not high enough. If they had been less than they are, I should not have accomplished what I have."

"What has been your experience as to working hours?"

"I have worked twelve and fourteen, at times even eighteen hours a day, particularly when I was working to establish this institution, but I paid for it dearly. I suffered a paralytic stroke which put me on my back for nine months, and in that time you see I not only suffered, but lost all I had gained by the extra hours."

How to Meet Great Emergencies

"You believe in meeting great emergencies with great individual energy?"

"There doesn't seem to be any way out of it. A man must work hard, extra hard, at times, or lose many a battle."

"You have mingled in public affairs here in Chicago, also, have you not?"

"Yes. I have always tried to do my share."

"You believe the chances for young men to-day are as good as in times gone by?"

"I certainly do. That is my whole doctrine. The duties devolving on young men are growing greater, more important, more valuable all the time. The wants of the world seem to grow larger, more urgent every day. What all young men need to do is to train themselves. They must train their hands to deftness, train their eyes to see clearly, and their ears to hear and understand. Look at the call there is going to be upon young men when this country will be organizing its new possessions and opening up new fields of activity. What the world needs is young men equipped to do the work. There is always work to be done."

"You think, in your own field, there is a call for energetic young men?"

"It never was greater. A young preacher who looks around him, studies the conditions, finds out just a few of the ten thousand important things that are going begging for someone to do them, and then proceeds to work for their accomplishment, will succeed beyond his wildest dreams.

"The world looks for leaders, it looks for men who are original, able and practical; and all I have got to say to a young man is simply to find out clearly all about a need in a certain direction, and then lead on to the alleviation in it. Money, influence, honor, will all follow along after, to help."

Notes

"A Leader of Young Manhood: Frank W. Gunsaulus," *Success* 2 (15 December 1898): 23–24; Reprinted as "The Power of Oratory; And Counsel by a Leader of Young Men" in *Talks with Great Workers,* 323–30; also as "An Inspiring Personality Wins a Noted Preacher Fame—Frank W. Gunsaulus" in *Little Visits with Great Americans,* 432–40.

1. Frank W. Gunsaulus, D. D. (1856–1921).

2. Philip Danforth Armour (1832–1901), American financier and philanthropist, gave financial support for the foundation of the Armour Institute of Technology. Dreiser wrote a magazine article, "Life Stories of Successful Men—No. 10: Philip D. Armour," *Success* 1 (October 1898): 3–4; reprinted in *Selected Magazine Articles,* 1:120–29.

3. Fisher Ames (1758–1808), American Federalist leader eloquently championed strong central government based on an aristocracy of "the wise and good and opulent." Daniel Webster (1782–1852), American statesman and orator.

4. Wendell Phillips (1811–84), American orator and reformer.

5. Henry Ward Beecher (1813–87), American clergyman. Phillips Brooks (1835–93), American bishop.

5

Champ Clark, the Man and His District

Photo by Frances B. Johnston

No one that has met the Honorable Congressman from the
Ninth Missouri would doubt that Champ Clark comes from a part of the
country as characterful as himself.[1] His broad face, stout body, keen, gray
eyes and restful manner mark him emphatically for the West. There is
something in the pursed lips, set against even teeth, the broad brimmed hat,
pushed genially back upon the forehead, the heave of the body by which he
rests now on one foot, now on the other, that shows him to hail from
a region where easy manners and aggressive independence are still the
rule in the individual, and not the exception. When he utters his slow,
measured, "I hope *you all* will excuse me," he settles conjecture. "*You
all*" is good *Missouri* for you. In the famous Pike County, where he

lives, you will hear nothing better than this. He gets his style from his constituents.

The Ninth Missouri is proud of Champ Clark. The whole state admires him, but the Ninth considers him a fine type of itself. There you will hear him spoken of by his good, old hidebound Democratic supporters as you hear fathers speak of their sons.

"Champ's a pretty able man," they will tell you, with a fine mental reserve. "He's as smart as a whip."

If you imagine this is poor praise, accuse Champ Clark of being a poor twig of Democracy. Then you will hear something which will make clear why he is invincible in his district. When Missourians of the old school like a man, they like him all over.

"Oh, Clark's got good friends out here," one said to me. "His best ones 'ud go through hell and water to save him, I guess. He's as smart a man as you'd want for that job."

To understand a political character of this sort, we must understand his district. The average Congressman at Washington, neatly dressed, smooth-mannered and pleasantly conversing upon broad American principles, savors little of the crude condition from which he has sprung. In the luxurious atmosphere of Washington, the rough county trailer walks a different man. He meets a class who may never have seen the rough district with which he is so familiar. He enters an entirely different world, a world where his position is accepted, where the means by which he has risen are unrecognized. Here he is a Congressman, pure and simple, with all the dignity that attaches to the office, with all the smallness that it may indicate.

Back of him may be, as in the present case, a country and a people wholly strange to the capital atmosphere. The land is of meagre population, of crude habitation, of old-fashioned ideas, of simple, almost primitive, amusements. The long roads lie untraveled save by the hardest necessity. The fields may be cultivated in the crudest way. The majority may not see a railroad train once in three weeks. A daily newspaper may be a rarity, except in the case of the best of the local families. The fathers are rough and husky—their one comfort their home, their one diversion, politics. The mothers are excellent housewives, whose world consists of husband and children. The children, hale, quiet-mannered youngsters, have a drawl of voice and manner which would make their city cousins stare. Often they are studious, and of that solid stuff which reinforces the cities with brain and brawn, and gives to the world men of mark. When you find such a district, you will sometimes find a man who represents it. Such a representative is Champ Clark.

The Honorable Congressman from the Ninth has a district which is as interesting as he is. It is one of the fifteen gerrymandered portions of

Missouri which have sent to Washington such men as Dockery, of Gallatin, Cowherd, of Kansas City, Bland, of Lebanon.

It was the Eighth, which adjoins Clark's district on the west, that, barring one term, kept Bland at Washington from 1873 until the day of his death. It is the Third that has done nearly as well by Dockery. The Ninth is one which is gerrymandered, but not in Clark's favor. It has a great many more Democrats than it needs to elect a Congressman.

"We was just a-wasting votes up here until we decided to help out the Thirteenth," one white-headed patriarch said to me, "so we threw out two counties and took in Gasconade and Crawford. They're naturally Republican, but when they're in with us they can't do much damage."

These two sad-fated Republican counties now cast their votes in vain. A rousing three thousand majority greets the Democratic nominee, whoever he may be, providing the Democrats are not quarreling among themselves, which happens not infrequently.

In this district the voters are known personally to the leaders, the leaders are solid men of the community. An element of individuality comes into play, and on which the leaders must count. The average citizen knows his own district as he knows his best horse. He can tell you just what it can do politically and financially. He is proud of its towns and its country districts, of its fertility and beauty. The man of the Ninth sees it in his mind's eye a long, straggling line of counties, shaped almost like the continent of Africa. He knows where the good towns are, where the rich valleys lie, where the streams run. He has heard of the political squabbles of this place, the financial difficulties of that. Jonesburgh, Montgomery County, is going to have a new opera house. So it is, to be sure. When you tell him that, it is of the same nature to him as information concerning his brother's eldest boy's success. It is all family information.

The residents of such a district are proud enough to want a good leader. It is the district they love, more than the Congressman who represents it, but when a Congressman arises, who, by the very qualities which they admire, distinguishes himself, who has somewhat about him of the atmosphere and the soil which they are accustomed to, that man comes to embody for them the spirit of their local world. His manners are the manners of the district; his sentiments are the sentiments of the district. He walks abroad shod as they are shod and strong as they are strong. He comes to have their failings, as well as their virtues, and at last he is their representative. No one can beat him. There is no need for any one to try.

It takes a sterling sort of people to make a sterling leader. The men must have independence, the women virtue. Out in the Ninth they have both. One still finds family life there operating almost upon a patriarchal basis. It is a region of large families, as well as of large convictions. The father who has nine stalwart sons is not a rarity.

"I just met Brother Weemans over here," said Congressman Clark while canvassing Gasconade County in 1896. It was during one of those long buggy rides over rough roads from one small town to another, and all sorts of topics were seized upon to relieve the tedium. "He's got nine strapping boys, and had 'em all there to shake hands with me. Said he wisht he had nine girls so he could make 'em all marry Democrats who would vote for me also. Good old man, Weemans is."

There are families much larger and just as loyal. They live and propagate in one region, and finally become exceedingly numerous and of one name. There is a family of Tates in Montgomery County, seventy or more strong, all living in one neighborhood, and all Democrats. A family of Homans in another section of the district is equally numerous and equally Democratic. Family feeling does not end with one household. It extends to the homes of every son and daughter, and to the homes of their children and their children's children in turn. Speak of the Swart family out there and you are thought to be referring to several scores of Swarts, scattered all over the district. Family reunions are common, and embrace such multitudes that camping out is resorted to, and a picnic indulged in while they last.

Among the members of families blood feeling is strong. They concern themselves with one another, not so much to praise as to regulate. You must be industrious and energetic; your children must be well trained and sent to school. Your wife must know how to cook and keep a good home. They gently advise to this end constantly. It is taken for granted that this is the ideal of all. Whole families ride together for miles over rough, almost impassible, roads, to get together and discuss these things. Christmas and Fourth of July are times of the largest reunions. Election periods are the times when principles are thrashed over and party spirit unifies.

Champ Clark has little, if any, blood kin, as the word is there, but a vast number of political and social friends who are close as blood could make them. Most of the Democrats of the nine counties claim a speaking acquaintance with him. Most of them have entertained him at one time or another. He has stopped at their gates, dined at their tables, slept for a night in their best spare bedrooms. He has talked politics with the fathers, encouraged and strengthened the political views of the sons.

Among his chief adherents you find men who have sacrificed not only time and labor, but hard earned money, in the cause of their political idol. In almost every case, they expect nothing and receive nothing. Their reward is the triumph of their affections and prejudices.

"I went to my brother Morg," said one of Clark's supporters, in describing the latter's first Congressional fight, "and begged him to let up on Clark. 'It doesn't make any difference to you,' I said. 'Why do you help my enemies? You know his enemies are my enemies. For God's sake, turn once now and help me.'"

"Did he?" I asked.

"Yes, he did."

"And why did you make such a fight for the man?"

"I liked him. He's my friend. He is a friend of all my friends."

In the nine counties there are but 153,000 people, 60,000 of whom are gathered into small towns. The remaining 93,000 are scattered over 3,000,000 acres of land. If all families were of the state's average size— five and one-half members—and these were evenly scattered over the district, there would be one such family to every 200 acres. As it is, with the large families prevailing in the country there are large tracts of rough, wooded land, low hills receding behind low hills, where you will scarce encounter a habitation. Throughout the entire district there are scarcely a hundred brick houses. You may travel for miles and miles and encounter nothing better than one-story log cabins, built of quarter sawed oak or hickory, and filled in between with plaster. Many cabins have mud floors. Plastered walls and ceilings are rare. Old style furniture abounds, great, crude walnut beds, old-fashioned rag carpets, piece quilts of the forties, clocks, coffee mills and stoves that have been in use anywhere from forty to a hundred years. Also old manners and old customs, to say nothing of a dialect, celebrated by Miss Craik as being common to Tennessee. These things are not the rule, but off the main-traveled roads, and on those little wagon tracks which follow the shallow beds of streams, you will find them.

The county seat of Montgomery County is Montgomery City, which has one railroad and a population of 2,000. It is said to be the best town on the Wabash Railroad between St. Louis and Moberly. It is a good place from a trade point of view. Cattle, poultry, hides, dairy products and cereals are shipped from here. There are well-to-do citizens, men who have from fifty to one hundred thousand dollars, and yet Montgomery is without gas or electric light. The streets are unpaved, the water supply is one of wells and cisterns, and the houses are nearly all of one story. As much might be said for Bowling Green, the county seat of Pike County, and the home of Congressman Clark, as well as of Herman, of Gasconade, Steelville, of Crawford, Warrenton, of Warren, and several other places. Some of these have electric lights and made roads. At Montgomery cordwood is piled in front of the stores.

This is the region of the Missourian simonpure. You will find many a Champ Clark loitering about the public square or moving with that easy grace so common to country towns. The big, broad-brimmed, soft felt hat, the long coat, and flat, broad-toed shoes are worn by doctors, lawyers and politicians. Another type, equally numerous, wears the broad-brimmed, soft, white felt hat and heavy, red-topped boots. They are the men of corduroy jackets, and corduroy trousers tucked away in their boots.

Such are the men, such is the region to which Champ Clark appeals for his election every two years. Here he returns after each session, and here holds political conferences. He has staunch supporters in almost every county, leaders who organize and work for him, and who see that every voter is gotten out and lined up in his favor. There is a district Congressional committee composed of nine men, one from each county, and every man a leader in his county. They are presided over by W. L. Gupton, of Montgomery, one of the shrewdest of the executive politicians, and a warm friend of Clark. These men say little and think a great deal. They give the enemy no opportunity to catch them napping. It is watch, watch, watch all the time, against factional uprisings within the party. Every now and then comes a Democrat to oust Clark from his position. Then Gupton and his associates look after Clark's fences and dig the pit for the enemy.

Champ Clark came to Missouri in 1875, from his "last job," as he called it, in West Virginia, where from 1873 to 1874 he had been president of the first normal school established in that state. From 1874 to 1875 he attended a law school at Cincinnati, Ohio, but that, as he has said, did not count. He was born in Kentucky, at Lawrenceburg, Anderson County, in 1850, and left that state when he entered Bethany College in West Virginia. Up to the time he arrived in Missouri, he had earned his living and paid his way by serving at intervals as hired hand on a farm, as clerk in a country store, as district school teacher, and what not, reading law at night. For one year he was principal of the high school at Louisiana, in the county where he now lives. Then he opened a law office at Bowling Green, the county seat of Pike, where he has practiced ever since, except while in Congress. He mixed in politics, and though not a man to be counted social. He made sufficient friends to start him on his career. He became first assistant prosecuting attorney, and then prosecuting attorney of Pike County. Later he was editor of the *Riverside,* now the *Louisiana Press,* and then ran successfully for the State Assembly. At the close of his term he felt able to try for the Congressional nomination. He began to look around him for those friends and that assistance which he has since retained and increased. His long residence in Bowling Green had gained him a reputation on which he could rest a plea for financial assistance to carry on the campaign in case he got the district nomination.

In 1890, when he first applied for the Congressional nomination of his district, Clark was forty years old, and thoroughly experienced in the politics of his county and state. He was poorer then than he is now. Of temperament more or less poetic he was inclined, because of his seeming narrow fate, to be morose. What were the small duties of a State Assemblyman to him? He felt he was fitted for larger duties. He had learning, he had ideals. He admired Aaron Burr and the invincible Benton.[2] If he wished to emulate the example of any man it was that of Benton, with his strength to follow an ideal to his own political destruction.

At this time Richard H. Norton was Congressman, and had been for several terms. He had served faithfully, but without distinction. He was neither a favorite nor an object of dislike. In an eastern district, with a strong party organization, Norton could have endured by mere force of successful precedence. In a district like the Ninth, however, which possesses so much individuality, it could be only a matter of time before unrest would manifest itself. The voters love their district too well not to want to hear of it in the national councils. When the average man represents it, his tenure of office is never settled. His fight for re-election is never closed.

In the present instance, the district Congressional committee which looks after the fences of the Congressman in office was neutral. The members knew something of Clark and liked him. When he inquired whether he could get the nomination, they were friendly enough to advise him to try. Four of the nine counties, they told him, would send up county delegations to the district convention, which would be solid for Norton. Four others he could probably secure for himself by a personal canvass. One county, Audrain, was doubtful. If he could go into Audrain and capture the primaries, so that the county delegation would be instructed to vote for him, he might enter the fight with some hope of winning the nomination. Since nomination here is equivalent to election, it may be imagined how hotly these preliminary movements are contested.

Clark invaded Audrain County, but after traveling it over several times, he realized that he could not carry the primaries, and so withdrew from the fight and returned to Bowling Green. He passed the intermediate two years until the next canvass, practicing law. Yet he was not idle politically. He had made up his mind to become Congressman, and he rummaged the entire district, picking up acquaintances, getting himself introduced and studying the political desires of his future constituents. All the old hard-shell Democrats were pleased with him. They saw in him the *representative* which Norton was not. Even on the district Congressional committee, a body supposedly organized to look after Norton's interest, were men who viewed the new aspirant with a kindly eye. Norton had been a compromise candidate. Factional squabbles in the party had brought him to the fore.

In his first canvass, Clark came close to the one man who has done him more good than any other in the district; the man on whose shrewdness and political sagacity, indeed his election to Congress has depended, namely, W. L. Gupton. He had known Gupton since 1881, when the latter was County Clerk of Montgomery. Since that day, however, Gupton had steadily risen, until in 1890, he was president of a small bank at Jonesburg, and a promising political leader. Gupton knew every person in his own county by name and history, and was fairly familiar with the principal Democrats of the other counties. When Clark approached Gupton to discuss the possibility of his getting the Congressional nomination, Gupton figured out that if he could carry the primaries of Audrain and have that county send up a solid Clark delegation to the district convention, he would win. Gupton proposed to get him four delegates from Montgomery County in addition, which would have given him forty-three to Norton's thirty-five votes in the district convention. However, as previously stated, after looking over Audrain, the canvass was not made.

After two years, however, Clark was better able to make a fight. He had met the sound, old Democratic farmers, and had been assured of their personal favor. Not much of a man to talk, there was yet something in his quiet, reserved manner which won people. When the time came for holding the primaries to elect the delegates to the convention which would name the Democratic candidate, Clark had so contrived that he was moderately sure of carrying Audrain. His own county, Pike and two others, Ralls and Lincoln, were, thanks to the sagacity of his political friend and adherent, David Ball, now a candidate for Governor of Missouri, considered safe. The other four counties were controlled by Norton's men. This left one county, Montgomery, uncertain. Norton reasonably supposed that this county would sent up delegates pledged to him. Clark, however, had Gupton there.

The policy adopted in this fight by Gupton was to concede everything apparently to Norton and so to ward off a thorough canvass until it was too late. His plan was to spring suddenly a majority of Clark Democrats at the primaries and have them choose only Clark delegates. This scheme would have worked well enough had not one of Gupton's men spoken of it to one who was considered a Clark Democrat, but, in reality, was a Norton Democrat. The news spread quickly, and the next day it was plain that the biggest fight of the canvass would take place right where everything was thought to be safe.

In Montgomery County the Democrats, irrespective of Norton's personality, were some for and some against Clark, owing to his record on the division of the courts. Montgomery, like many another county, had for years been torn with dissension over the question of whether the county seat should remain at Danville or be removed to Montgomery City. The former place was and still is the county seat, but Montgomery City is by far the largest town in the county. It has the railroad, the population, the trade. Danville has the court-house. For long Montgomery had schemed to get the court-house. It had looked to it that such State Assemblymen as it could elect were men pledged to fight for the change at Jefferson City. On the contrary, Danville and the other towns of the county, jealous of Montgomery City, were equally determined to frustrate its ambition. The fight was carried into the State Legislature, where Clark, then Assemblyman, voted to keep the courts undivided and the prestige of Danville whole. This angered the citizens of Montgomery City, and so now, when he came to win the county against Norton, he found many Democrats who remembered his vote for Danville.

There was no such feeling against Norton. He had never been in the State Assembly, and had always dodged the squabble between the two towns, giving aid and comfort to neither. If the question came up now, he was sure to lose one faction or the other by being compelled to take a stand.

If Montgomery City and its faction were against Clark, Danville and its sympathizers were for him. As a matter of fact, even the Montgomery City faction liked him, but they wanted to punish him.

"I want to see you go to Congress, Clark," said a sound old Democrat of Middletown, who belonged to the Montgomery City faction. "You're the better man, and I like you, but, by the Lord! I'm going to punish you. I'll lick you in this precinct if I can." Over in Danville, Clark had an earnest supporter in A. H. White, a sound Democrat of the old school and the oldest resident of the town.[3] When the primaries were held there, this man organized the Clark forces in such a way, and so artfully worked in the prejudices against Montgomery City, that Clark delegates were elected from that quarter. In Montgomery City and the rest of the county, the honors were fairly divided, Norton getting about as many delegates as the new aspirant. The old Middletown Democrat was as good as his word and punished his favorite thoroughly by carrying the precinct for Norton. Crawford County sent up a contesting delegation, one crowd being for Clark, the other for Norton. When the district convention met, it was found that if the Clark delegation from Crawford were seated, Clark would be nominated, and if the Norton delegation received the preference, then Norton would get the nomination. There was considerable bickering, and finally both delegations were seated, the Norton faction nominating Norton and the Clark faction Clark. Both sides recognized that this would never do, and so they finally decided to appeal to the Democratic State Central Committee. This body heard both sides, and decided to call another primary all over the district on the same day and leave it to the Democrats to decide for themselves. When this decision was reached, it was seen at once that the candidate who could carry Montgomery County would be elected. Both candidates resolved to make their fight here, and both invaded that characterful region at once. Such wagon traveling, such stump speaking, such hand-shaking the county had never before witnessed. Both candidates rode back and forth over the county, spoke in every cross-roads school, addressed every barn-yard, invaded every household. The scattered firesides resounded with political contention. Clark lived in a buggy, traveling the rough roads by night and dozing in his seat. His voice was hoarse, his temper sad. The gray days, the rain, the

Along the Missouri River.

slush, the cold, weighed upon him. He tried to be hopeful, he wondered at the vainness of the thing.

"If there was a man, woman or child in Montgomery County that did not know Clark by sight and voice," said Brother White to me, looking back over the contest, "it was because they took to the woods when he was around. Such another campaign there never was."

Clark had the district's heart. They saw in this strong, slow-speaking man their own kind, their own flesh and blood. Here was the good old Ninth walking around on two legs. They couldn't resist the influence of his presence. When it came to the primaries, the big-bodied Democrats wandered out in their heavy boots and slouch hats and registered a vote for Clark. He won handsomely, and was elected.

So Clark went to Congress. It was not long before the "big Piker," as he is called, went before Tammany Hall and told them of the manhood and the spirit of the West.[4] The whole country heard of it, but particularly the Ninth. It was pleased beyond measure. When he entered the House, that body was astonished at his wit and oratorical power. His bright humor, his quips and jests, and, above all, his chunks of Pike County philosophy caused his speeches to be widely quoted and widely read.

Clark lives in a small house at Bowling Green, as modest as any in the district. When he visits or campaigns in the various counties, at every Democratic household he is welcome. He has a buggy furnished him by every admirer to carry him to the next stopping place.

"How do you do, Mr. Clark?" said the mother of one of these Democratic households when he appeared unexpectedly at the door, during the campaign.

"I'm sick," was his reply.

"What can I do for you?" she asked.

"You can give me a bed," he muttered.

He was ushered at once into one of the big bedrooms, and, without a word, stretched himself and went to sleep, leaving when he was rested to make a speech farther on.

One of the elements of his strength lies in the fact that he is really vain and boastful of his constituents. He is known throughout the district to glory in the friendship of those stout old characters who are esteemed in their section for probity and honor.

"Clark blows so," said a resident of Gasconade County, "he never gets tired of telling about his constituents. He's got a man over in Pike with a beard seven feet and six inches long, and keeps it tied up. Clark never gets tired of telling how that fellow votes for him all the time. There's another man with nine sons who votes for him—sons and all—and he blows about them."

He mused over this, and then relented sufficiently to add "and well he arter."

For all his standing, Clark has his hours of depression. There are times in the midst of the toil of a campaign when he thinks fate is against him. One of his friends in Warren tells how he carried him in his buggy from one side of the county to the other. The weather was cold and wet, the road a quagmire, and the night wearisome. Clark folded his hands and held his peace.

"I never saw such a depressed man," his friend reported. "He seemed to think he couldn't win. 'It's no use,' he said, 'they won't come out. The Democrats around here don't care. I've toiled over the whole district, and haven't met a decent-sized crowd yet.' He felt as if there was no hope."

"How did he come out in the end?"

"Won by 3,000. There never was any chance of his losing."

The rain, the wariness, the single lights through the far-off trees had probably somewhat to do with this gloomy frame of mind.

NOTES

"Champ Clark, the Man and His District," *Ainslee's* 5 (June 1900): 425–34.

1. Champ Clark (1850–1921) was a well-known Congressman from Missouri, where in St. Louis from 1892 to 1894 Dreiser worked as a reporter for the *Globe-Democrat* and then for the *Republic,* a Republican paper.

2. Aaron Burr (1756–1836), 3rd Vice-President of the United States (1801–5). Thomas Hart Benton (1782–1858), American politician.

3. Arch Herndon White was the father of Dreiser's first wife Sara Osborne White, nicknamed Jug. Dreiser fictionalized his father-in-law as Samuel Howdershell in "Rella," one of the portraits in *A Gallery of Women,* 2 vols. (New York: Liveright, 1929). Dreiser also published a magazine article featuring A. H. White, with illustrations by William J. Glackens, in "A True Patriarch: A Study from Life," *McClure's* 18 (December 1901): 136–44; reprinted as "A True Patriarch" with many stylistic alterations in *Twelve Men* (New York: Boni and Liveright, 1919), 187–205. More recently the article was reprinted as "A True Patriarch: A Study from Life" in *Selected Magazine Articles,* 1:181–92.

4. Tammany Hall originally was the headquarters of the Tammany Society, a political organization in New York City. Hence it refers to a political organization seeking municipal control by methods associated with corruption and bossism.

6

Thomas Brackett Reed:
The Story of a Great Career

THE TRUE STORY OF THE CAREER OF THAT REMARKABLE AMERICAN, Thomas Brackett Reed,—the story of the forces which have dominated his life and of the hopes and ambitions which have swayed him,—has never before been told.[1] The Maine statesman has been written *about* fully as much as any other man in public life, and from his own pen have come many interesting contributions to the virile literature of the day; and yet his secret personality, the true Thomas Brackett Reed, has escaped.

To get this, to induce him to talk of himself, was the purpose of my recent visit to him in New York, where his great talents are now finding expression in the practice of the law.

"Had you thought anything, Mr. Reed," I asked, "of retiring from politics before you took the step last fall?"

A merry twinkle changed the seriousness of his look, as he answered, "Election time has frequently brought me that thought."

"But more seriously?" I ventured.

∞

"I have always been ready to step down and out; not that I was dissatisfied, but willing to do so, if affairs more urgent or more suited to my abilities offered."

"How did you feel when the entire Democratic press of the country had pounced upon you for what it called your tyrannical method of interpreting the rules of the house of representatives?"

"Oh," replied the ex-speaker, promptly, "you mean, whether I was disturbed by the uproar? Well, I had no feeling except one of entire serenity, and the reason was simple. I knew just what I was going to do if the house did not sustain me."

Then he raised his eyes, and, with a characterful twist of the mouth which those who have once seen do not soon forget, added: "When a man has decided upon a plan of action for either contingency, there is no need for him to be disturbed, you know."

"And may I ask what you had determined to do, if the house did not sustain you?"

"I should simply have left the chair, resigned the speakership, withdrawn from the house, and given up my seat in congress. There were things that could be done, you know, outside of political life. For my part, I had made up my mind that, if political life consisted in sitting helplessly in the speaker's chair, and seeing the majority powerless to pass legislation, I had had enough of it."

"Do you object to speaking of the circumstances which formed your political opinions and ambitions?"

"You mean my early life, I suppose. Well, one biographer has traced my line back to George Cleeve, who built the first white man's habitation ever erected in the territory now included in Portland's boundaries."

∞

Mr. Reed did not trouble himself to finish the story, which is interesting. The settlement was called "Stogumnor," in tender memory of an English field of that name, and its founder's life was one of ceaseless conflict, now with the redskins and now with the white neighbors of other settlements, so that Cleeve left behind him the impress of a bold, vigorous pioneer. His daughter became the wife of Michael Milten, whose two daughters in turn were married to two brothers named Brackett. One of the Brackett daughters was espoused by a fisherman named Reed, whose descendant Thomas Brackett Reed is. Much of the nerve and daring that animated his stern old fighting settler-ancestor, George Cleeve, has evidently been inherited by him. I soon brought him around to his boyhood days.

"Literature and old romances attracted me most," he said; "much more than text-books. A spare young man, Master Moses Lyford, was my teacher, the best disciplinarian I ever knew."

"He must have imparted some of that quality to you," said I.

"Possibly. He had the art of holding a turbulent school by finding out what was the particular spring he could touch to control every one of his lawless boys. His 'pull' on me was dismissal. By simply holding that threat over me at critical moments, he conquered. You see I had a sort of inborn idea that school was a great thing for me, and I also knew that my parents were too poor to be able to send me anywhere else, so I kept straight along as best I could. He had a way of letting every boy who had no demerits ring his bell before leaving the class. Once, for three days, I did not ring that bell. So he came to me. 'Tom,' he said, 'is it an inadvertence?' 'No, sir.' 'Did you break the rules?' 'Yes, sir.' 'Why?' 'Because they were too hard.' 'Well, boy, you know what you can do if the rules are too hard; you can leave school.' I hung my head, and he went away, saying, 'Never let me hear of this again, Tom.' 'No, sir,' I replied, and I meant it."

"How did you get along at Bowdoin?"

"Only fairly well. I neglected some things."

"Were you well supplied with money?"

"No. I paid my own way. I spent a little too much time on light literature, and it nearly cost me my sheepskin."

∞

The truth is that his college experience was rather hard. His life-struggle began with the first year there, and he had to earn enough to pay his way as he went along. His attendance at class recitations during the first term of his freshman year was regular, but he found it necessary to remain out the next two terms and earn some money by teaching. He kept up his studies, however, without an instructor.

"All through the first part of my college course," he said to a friend, "I devoted a great deal of time to literature, to the neglect of other studies; a garret in the house of one of my mother's relations became my mecca. It was packed full of books, especially novels, and thither I went, twice a week, loading myself with novels, which I spent days, and the best part of my nights, reading. They were mostly trashy, imaginative stuff, but gave me delight and some information. I believe, I gained my knowledge of words from them; anyhow, they gradually waked me to a knowledge of higher and really important literature."

Graduation was little more than a year off when, the contents of the garret being exhausted, the young man realized, to his confusion, that his class standing was very low. His position in the graduating class depended on the average of his class ratings for the four years. None of the sixteen junior parts, given out during the junior year, had reached him. Also, the English orations, which should have numbered sixteen, were, for his senior year, reduced to twelve. This stiffened the contest, and to get one meant a struggle. Yet every ambitious and spirited boy entered the contest. Reed was one. Eleventh hour as it was, he laid aside poems and romances.

"From that time on until commencement I toiled," he said; "I got up at five every morning, and went promptly to bed at nine every night. I did not like it, and felt every morning that I could sleep a month undisturbed. When the time came, I was so scared, after taking the examination, that I was afraid to go and hear the result. Finally, one of the boys came to my room and told me that I stood fifth, and I was then as happy as I have ever been, before or since."

"Did that win you the privilege of delivering one of the orations?"

"Yes. It was the hardest year of my life. If ever I measured the limit of my capacity, I did that year."

His oration was entitled "The Fear of Death," and it won the first prize for English compositions. It was Mr. Reed's first attempt at oratory, and he says that his emotions, when he felt every eye upon him and realized that profound stillness prevailed, were most disturbing, yet his words aroused deep interest.

∞

"What did you do after graduation?"

"Let me see. I engaged in school-teaching. I became assistant teacher in the Boys' High School in Portland. After a year, I resigned and went into the law office of Howard and Stroul, Portland, where I studied for two years."

"How much was a teacher's salary at that time?"

"I can't speak for every one. Mine was thirty dollars a month."

His old comrades delight in telling, what he will not, how he once found it necessary to chastise a boy who was about his own age. He, as teacher, had been cautioned against whipping any one without first consulting the members of the committee of the district. But Reed was Reed even in those days. The committee had not sustained his opinion in several previous cases, when consulted, so he decided to act without them. He was fast losing his authority and proposed to retrieve it, which he did in fifteen of what he calls "the most exciting minutes of my life." It was a close victory, which a single pound more of avoirdupois added to the youth might have decided against the teacher.

"Finding the law poor picking, at first," he said, "I went to California."

Mr. Reed acknowledged that he went in the steerage, *via* Cape Horn. "I had no money to spare," he said, "so I went on a sailing vessel. I taught school at Stockton, and studied law again at San José. There was not very much out there for me, so I returned to Portland in 1864 and obtained an appointment as an acting assistant paymaster in the navy, in which capacity I served for a year."

∞

One of the most interesting incidents of Reed's career in California is told by Robert P. Porter, and vouched for by the ex-speaker. It was in 1863, during the Civil War, when the Legal Tender Act was much discussed in California, where a gold basis was then maintained, that Wallace, whose office adjoined the one in which Reed was studying, happened in one day and said: "Mr. Reed, I understand you want to be admitted to the bar. Have you studied law?" "Yes, sir, I studied law in Maine, while teaching." "Well," said Wallace, "I have one question to ask. Is the Legal Tender Act constitutional?" "Yes," said Reed. "You shall be admitted to the bar," said Wallace. Tom Bodley, a deputy sheriff, who had legal aspirations, was asked the same question, and he said "No." "We will admit you both," said Wallace, "for anybody who can answer, off-hand, a question like that, ought to practice law in this country."[2]

"How did you come to get into politics?"

"Oh, I became a little known, locally. There was nothing against me. I had a good many personal friends. One of these was Judge Nathan Webb, the county attorney at that time, who knew me as his opponent in a number of cases. He had a fancy for me, and wanted to see me get along in the world; so, when convention time came around, he proposed my name for the state legislature. He not only proposed it, but amused himself with a hearty fight on my behalf, and, after six ballots, had me nominated. I really knew nothing about it until the next morning, when I read in the papers that I was on the ticket. I at first decided to decline, because my law practice was growing, and to go to the state capital meant to neglect it. But Webb came around, and urged me so kindly to take it that I consented. He said the experience would broaden me."

"Did it?"

"Yes, but my law business went by the board."

"How long were you in the state legislature?"

"I was two terms in the house. Then I was elected to the state senate. Afterwards, I became attorney-general of Maine, and then city solicitor of Portland. After that I was elected to congress—in 1876."

∞

"How did you get on in congress?"

"Well, that is for other people to say,—a matter of record. We can hardly talk of that."

Still, Mr. Reed did not object to acknowledging some of the current gossip concerning his distinguished career in the national house. When he went up from Portland, he was escorted by one of his colleagues to a seat. His massive figure, and his reputation as a wit and orator, interested older members. S. S. Cox was one of those who knew of this.[3] He turned to William P. Frye, then a member from Maine, and said:—

"Well, Frye, I see your state has sent another intellectual and physical giant here."

"Whom do you mean?"

"This man Reed, who must be even now cracking a joke, for I see they are all crowding about him."

In a later congress, his power of sarcasm and of insinuating inquiry furnished the electoral inquiry committee and the public with the most dramatic scenes that occurred at any of its sessions. By cross-examining one clever scoundrel for two whole days, he at length compelled him to admit that he was a forger. In the fifty-first congress he took the speaker's chair.

Concerning the memorable stand he took in that congress regarding the counting of a quorum, I asked:—

"You never had a doubt in your own mind that the position taken was in perfect accordance with justice and common sense?"

"Never for a moment. Men, you see, being creatures of use and wont, are naturally bound up in traditions. While every court which had ever considered the question had decided one way, we had been used to the other. Fortunately for the country, there was no wavering in our ranks."

∞

"When the members of the minority were raging on the floor together and the uproar was at its worst, how did you feel?"

"Just as you would feel," was his reply, "if a big creature were jumping at you and you knew the exact length and strength of his chain, and was quite sure of the weapon you had in your hands. I felt I was right. I knew I could live outside of congress. So I could afford to strike for the principle."

"Do you believe the country is following the right path in seeking foreign territory?"

"No interest can attach to my opinion on that now. I am not now in politics."

"You cannot fairly say that your views are not of public interest, though."

"Well, I believe our life as a nation will not be benefited by adding foreign territory."

"Some point to England," I said, "as an example of how a great and enlightened power ought to extend its beneficent influence."

"We are not like England, and cannot be," he replied. "That country has two kinds of colonies,—those inhabited by peoples of a radically different civilization and of barbaric customs, in some instances, and those made up of colonial Englishmen, equal in every respect to the men of the mother country. The secret of England's colonial success is that she is satisfied with the mere name of empire. She certainly gets nothing more than that. It is give, give, give, on her part. She yields to her colonies' wishes and fights for them, without gaining anything but a great name. For instance, we should have settled the Bering Sea question in our favor, if it had been between us and England alone. Canada complained, and England yielded to her. So we lost."

∞

"It is a question whether we are satisfied with the honor of having colonies and are willing to pay for it. Remember, we have great enthusiasm for unity and nationality as regards the combined states. England has nothing like this. Her people glory in the thought of empire. To them, it is a very tangible and satisfactory thing. They have an empress-queen, which makes the thought something real. The colonies glorify her, and they can see it. Here we have a new president every four years, with half the people opposed to him, and so colonial possessions cannot find glorious representation in him. The people may grow tired and arbitrary toward the colonies. That will injure us more than anything else."

"You are well experienced in this world's affairs," I ventured. "What do you take to be the object of life? Money?"

"No."

"Individual happiness?"

"Not wholly. Right action. A man should take a part in the affairs of his fellow men and live up to the dictates of his conscience in acting. He should be of some use. If he has desires, all the better. A desire for anything that will help others and satisfy you is a good thing. A man has a right to desire money or place or public praise, but he has no right to any selfish feeling in the matter. He ought to desire to be liberal and earn his reward by service of some kind."

"Do you think the world offers as much to individuals as it ever did?"

"If we can trust history, it does. The literature of earlier times seems more complaining than our own. Men were just as dissatisfied a thousand years ago as they are now. Man seems always to have craved a great deal more than he could obtain. Individually, I think, the age is richer with opportunities than for ages. The system under which we live is somewhat defective, and many suffer by it; but it is changing and the world grows better. The unselfish man will find enough, I fancy, if he honestly fulfills his duty to his fellow men. It is all a question of peace of mind, and that can be obtained in various ways,—the best one, by doing right."

NOTES

"Thomas Brackett Reed: The Story of a Great Career," *Success* 3 (June 1900): 215–16.
   1. Thomas Brackett Reed (1839–1902).
   2. The Legal Tender Act is a legal provision that money which is valid for the payment of debts must be accepted for that purpose when offered. Lewis [Lew] Wallace (1827–1905), California lawyer, politician, general, and novelist.
   3. Dreiser mentions S. S. Cox, United States Senator and uncle of H. Barrington Cox, electrical scientist and inventor, in his magazine article "A Vision of Fairy Lamps: H. Barrington Cox," included in this collection.

7

A Doer of the Word

NOANK IS A LITTLE PLAYED-OUT FISHING TOWN ON THE SOUTHEASTERN coast of Connecticut, lying half way between New London and Stonington. Once it was a profitable port for mackerel and cod fishing. To-day its wharves are deserted of all save a few lobster smacks. There is a shipyard, employing three hundred and fifty men, a yacht-building establishment, with two or three hired hands; a sail loft, and some dozen or so shops or sheds, where the odds and ends of fishing life are made and sold. Everything is peaceful. The sound of the shipyard axes and hammers can be heard for miles over the quiet waters of the bay. In the sunny lane which follows the line of the shore, and along which the few shops straggle in happy-go-lucky disorder, may be heard the voices and noises of the workers at their work. Water gurgling about the stanchions of the docks, the whistle of some fisherman as he dawdles over his silent labor, the whirr of the single sewing machine in the sail loft, often mingle in a pleasant harmony and invite the mind to repose and speculation.

I was sitting one day in the shed of the maker of sailboats, where a half-dozen characters of the village were gathered, when some turn in the conversation brought up the nature of man. He is queer, he is restless; life is not so very much when you come to look upon many phases of it.

"Did any of you ever know a contented man?" I inquired.

There was silence for a moment, and one after another met my revolving glance with a thoughtful, self-involved and retrospective eye.

Old Mr. Main was the first to answer.

"Yes, I did."

"So did I," put in the sailboat maker, as he stopped in his work to think about it.

"Yes, and I did," said a dark, squat, sunny, little old fisherman, who sold cunners for bait in a black little hut next door.

"Maybe you and me are thinkin' of the same one, Jacob," said old Mr. Main, looking inquisitively at the boat builder.

"I think we've all got the same man in mind, likely," returned the builder.

"Who is he?" I asked.

86

"Charlie Potter," said the builder.

"That's the man!" exclaimed Mr. Main.

"Well, I reckon Charlie Potter is contented, if anybody be," said an old fisherman who had hitherto been silent.

The unanimity of opinion struck me forcibly.

"So you really think he is contented?" I asked.

"Yes, sir! Charlie Potter is a contented man," replied Mr. Main, with convincing emphasis.

"Well," I returned, "that's rather interesting. What sort of a man is he?"

"Oh, he's just an ordinary man," put in the boat builder.

"I know; but what does he do for a living?"

"He preaches," said Mr. Main.

"Anybody can be contented when he is getting paid so much a year for being so," I said, more to draw out the information I desired than to cast a slur on the ministerial profession. "A preacher is expected to set a good example."

"He ain't a regular preacher," said Mr. Main, rather quickly. "He's just kind of around in religious work."

"You can't say anything like that of Potter, anyhow," interrupted the boat builder. "He don't take any money for what he does. He ain't got anything."

"What does he live on?"

"I don't know. He used to fish for a living. Fishes yet once in a while, I believe."

"He makes models of yachts," put in one of the bystanders. "He sold the New Haven Road one for $200 here not long ago."

A vision of a happy-go-lucky Jack-of-all-trades arose before me.

"What makes you all think he is contented?" I inquired. "Is he a good man?"

"Yes, sir!" said Mr. Main, with something of pathetic emphasis in his voice. "Charlie Potter is a good man."

"You won't find anybody with a kinder heart than Charlie Potter," added the boat builder. "That's all that's the trouble with him. He's too good."

"If he wasn't that way, he'd be a darned sight better off than he is," said a thirty-year-old helper from a far corner of the room.

"What makes you say that?" I queried. "Isn't it better to be kind-hearted and generous than not?"

"It's all right to be kind-hearted and generous, but that ain't sayin' that you've got to give your last cent away and let your family go hungry."

"Is that what Charlie Potter does?"

"Well, if he don't, he comes mighty near to it."

"There's no doubt but that's where Charlie is wrong," put in old Mr. Main. "He don't stop to think of his family."

"What did he ever do that struck you as being over-generous?" I asked of the young man who had spoken out of the corner.

"That's all right," he replied in a rather irritated and peevish tone; "I ain't going to go into details now, but there's people around here that hang around after him, and that he give to, that he hadn't orter."

"I believe in lookin' out for Number One, that's what I believe in," interrupted the boatmaker, laying down his rule and line. "This givin' up everything and goin' without yourself may be all right, but I don't believe it. A man's first duty is to his wife and children, that's what I say."

"That's the way it looks to me," put in Mr. Main.

"What did Potter ever do that seemed wrong in this way?" I asked of the boatmaker.

"What didn't he do?" he returned, addressing the company in general. "Look at the time he worked over there on Fisher's Island, at the Ellesbie farm—the time they were packing the ice there. You remember, Main, don't you?"

Mr. Main nodded.

"What about it?"

"What about it! Why, he give his rubber boots away, like a darned fool, to that old drunken Jimmy Harper, and worked around on the ice without any shoes himself. He might have took cold and died."

"What did he do it for?"

"Charlie's naturally big-hearted," put in the little old man, who sold cunners, meekly. "He's got the biggest heart I ever see in a livin' being."

"The other fellow didn't have any shoes fit to wear, but he never would work, anyhow," added the boatmaker.

They lapsed into silence, while the latter returned to his measuring, and then out of the drift of thought came this from the helper in the corner:

"Yes, and look at the way Bailey used to sponge on him. Get his money Saturday night and drink it all up, and then Sunday morning, when his wife and children were hungry, go cryin' around Potter. Dinged if the man wouldn't take the food right off his breakfast table and give it to him. I don't think that's right."

"Why isn't it?" I asked.

"'Cause he had his wife and children to take care of—that's why."

Another lull, and then, as I was leaving the room to give the matter a little quiet attention, I remarked to the boatmaker:

"Outside of his foolish giving, you haven't anything against Charlie Potter, have you?"

"No," he replied, in apparent astonishment. "Charlie Potter's one of the best men that ever lived. He's a good man."

I smiled at the inconsistency and went my way.

A day or two later the loft of the sailmaker happened to be my lounging place, and thinking on this theme, now uppermost in my mind, I said to him:

"Do you know Charlie Potter?"

"Well, I might say that I do. He lived here for over fifteen years."

"What sort of a man is he?"

He stopped in his stitching to look at me and say with feeling emphasis: "Charlie Potter is a good man."

"What has he done that makes him so popular with all of you people?"

"Well," he said, ceasing his work as if the subject were one of extreme importance to his mind, "he's a peculiar man. He believes in giving everything that he has away. He'd give his coat off his back if you'd ask him for it."

He looked away as if he expected some objection to be made to this, but hearing none, he went on:

"Some folks condemn him for one thing and another, but I always thought the man was nearer right than most of us. I've got a family myself—but then so's he, for that matter. It's pretty hard to live up to your light always."

"You say he's so good. Do you remember any one thing that he ever did that struck you as being pre-eminently good?"

"Well, now, I can't say. He was always doing things one way and another. He gave to everybody around here that asked him, and to a good many that didn't. I remember once"—and a smile gave evidence of a genial memory—"he gave away a lot of pork to some colored people back here—two or three barrels, maybe. My, how his mother-in-law did go on about it. She was living with him then."

"She didn't like to give it to them, eh?"

"Well, I should say not. She didn't set with his views exactly. He took the pork—it was right in the coldest weather we had that winter—and hauled it back about seven miles here, where they lived, and handed it all out himself. Charlie's too good, that way. It's his one fault, if you might so speak of it."

I smiled as the evidences went on. Houseless wayfarers, stopping to find food and shelter under his roof, an orphan child carried seven miles on foot from the bedside of a dead mother and cared for all winter—three children, besides two of his own, being raised out of a sense of affection and care for the fatherless.

One day in the local post office I was idling a half hour with the postmaster, when I again inquired:

"Do you know Charlie Potter?"

"I should think I did. Charlie Potter and I sailed together for something over eleven years."

"How do you mean sailed together?"

"We were on the same schooner. This used to be a great port for mackerel and cod. We were wrecked once together."

"How was that?"

"Oh, we went on rocks."

"Any lives lost?"

"No, but there came mighty near being. We helped each other in the boat. I remember Charlie was the last one in that time. Wouldn't get in until all the rest were safe."

A sudden resolution came to me.

"Do you know where he is now?"

"Yes; he's up in Norwich, preaching or doing missionary work. He's kind of busy all the time among the poor people, and so on."

"Do you know how he manages to live?"

"No, I don't, exactly. He believes in trusting to Providence for what he needs. Got an idea the Lord will send whatever he needs."

"He works, though, of course?"

"Oh, yes. There's nothing lazy about Charlie. He's a good worker. When he was in the fishing line there wasn't a man worked harder than he did. They can't anybody lay anything like that against him."

"I wish I knew him," I said.

"Well, you could, if you went up to see him. He's one of the finest men that way I ever knew."

I caught a boat for New London and Norwich at one-thirty that afternoon, and arrived in Norwich at five. The narrow streets of the thriving little city were alive with people. Through the open door of a news-stall I called to the proprietor:

"Do you know any one in Norwich by the name of Charlie Potter?"

"The man who works around among the poor people?"

"That's the man."

"Yes, I know him. He lives out on Summer Street, Number Twelve, I think. You'll find it in the city directory."

The ready reply was rather astonishing. Norwich has something like 30,000 people.

I walked out in search of Summer Street and found beautiful lanes climbing upward over gentle slopes, arched completely with elms. Some of the pretty porches of the cottages extended nearly to the sidewalk. Hammocks, rocking-chairs on verandas, benches under the trees—all attested the love of idleness and shade in summer. Only the glimpse of mills and factories in the valley below evidenced the grimmer life which gave rise to the need of a man to work among the poor.

"Is this Summer Street?" I inquired of an old darky who was strolling cityward in the cool of the evening. An umbrella was under his arm and an evening paper under his spectacled nose.

"Bress de Lord!" he said, looking vaguely around. "Ah, couldn't say. Ah know dat street—been on it fifty times—but Ah never did know de name. Ha, ha, ha!"

The hills about echoed his hearty laugh.

"You don't happen to know Charlie Potter?"

"Oh, yas, sah. Ah knows Charlie Potter. Dat's his house right ovah dar."

The house in which Charlie Potter lived was a two-story frame, over-hanging a sharp slope, which descended directly to the waters of the pretty river below. For a mile or more, the valley of the river could be seen, its slopes dotted with houses, the valley itself lined with mills. Two little girls were upon the sloping lawn to the right of the house. A comfortable-looking man was sitting by a window on the left side of the house, gazing out over the valley.

"Is this where Charlie Potter lives?" I inquired of one of the children.

"Yes, sir."

"Did he live in Noank?"

"Yes, sir."

Just then a pleasant-faced woman of forty-five or fifty issued from a vine-covered door.

"Mr. Potter?" she replied to my inquiry. "He'll be right out."

She went about some little work at the side of the house, and in a moment Charlie Potter appeared. He was short, thick-set, and weighed no less than two hundred pounds. His face and hands were sunburned and brown like those of every fisherman of Noank. An old wrinkled coat and a baggy pair of gray trousers clothed his form loosely. Two inches of a spotted, soft-brimmed hat were pulled carelessly over his eyes. His face was round and full, but slightly seamed. His hands were large, his walk uneven, and rather inclined to a side swing.

"Is this Mr. Potter?"

"I'm the man."

"I live on a little hummock at the east end of Mystic Island, off Noank."

"You do?"

"I came up to have a talk with you."

"Will you come inside, or shall we sit out here?"

"Let's sit on the step."

"All right, let's sit on the step."

He waddled out of the gate and sank comfortably on the little, low doorstep, with his feet on the cool bricks below. I dropped into the space beside him, and was greeted by the sweetest, kindliest look I have ever seen in a man's eyes. It was one of perfect friendship and affection—void of all suspicion.

"We were sitting down in the sailboat maker's place at Noank the other day, and I asked a half-dozen of the old fellows whether they had ever known a contented man. They all thought a while, and then they said they had. Old Mr. Main and the rest of them agreed that Charlie Potter was a contented man."

I looked into his eyes, and if there were not misty tears of delight and affection being vigorously restrained, I was very much mistaken. Something seemed to hold the man in helpless silence as he gazed vacantly at nothing. He breathed heavily, then drew himself together, and lifted one of his big hands, as if to touch me, but refrained.

"Say, brother," he said, confidentially, "I *am* a contented man."

"Well, that's good," I replied, taking a slight mental exception to the use of the word brother. "What makes you contented?"

"I don't know," he replied, "unless it is that I've found out what I ought to do. You see, I need so very little for myself that I couldn't be very unhappy."

"What ought you to do?"

"I ought to love my fellowmen."

"And do you?"

"Say, brother, but I do. I love everybody. There isn't anybody so low or so mean but I love him. I love you, yes, I do. I love you."

He reached out and touched me with his hand, and I thrilled as I have not over the touch of any man in years. The glance that accompanied it spoke as truthfully as his words.

We lapsed into silence. After a while I said:

"It is very evident you think the condition of some of your fellowmen isn't what it ought to be. Tell me what you are trying to do. What method have you for improving their condition?"

"All that some people have is their feelings," he replied, "nothing else. Take a tramp, for instance, as I often have. When you begin to sum him up to see where to begin, you find that all he has in the world, besides his pipe and a little tobacco, is his feelings. It's all most people have, rich or poor, though a good many think they have more than that. I try not to injure anybody's feelings."

He looked at me as though he had expressed the solution of the difficulties of the world, and the wonderful, kindly eyes beamed in charity upon the scene.

"Very good," I said; "but what do you do? How do you go about it to aid your fellowmen?"

"Well," he answered, unconsciously overlooking his own personal actions in the matter, "I try to bring them the salvation which the Bible teaches. You know I stand on the Bible, from cover to cover."

"Yes, I know you stand on the Bible, but what do you do? You don't merely preach the Bible to them. What do you do?"

"I go wherever I can be useful. If anybody is sick or in trouble, I'm ready to go. I'll be a nurse. I'll work and earn them food. I'll give them anything I can—that's what I do."

"How can you give when you haven't anything? They told me in Noank that you never worked for money."

"Not for myself. I never take any money for myself. That would be self-seeking. The Lord doesn't allow a man to be self-seeking."

"Well, then, how do you get money to do with? You can't live and do without money."

He had been looking away across the river and the bridge to the city below, but now he brought his eyes back and fixed them on me.

"I've been working now for twenty years or more, and, although I've never had more money that would last me a few days at a time, I've never wanted for anything. I've run pretty close sometimes. Time and time again, I've been compelled to say, 'Lord, I'm all out of coal,' or 'Lord, I'm going to have to ask you to get me my fare to New Haven to-morrow,' but in the moment of my need He has never forgotten me. Why, I've gone down to the depot time and time again, when it was necessary for me to go, without five cents in my pocket, and He's been there to meet me. Why, He wouldn't keep you waiting when you're about his work. He wouldn't forget you—not for a minute."

I looked at the man in open-eyed amazement.

"Do you mean to say that you would go down to a depot without money and wait for money to come to you?"

"Oh, brother," he said, with the sweetest light in his eyes, "if you only knew what it is to have faith."

He laid his hand softly on mine.

"What is car fare to New Haven or to anywhere to Him!"

"One instance," I said.

"Why, it was only last week, brother, that a woman wrote me from Malden, Massachusetts, wanting men to come and see her. She's very sick with consumption, and she thought she was going to die. I used to know her in Noank, and she thought if she could get to see me she would feel better.

"I didn't have any money at the time, but that didn't make any difference.

"'Lord,' I said, 'here's a woman sick in Malden, and she wants me to come to her. I haven't got any money, but I'll go right down to the depot, in time to catch a certain train, and while I was standing there a man came up to me and said, 'Brother, I'm told to give you this,' and he handed me ten dollars."

"Did you know the man?" I exclaimed.

"Never saw him before in my life," he replied, smiling genially.

"And didn't he say anything more than that?"

"No."

I stared at him, and he added, as if to take the edge off my astonishment.

"Why, bless your heart, I knew he was from the Lord, just the moment I saw him coming."

This incident was still the subject of my inquiry when a little colored girl came out of the yard and paused a moment before us.

"May I go down across the bridge, papa?" she asked.

"Yes," he answered, and then as she tripped merrily away, said:

"She's one of my adopted children." He gazed between his knees at the sidewalk.

"Have you many others?"

"Three."

"Raising them, are you?"

"Yes."

"They seem to think down in Noank, that, living as you do, and giving everything away, is satisfactory to you, but rather hard on your wife and children."

"Well, it is true that she did feel a little uncertain in the beginning, but she's never wanted for anything. She'll tell you herself that she's never been without a thing that she really needed, and she's been happy."

He paused to meditate over the opinion of his former fellow townsmen, and then added:

"It's true, there have been times when we have been right where we had to have certain things pretty badly before they came, but they never failed to come."

While he was still talking, Mrs. Potter came around the corner of the house, and out upon the sidewalk. She was going to the Saturday evening market in the city below.

"Here she is," he said. "Now you can ask her."

"What is it?" she inquired, turning a serene and smiling face to me.

"They still think, down in Noank, that you're not very happy with me," he said. "They're afraid you want for something once in a while."

She took this piece of neighborly interference as I have never seen the same kind of gossip taken before.

"I have never wanted for anything since I have been married to my husband," she said. "I am thoroughly contented."

She looked at him, and he looked at her, and there passed between them an affectionate glance.

"Yes," he said, when she had passed, after a pleasing little conversation, "my wife has been a great help to me. She has never complained."

"People are inclined to talk a little," I said.

"Well, you see, she never complained, but she did feel a little bit worried in the beginning."

"Have you a mission or a church here in Norwich?"

"No, I don't believe in churches."

"Not in churches?"

"No, the sight of a minister preaching the word of God for so much a year is all a mockery to me."

"What do you believe in?"

"Personal service. Churches and charitable institutions and societies are all valueless. You can't reach your fellowman that way. This giving of a few old clothes, that the moths will get anyhow, that won't do. You've got to give something of yourself, and that's affection. Love is the only thing you can really give in this world."

"Money certainly comes handy sometimes," I ventured.

"When you give it with your own hand and heart. Ah!" he exclaimed, with sudden animation, "the tangles men can get themselves into, the snarls, the wretchedness! Troubles with women, with men that they owe, with evil things they say and think, until they can't walk down the street any more without peeping about to see if they are followed. They can't look you in the face; can't walk a straight course, but have got to sneak around corners. Poor, miserable, unhappy—they're worrying and crying and dodging one another!"

He paused, lost in contemplation of the picture he had conjured up.

"What to do about it?" I asked.

"You can't reach 'em with old clothes and charity societies," he said. "You've got to love them, brother. You've got to go to them and love them, just as they are, scarred and miserable and bad-hearted.

"Why, one night I was passing a little house in this town, and I heard a woman crying. I went right to the door and opened it, and when I got inside, she just stopped and looked at me.

"'Madam,' I said, 'I have come to help you, if I can. Now you tell me what you're crying for.'

"Well, sir, you know she sat there and told me of how her husband drank and how she didn't have anything in the house to eat, and so I just gave her all I had, and I told her I would see her husband for her, and the next day I went and hunted him up, and I said to him, 'Oh, brother, I wish you would open your eyes and see what you are doing. I wish you wouldn't do that any more. It's only misery you are creating.' And, you know, I got to telling him about how badly his wife felt about it, and how I intended to work and try and help her, and bless me, if he didn't up and promise me before I got through that he wouldn't do that any more. And he didn't. He's working to-day, and it's been two years since I went to him, nearly."

His eyes were alight with his appreciation of the value of personal service.

"Yes, that's one instance," I said.

"Oh, there are plenty of them," he replied. "It's the only way. Down here in New London, a couple of winters ago, we had a terrible time of it. Cold—my, but that was a cold winter. Things got so bad there that I finally went to the mayor and told him that if he'd give me the little money they were talking of spending, that I'd feed the hungry for a cent and a half a meal."

"A cent and a half a meal?"

"Yes, sir. They all thought it was rather curious, but they gave me the money, and I fed 'em."

"Good meals."

"Yes, as good as I ever eat myself," he replied.

"How did you do it?" I said.

"Oh, I can cook," he replied. "I just went around to the markets, and told them what I wanted—heads of mackerel, and the part of the halibut that's left after the rich man cuts off his steak—it's the poorest part that he pays for, you know. And I went fishing myself two or three times—I'm a good fisherman, you know—oh, I can catch fish, and I made fish chowders, and fish dinners, and really I set a very fine table, I did, that winter."

"A cent and a half a meal!"

"A cent and a half a meal. That's all it cost me. The mayor himself said he was surprised at the way I did it."

"There wasn't any personal service in the money they gave you?" I said.

"Yes," he said, with unconscious simplicity. "But they gave through me, you see. I gave the personal service. That's the way. Don't you see?"

I smiled, and in the drag of his thought he took up another idea.

"I clothed them that winter, too—went around and got barrels and boxes of old clothing. Some of them felt a little ashamed to put on the things, but I got over that all right. I was wearing them myself, and I just told them, 'Don't feel badly, brother. I'm wearing them out of the same barrel with you—I'm wearing them out of the same barrel.' Got my clothes entirely free that winter."

"Can you always get all the aid you need for such enterprises?"

"Usually, and then I can earn a good deal of money when I work steadily. I can get a hundred and fifty dollars for a little yacht, you know, every time I find time to make one; and I can make a good deal of money out fishing. I went out fishing here on the Fourth of July, and caught two hundred blackfish—four and five pounds almost, every one of them."

"That ought to be profitable," I said.

"Well, it was," he replied.

"How much did you get for them?"

"Oh, I didn't sell them," he said. "I never take money for my work. I gave them all away."

"What did you do," I said, laughing, "advertise for people to come for them?"

"No," he said, "my wife took some and my daughter, and I took the rest, and we carried them around to people that we thought would like to have them."

"That was profitable!"

"Yes, they were fine fish."

We dropped the subject of personal service at this point, and I expressed the opinion that his service was only a temporary expedient. Perhaps those he aided were none the better for accepting of his charity.

"I know what you mean," he said. "But money is the only dangerous thing to give—but I never give money—not very often. I'd rather give food and clothing. You've got to reach the heart, you know. You've got to make a man over in his soul, if you want to help him, and money won't help you to do that, you know."

"Make them over. What do you mean? How do you make them over?"

"Oh, in their attitude, that's how. You've got to change a man and bring him out of self-seeking if you really want to make him good. Most men are so tangled up, and so worried over their seekings, that unless you can set them to giving it's no use. They don't know what they want. Money isn't the thing.

"Why half of them wouldn't understand how to use it if they had it. Their minds are not bright enough. Their perceptions are not clear enough. All you can do is to make them content with themselves. And that, giving will do. I never saw the man, or the woman, yet, who couldn't be happy if you could make them feel the need of living for others."

He rubbed his hands as if he saw the solution of the world's difficulties very clearly, and I said to him:

"Well, now you get a man out of the mire, and saved, as you call it, and then what?"

"Well, then, he's saved," he replied.

"I know. But must he go to church, or conform to certain rules?"

"Nothing to do except to be good to others," he returned. "Charity is kind, you know. 'Charity vaunteth not itself, is not puffed up with pride. . . . '"

"Well," I said, "and then what?"

"Well, then the world would come about. All the misery is in the lack of sympathy one with another. When we get that straightened out we can work in peace. There are lots of things to do, you know."

"Yes."

"I'm an ignorant man myself," he went on, "and I'd like to study. My, but I'd like to look into all things, but I can't do it now. We can't stop until this thing is straightened out. Sometime, maybe," and he looked peacefully away.

"By the way," I said, "whatever became of the man to whom you gave your rubber boots over on Fisher's Island?"

His face lit up as if it were the most natural thing that I should know about it.

"Say," he exclaimed, in the most pleased and confidential way, as if we were talking about a mutual friend. "I saw him not long ago. And, do you know, he's a good man now—really, he is. Sober and hard-working. And, say, would you believe it, he told me I was the cause of it—just that miserable old pair of rubber boots—what do you think of that?"

I shook his hand, at parting, and as we stood looking at each other in the shadow of the evening, I asked him:

"Are you afraid to die?"

"Say, brother, but I'm not," he returned. "It hasn't any terror for me at all. I'm just as willing. My, but I'm willing."

He smiled and gripped me heartily again, and, as I was starting to go, said:

"If I die to-night, it'll be all right. He'll use me just as long as He needs me. That I know. Good-by."

"Good-by," I called back.

He hung by his fence, looking down upon the city. As I turned the next corner I saw him awakening from his reflection and waddling stolidly back into the house.

NOTES

"A Doer of the Word," *Ainslee's* 9 (June 1902): 453–59. Reprinted in *Twelve Men* (New York: Boni and Liveright, 1919), 53–75; also reprinted as a short story in *The Best Short Stories of Theodore Dreiser,* ed. with an introduction by Howard Fast (Cleveland: World, 1947). The collection was republished with a new introduction by James T. Farrell (Cleveland: World, 1956).

Part II
Science, Technology, and Industry

1

A Prophet, but Not without Honor

The lair of the forecaster.

To BE A PROPHET WITH HONOR IN ONE'S OWN COUNTRY, ONE MUST BE AN official weather prophet. There are other ways, but this is the safest. To no other form of forecasting does government lend its aid and approval, and science its instruments. Neither are salaries attached to any other form of predicting. On the contrary, prophets are usually a mark for the scribes and pharisees, and scoffers in general. If their prediction come out correct they are apt to be accused of some unholy alliance with unseen and noxious forces, and if they fail contumely and scorn are heaped upon them. Such at least was the case a hundred years ago, and things have not changed much. Their way is hard and without reward except as government weather

101

prophets. If the old Hebrew seers were alive there is little doubt but they would all be weather forecasters.

New York has the first of the great weather stations in the United States, and consequently the first of the weather prophets. It is considered second to the central one of the Bureau in Washington, but this is more official form than reality. It is situated in a little circular eyrie of steel and glass perched on the top of the tower of the building of the Manhattan Life Co., on Broadway, below Wall street, and it is a high, storm-beaten, gusty perch indeed. The prophet, who from its inner sanctuary dispenses sunshine, wind and rain, is Elias B. Dunn, commonly denominated Farmer by the heathen scribes of New York, but whose legal title is Local Forecast Official. Here, with a staff of six or eight expert assistants, his observations, which are of interest to a very large section of our continent, are made and recorded. Here, also, are received from no less than one hundred and twenty-five stations scattered over the United States, British Columbia, Canada and Nova Scotia the reciprocal reports upon which he bases his daily forecasts for thirty-six hours ahead. These are the forecasts which appear in the daily papers and which are announced hour by hour, from the tower itself, by means of signals, flags and lights. It is an interesting Bureau, and an interesting life.

Although the Weather Bureau is still a comparatively new branch of the public service, it is one in which all classes are personally interested. The dweller in the city may have lost faith in the predictions to a certain extent, but deciding for him whether he shall or shall not take his umbrella down town in the morning is not the chief aim and end of the Bureau. The hundreds of thousands of farmers, stock raisers, fruit-growers, sea-faring men, tradesmen and others, whose callings depend seriously upon the weather, consult its reports more attentively as a matter of business, and as a result have more faith. Your city clerk and small merchant forget from day to day whether the long distance 36-hour forecast came true or not, but not so the others. Long before the arrival of a great gale, snowstorm, blizzard, or cold wave, they are warned of its approach and take the necessary precautions to avoid loss and escape danger. Crops are housed or guarded, cattle and sheep are sheltered, vessels stay in port instead of venturing out to sea, and outdoor work that would be ruined by a storm is so arranged that loss is avoided.

Of course the Weather Bureau has its critics, who assert that much of its work is useless, and that a very large proportion of its predictions are faulty.

So learned a person as Professor Thomas Russell, United States Assistant Engineer, in his late work on meteorology plainly states that the chief use of a weather bureau is historical rather than predictive. "In recent years," says he, "there has been developed a great deal of interest in

Signal Tower of the New York Weather Bureau.

scientific weather observations. But the hopes that were once entertained that a precise knowledge of coming weather could be gained from the weather may have not been fully realized. Cases are comparatively rare in which it can be used in predicting the weather. There are not more than six to twelve occasions in the course of a year for any part of the country where successful predictions can be made, and for some cases successful predictions are never possible."

This kind of criticism is unavoidable, perhaps, where a territory so vast is covered, and interests so varied have to be served. But even these fault-finders are not blind to the valuable services it renders in the great emergencies already referred to, and especially in foretelling the devastating storms that occur at the change of every season, as well as the dreaded tornadoes and cyclones of midsummer. Every year shows an increase in the efficiency of the Bureau.

Forecaster Dunn has an answer, also, which carries weight. As he said to me not long since: "Weather predictions can be made with confidence and they usually come out true. The percentage of successful predictions is from eighty-five to ninety-five during a whole year. For shorter periods a hundred per cent. of successful forecasting is not at all unusual. It is as near being an exact science as anything can be, because it is founded upon observation and experience. You must remember that the United States Weather Bureau was founded only twenty-eight years ago. When it began, the country was divided into great sections. Here in the East there were the North, Middle and South Atlantic group of States, for which separate probabilities were announced. That was when the Weather Bureau was controlled by the War Department. Now under the Agricultural Department's management, forecasts are made for each State in the Union, and for divisions of the larger States. Again, in twenty-five great cities throughout the country there are what are called local forecasters, who make predictions for that one city. In my own case I succeed or fail in my predictions of rain, according as rain falls in my rain register outside, so that I may say I only predict for a space one foot square at this particular spot. If I announce rain for New York and it rains over half the city, but not in my pan, I must score myself with a failure. Again it may rain slightly in my pan, but not over all New York, and though my prediction may be verified, 'Old Subscriber' who keeps track of the rain as regards his doorstep inwardly rejoices that I have failed in another prediction. So it goes."

There is no room to explain here, even briefly the wonderful and exact physical geographical facts upon which the science of forecasting is based, but a half hour's investigation at the proper sources will convince anyone that with the means at the Weather Bureaus' hand predictions can be made with certainty. It is all a science of air—the cold which waves from the arctics toward the equator and the heat which moves from the equator toward the arctic regions. It is the meeting and interflowing of these differently tempered airs, combined with the rotation of the earth which produces all the phenomena of changing heat and cold, sunshine and rain, calms and storms.

The reason that predictions sometimes fail is that wind is the most capricious of elements, and has a trick of doing the unexpected. "Thou hearest the sound thereof, but canst not tell whence it cometh nor whither it goeth" is about as true to-day as when "Mary's Son walked beneath the palms of Palestine." You may know where the ranges of mountains are and how much they will deflect a storm, and you may have the flat exposure of lakes and seas to assure you of a straight procedure as a rule, but once in a while the winds will change their course without evident cause. The reason could be discovered, of course, after much investigation, but the prediction fails for the nonce.

The New York office is as thoroughly equipped to cope with the problem as any office well can be. From his aerial platform, three hundred and eighty-four feet above the ground, its prophet can look down upon the gilded cross at the top of Trinity Church spire across the way, or sweep the horizon encompassing a tremendous view of Greater New York, including Brooklyn, Jersey City, Staten Island, Westchester county, the North and East rivers, the Harlem, Long Island Sound and the harbor and bay. On the back part of the great building, and some distance from the tower proper in which are the Bureau offices, is an observatory, built of open work iron beams, like a lighthouse, with a closed chamber on top, where are placed the self-registering instruments for measuring the velocity and direction of the wind, the temperature and general atmospheric conditions. All these instruments, by means of electric wires, communicate automatically with Mr. Dunn's office in the tower proper, and upon them he bases the weather maps, there prepared.

The tower proper is divided into a half dozen circular rooms or floors, one above the other, which are connected by a spiral stair. One of these is the main offices, where the historical records are compiled and kept, another is the office of the forecaster, with its dozen instruments connected by wire with the observatory in the rear. A third is a typesetting room where the reports of the office are set up, and a fourth is the Bureau printing office. There is considerable work to do and the Bureau presents a scene which may well confuse the average citizen who is wont to study the western sky at night, or depend on the twinges of divers muscles and corns for indications of a change in the weather.

NOTES

"A Prophet, but Not without Honor," *Ainslee's* 1 (April 1898): 73–79. Signed "Edward Al."

2

Where Battleships Are Built

Uncle Sam's Latest Battleship—"Alabama"

Wᴛʜɪɴ ᴛʜᴇ ʟɪᴍɪᴛs ᴏғ ᴛʜᴇ ᴄɪᴛʏ ᴏғ Pʜɪʟᴀᴅᴇʟᴘʜɪᴀ, ɴᴏᴛ ᴀ ɢʀᴇᴀᴛ ᴅɪs-
tance from the commercial heart, and yet not a great distance from the
suburbs of the city lies a tract of thirty-one acres, on the eastern shore of the
Delaware which is devoted entirely to the construction of ships. One
invades this region of construction not without a sense of diffidence, for
it is a realm of roaring machinery, a region traversed by strange, self-
propelling engines, and filled with thousands of men. Great warships
representing each in itself millions of dollars of expenditure, stand huge
and skeleton-like in immense stocks or frames of wood. In docks of the
largest proportions half, or almost wholly completed vessels ride quietly at
anchor, and throughout the grounds huge piles of the various materials of
construction lie scattered. A section that would strike one as an ordinary
lumber yard, proves to be composed wholly of orderly piles of inch thick
steel plates. Yet another section is filled with cars of rough iron, which at a
distance might pass for wood. Great, long, narrow shops extend in random
directions, from which issue a variety of sounds, the roar of machinery, the
clash and clatter of a boiler shop, the rumbling of a region of smiths and

106

forges, and yet another of huge punching presses, where plates of steel are punctured for purposes of bolting, with a rapidity that in a sense passeth all understanding. It is a realm of bustle and hurry, of vast undertakings and great materials altogether, a city of machines supervised by thousands of men, where things are not measured by the hundreds, but the thousands and tens of thousands of dollars, and this is the region of naval construction, the site of the Cramps ship yards.

The establishment is rather a secret and exclusive affair on the whole, and the stranger is not admitted except on order. To the visitor first entering, it is all a realm of confusion, the centre of which is formed by immense skeleton hulks round which the disorder ranges. By slow degrees dimensions are suggested however, and some idea of the immense amount of work being done comes out of it all. The eye is instantly attracted by the sight of men moving in groups of six and more, an anomaly that is only clear when it is learned that as a rule men work here in small gangs or groups, so many being required at each different machine. Swinging cranes lumber by on tracks along which they propel themselves, carrying aloft in great iron claws immense plates of steel or other masses, which are thus transferred from one point to another. Conspicuously at the water edge rides a huge floating derrick, with its name, *Atlas*, loudly painted upon its head. Within the conglomeration of immense shops, which are scattered about the great open area called the yard, thousands of men and boys are at work, confusedly mingled with the vast extent of intricate machinery contained within their walls. Forging rooms, boiler rooms, joiner houses, machine shops, planing rooms, dawn upon the visitor, one after another. I found afterward, when I was partly free of the nightmare of iron and steel, that it was even more subdivided than I had thought. Presented in order the various sections might be enumerated as: (1) A building 1164 feet long, with an average width of 72 feet, partly three, and partly two stories high, which included under one roof joiner and pattern shop, machine and erecting shop, ship sheds, two mould lofts, roll shop, scribe board and bending shed. (2) A boiler shop 387 feet long by 112 1/2 feet wide, the most extensive in America, and one of the largest and best equipped in the world. (3) A machine shop and most extensive foundry in America, arranged in a quadrangle and covering an entire block of great area. (4) A power house in which are assembled extensive hydraulic, pneumatic and electric plants, whose power is distributed throughout the ship yard and the shops, by means of pipes or wires as the case may be, and applied to the operation of portable drills, slotters, riveters, calking machines, lighting, ventilation, blowing furnace fires, operating bending and sloping machines, and otherwise generally used. (5) Five large building slips, having a capacity of over six hundred feet in length by seventy-five feet in width. (6) Five wet docks, having wharfage ranging from 600 to

1,000 feet in length each. (7) A complete railway system, connecting with the great railways of the city, and penetrating every part of the ship yard and shops. (8) A six story building without the walls, at Beach and Ball streets, containing the administrative offices of the company, as well as the construction and steam engineering draughting room, and a restaurant for the accommodation of the officers of the company and members of the executive staff. (9) An extensive pipe shop, equipped for the manufacture of every variety of pipe required in the steam and water connections, and drainage and ventilating system of ships and their machinery. (10) A large brass foundry fully equipped for the manufacture of every variety of brass, bronze, manganese bronze and white metal castings, and which operates for itself a traveling crane of twenty-five tons, as well as melting and pouring facilities sufficient for single castings of fifty thousand pounds weight. (11) An ordnance plant where are manufactured breech-loading, rapid-firing cannon of four-inch calibre, as well as projectiles for them of all the varieties required in the service afloat and ashore. (12) A basin dry dock, 462 feet long and 72 feet wide. (13) A marine railway capable of hauling out vessels of 10,000 tons burden, and (14) the derrick, *Atlas,* the largest and most powerful of its kind in the world.

There are besides about ten acres of out-door storage space for material, provided with derricks both stationary and locomotive, which are used for handling and shifting heavy plates, shapes, castings and forgings. The company is also permitted to use the United States dry dock at the League Island Navy Yard, for docking and repairing vessels that may be too large for the company's Palmer street dock.

These facilities enumerated, together with many smaller and auxiliary shops and appliances, constitute a ship yard of a capacity equal to any in the world, and superior to all save two or three of the most important yards in Great Britain. Such a state of development has it reached as present that it is no longer a mere manufactory in private hands, but the greatest naval arsenal in the Western Hemisphere, recognized by the government and the people as a public institution and so of the first importance to the sea-power of the nation.

The entire ship yards are divided into two great general divisions, of which the first is the engineering department, in charge of Edwin S. Cramp, and the second the construction department, under Mr. Lewis Nixon.[1] By the first all machinery and motive power for the vessels is constructed as well as stationary engines and mining machinery. These include the enormous boiler shop, and the ordnance department. By the second construction of hulls, fittings and all parts of the ship except the motive power are operated. The vast detail of the yard is thus about equally divided. The two general departments are in turn subdivided into forty minor ones, with as many heads of departments, who answer to the chiefs of the general division in all things.

The order in which contracts are executed is simple enough and will make clear in a rough way the great system which regulates the yard. A government or a corporation upon deciding to build a vessel calls for plans and specifications. At the Cramp yards there is a department employing a score of experts whose time is devoted to preparing such plans and specifications. To one department is allotted the task of preparing all specifications of the ship proper exclusive of motive power. To another, the engineering department, all details of such machinery as will be productive of the greatest speed. Once these plans are accepted and the contract closed, the various manufacturing departments are given orders for such parts of the material as those departments manufacture. The entire ship is parceled out, and the manufacturing proceeds apace. In nearly all cases such parts when completed are stamped with the name of the vessel for which they are intended, and are sent to the company store room, which is a sort of giant wholesale house, with which all departments deal. Here is collected all the materials of which a ship may be constructed. The various manufacturing departments are constantly supplying its counters with every possible articles of use from brass headed tacks and such other small hardware, to immense plates, wheels, boilers and so on. At its counters slips of paper calling for certain material and signed with the name of the head of a department, is substituted for money. There is no direct dealing between any of the departments, and when anything is desired anywhere, it is always bought at the store.

No sooner is the contract for the construction of a vessel closed, than duplicate specifications are placed in the hands of the officers of construction and the keel is laid. The great stock to hold the hull of the new vessel is begun and hundreds of expert workmen are put to work, laboring according to direction of their superiors. Orders are presented at the store room for everything needed to begin the work, and as that is a source of never-failing supply, the work goes steadily forward. The storeroom may be out of certain materials and of course delay follows, but it is the endeavor of the company to keep its wholesale house constantly ready to supply every demand.

In passing, I should like to indicate the interest which attaches to the business methods employed in this department. I occupied a keg behind the counter for several hours one afternoon, and contemplated the stream of sooty-faced, blue-jacketed, oil stained purchasers, who paid their way with slips of paper. Some departed with such things as lamps, oil, brass fixtures, lead, nails, and other such small materials as an individual might carry without overburdening himself. Still others paid in their orders with requests that the goods be delivered at once. One of the orders called for the brass fixtures appropriate to some part of the engine room of the *Alabama* and these the salesman told me were valued at five thousand dollars. They were quickly sent out as one order. An order for the delivery of a number of steel plates aggregating in cost as high as ten thousand dollars is not uncommon. The business transacted at the company store in one day is seldom less than thirty thousand dollars and very often much more. The stream of buyers is unbroken from morning till night. It is needless to say that the order slips thus taken as money, simplify the book-keeping of the company and serve as vouchers for every dollar's worth of material used.

As a rule the construction of an armored vessel is a work covering a period of four or five years. That of commercial vessels, such as the *St. Louis* and *St. Paul* takes slightly less than two years. The time required for other vessels varies from six months to two years. At the launching of the steamer *Miama*, which took place in October of last year, the Cramps won laurels, and made a record for building a ship in less time than has ever been known before. The vessel was constructed for Henry M. Flagler, and in less than six months from the time the keel was laid, the vessel was equipped and ready for service.[2] While not as large as some of the trans-atlantic liners, she is equal, if not superior, in fittings to most of them. The old United States navy which did service during the War of the Rebellion was partially built by the Cramps Company. The famous ironclad steam frigate *New Ironsides,* which was long employed in the blockading fleet off Charleston, was built at the Kensington yard. The monitors *Yazoo* and *Tunxis,* as well as the three thousand five hundred ton steam frigate *Chattanooga,* were also constructed by the Cramps during the war. The famous protected cruisers of to-day were modeled almost exactly on the *New Ironsides.*

Of the new navy the protected cruisers *Baltimore, Philadelphia, Newark, Columbia* and *Minneapolis;* the armored cruisers *New York* and *Brooklyn,* the gunboat *Yorktown,* the dynamite cruiser *Vesuvius,* the battle-ships *Indiana* and *Massachusetts* and the sea-going battleship *Iowa,* have been built at and launched from these yards since 1886. There have been as many as five warships in the stocks at one time, with nearly six thousand men at work, and eight million dollars worth of prepared material ready at hand. The *Alabama* now in process of construction is the last on the list—a battleship of the first class.

At the present writing there are but two war vessels in the stocks, though as a rule there are four and five. These are the battleship *Alabama,* being built for the United States Government, and the cruiser *Kasagi,* under construction for Japan. Most of the hull work on these has been finished, and the work of putting in place the steel-protected deck of the *Kasagi* is now being done. The latter is to be completed in December of the present year, while the *Alabama,* owing to the failure of our Government to furnish the armor and its accessories within the time, will be delayed until some time in 1900. The price paid the Cramps Company by Japan for *Kasagi* is two million dollars. That paid by the United States for the *Alabama,* two million six hundred and fifty thousand dollars.

NOTES

"Where Battleships Are Built," *Ainslee's* 1 (June 1898): 433–39. Signed "Edward Al."

1. Edwin S. Cramp was a descendant of William Cramp (1807–79), American shipbuilder, who pioneered in steam and ironclad ship construction. William Cramp founded the Cramps Company, which Dreiser mentions earlier in the article.

2. Henry Morrison Flagler (1830–1913), American capitalist, led the development of Florida as a luxury resort region.

3
The Making of Small Arms

CONNECTICUT IS CERTAINLY THE HOME OF THE MAKER OF WEAPONS. THE State has within its limits a numerous company of manufacturers of small arms, whose factories are the centre and life of many of its towns. It leads the union in the number of rifles and shotguns turned out, and the bulk of ammunition fired from Alaska to Panama is made at one of the big manufactories of Bridgeport. At New Haven, within a mile of the historic

The Outpouring at Noon

grounds and buildings of Yale University, are the thirty acres of grounds and buildings occupied by the Winchester Arms Company, where the new navy rifle known as the Lee Straight Pull is being manufactured for the Government, under pressure of the present emergency, by tens of thousands.[1] It is a rapid fire gun, from which five shots known to carry two miles in fair weather, may be delivered without taking the gun from the shoulder. It is loaded by inserting a clip containing five smokeless powder cartridges, and is always ready for rapid fire, as the time consumed in opening the breech and inserting a clip is rather short, when five shots are instantly ready for delivery. In addition, brass shells for the smaller forms of navy cannon are being turned out in great number, and, of course, all forms of rifles and ammunition sold to the lay public during the ordinary piping times of peace. It is an enormous concern, as measured by ordinary industries, and one which in time of war rises to the first importance.

As to location, all know that New Haven is about seventy miles from New York, on the northern shore of Long Island Sound. The city, favored by a broad, quiet harbor, has one hundred thousand population, and for nine months of each year the transient residence of the classmen of Yale. It is a well-built, cleanly place, with a kind of classic air loaned to it by the old and architecturally reminiscent buildings of the University, and reminds one in spots of the college towns of Europe. The armory and departments of the Winchester Company are located at the southwestern edge of the city, not quite within nor yet without the limits. They form a sort of village in themselves, wherein twenty-three hundred men and women are at work all day long, and wherein the click and beat of machinery join with the clatter and roar of large and small arms, so that it might be said that these workers dwell in the midst of alarms. The exterior is plain after the manner of all manufactories, consisting of long, narrow, four-story red brick buildings, which range as nearly as possible about a square internal space, filled with low-roofed store-rooms, foundries, smithies, testing departments, and so on. The whole is as safely shut to the stranger as are the walls of a penitentiary, and the several gates stand closed and guarded, during all but the hours of entry and departure. Hundreds of cottages in the immediate vicinity owe their existence to the employment furnished within, and the entire city hangs more or less on the prosperity of the great concern which distributes a million a year in wages. It is the largest of arms companies in America, and carries in times of war the heaviest government contracts.

An idea of the immensity of the industry can be had from a simple list of the various departments which are twenty in number, and in each of which from one to three hundred men are employed. They are (1) a drawing and annealing department where wrought iron is received in ingots and sent away in circular bars, the shape of an ordinary gun barrel; (2) a forging department, where the swell at the breech end of all barrels is stamped to a required shape by steam-hammer, and afterward straightened cold; (3) a department of turning and drilling machines, where the barrels are rough-bored; (4) a rifling department, where all rough-bored barrels secure their right to the name of rifle; (5) a breech-forging department, where all the mechanism of the breech is by a series of forgings, drillings, and so on, prepared for its union with the stock; (6) a stocking department, where blocks of wood are slightly sprung in turning and brought back to the necessary condition of accuracy; (7) a grinding department, where hundreds of sandstone wheels are employed in removing the roughness and marks of turning from the outer surface of the barrel; (8) a polishing department, which supplements the work of grinding, and (9) a proving room, where the barrels are tested with heavy charges of powder and shot for any sign of weakness.

The remaining half of the process of rifle constructing is carried forward in nine departments, which, briefly are, the assembling room, manipulation department, targeting alley, stability or heat-testing room, the departments of temperature, velocity, accuracy and penetration, and the departments of inlaying, packing and stuffing.

The whole work is governed by a large office corps, the power is supplied by an immense engine and boiler house, and a system of railway tracks penetrates the yards, connecting the works with the great metropolitan centres of the world.

The first operation in the manufacturing of a rifle is of course the formation of the barrel. For this purpose plates one foot in length and weighing ten pounds are heated to a white heat and then passed between three sets of rollers, each of which lengthens the barrel, reduces its diameter, and assists in forcing it to the proper size and taper. Four persons are employed at each set of rollers, and there being forty sets, the number of men at work present an interesting sight. Each gang consists of a foreman, who sees to the heating of the scalp and barrels; the straightener, who straightens the barrel after it passes through the roller; the catcher, who stands behind the roller to catch the barrel when it passes through, and the fireman. The rollers weigh several tons each, and forty sets are capable of turning out eight thousand barrels per day, one per cent. of which burst in the proving house.

The barrel when rolled is left much larger in the circumference, and smaller in the bore, than it is intended to be when finished, in order to allow for the loss of metal in the various finishing operations. When it passes into the roller the scalp weights ten pounds; when it comes from the roller the barrel weighs a little over seven; when completed it weighs but four and a half; so that more than one-half the metal originally used is lost in the forging, or cut away by the subsequent process.

The first of these latter is the boring-out of the interior of the barrels by boring machines, to which an immense department is devoted. The machines, which consist of square, solid frames of iron, in which the barrel is fixed are set close together. They occupy a room that is darkened with the shadow of moving belts and wheels. A slowly progressing and rotating augur advances through the barrel, enlarging the cavity as it proceeds. After it has passed through, another augur, a trifle larger, is substituted in its place, and so the calibre of the barrel is gradually enlarged to nearly the required size. The number of borings required has been cut down from six to three, and a still greater reduction is expected with steadily improving machinery.

After the boring of the barrel, it is removed to a department of lathe machines. Fastened in one of these, it slowly revolves, bringing all parts of the exterior surface under the action of a tool fixed firmly in the right position for cutting down the barrel to its proper form.

A curious and interesting part of the work follows when the barrel is straightened. This straightening takes place continually in every stage of the work, from the time the barrel emerges from the chaotic mass produced by heating the scalp, until it reaches the assembling room, where the various parts of the rifle are put together. As you enter the boring and turning room, you are struck with surprise at observing hundreds of workmen standing with rifle barrels in their hands, one end held up to their eyes, and the other pointing to some one of the innumerable windows of the apartment. Watching them a few moments, however, you will observe, that after looking through the barrel a half-minute, and turning it round in their fingers, they lay it down upon a small anvil standing at their side, and strike upon it a gentle blow with a hammer, and then raise it again to the eye. The thing that is really done is the holding of the barrel up directly to the pane of glass, which is furnished with a transparent slate, having two parallel lines drawn across it. These lines are reflected through the bore of the barrel to the eye—the inner surface of the barrel being in a brilliantly polished condition from the boring. When the barrel is placed at the proper angle, there are two parallel shadows thrown upon opposite sides of the inner surface, which by a slight movement of the barrel can be made to come to a point at the lower end. The appearance which these shadows assume determines the question whether the barrel is straight or not, and if not, where it requires straightening. Each workman is obliged to correct his own work, and afterward it is passed into the hands of the inspector, who returns it to the workman if faulty, or stamps his approval if correct.

The next process is that of grinding, for the purpose of removing marks left upon the surface by the tool in turning, and of still further perfecting its form. For this operation immense grindstones rotating at the rate of four hundred times a minute are used. They are fed with water, and covered to keep the stream from flying about the room. The barrel is then fitted upon an iron rod which is controlled by machinery, and here it slowly revolves, directed by a workman whose duty it is to see that the action of the stone is brought equally upon all parts.

There are twelve sets of stones in the grinding-room in constant operation. These stones, when set up, are about eight feet in diameter, and are used or worn down to within twelve inches of the centre. They last about ten days.

When a barrel has been rough bored, as the first boring is called, and before the exterior has been ground smooth or polished, it is removed to the proving-room, a small, solid-built hut unconnected with any other building. The character of this hut excites immediate attention, not alone for its massiveness of wall and roof, but for the tremendous explosions which take place within regularly every three minutes during the day. The spectator lingering for a few moments observes that the occupant of the hut, a man with smoke-stained face and grimy apron, appears at the door with a bugle in hand, upon which he blows a goodly blast. No sooner does the sound of the horn begin to die away than it is followed by a ground-shaking explosion which takes place within. A cloud of dense white smoke spreads with the sound, and in a moment completely envelopes hut and occupant from view. This interesting procedure is the outward and visible sign of the inner English Government test which is taking place. A score of rough-bored barrels are locked to a firing table which the solid walls surround, loaded with a charge of powder and lead twice as great as could be put into the shell the barrel is chambered for and fired. The blowing of a bugle blast at the door is a warning to all drivers of horses nearby, to rein in nervous ones. With the clearing of the smoke the barrels are removed and carefully inspected, and if any one shows the slightest trace of strain or other imperfection, it is condemned.

All barrels so tested are returned to the rough-boring department, where it is once more straightened and given a second rapid boring to remove the possible roughness. Again straightened, it is given what is known as the "lead test," a process that never fails to disclose any imperfection in the interior of the barrel. In making this test the barrel is held in a vise, and a plug of lead, the exact size of the bore, placed in it at the breech and expanded or upset, until it binds lightly and evenly all around the bore. The plug is then gradually pushed through the barrel with a copper rod by the expert conducting the test. The slightest variation in the diameter of the bore is instantly disclosed by the different pressure required to push the plug through the barrel.

In all shooting cartridges of different or like calibres, containing different weights of powder or lead, require a different "twist" or revolving movement to carry them forward against the wind to the best advantage. Accordingly one of the most difficult things to determine in making rifle barrels is the *twist* or *rifling* required to shoot a given cartridge to the best advantage. A perfect twist is one which will spin a bullet fast enough to keep it *point on* to the limit of its range, and make its pathway through the air as near a straight line as possible. If the twist is too slow the flight of the bullet will be untrue, and it will "tumble" or "keyhole," as it is called when a bullet passes through the air in a lengthwise position instead of point on. On the contrary, if the twist is too sharp or quick the bullet is spun so rapidly that it is unsteady in its flight and wobbles like a top when it first begins to spin. Perfect rifling is intended to give a perfect twist, and this work forms the next great department to which the barrel after grinding and polishing takes its way.

The gun barrel, after arriving here, is placed in a horizontal position in an iron frame and clamped firmly. The instruments which perform the rifling are three short steel cutters placed within three apertures situated near the end of an iron tube. The cutters upon this iron tube are narrow bars of steel, having upon one side three diagonal protuberances of about one-sixteenth of an inch in height and half an inch in width, ground to a very sharp edge at the top. It is these which produce the rifling. The iron tube to which they are attached, is in turn fixed upon a small iron rod attached to the machine. This rod, slowly revolving, is driven through the bore, and the cutters of steel, revolving with it mark and deepen the corrugations seen in the perfected barrel—in other words, rifle the barrel. It takes some twenty minutes to rifle a barrel, and there are hundreds of rifling machines in constant operation. This process is the last which takes place within the barrel, and it leaves the bore in a highly polished and brilliant condition.

There are forty-nine pieces used in the making of a rifle, which have to be formed and finished separately; only two of these, the sight and cone seat, are permanently attached to any other part, so that a rifle can, at any time, be separated into forty-seven parts by simply turning screws and opening springs. Most of these parts are struck in dies and then finished by milling and filing. The process of this manufacture is called swaging, *i.e.*, the forming of irregular shapes in iron by means of dies, one of which is inserted in an anvil in a cavity made for the purpose, and the other placed above it in a trip-hammer, or in a machine operated in a manner akin to that of a pile-driver, called a drop. Cavities are cut in the faces of the dies, so that when they are brought together with the end of a flat bar of iron, out of which the article is to be made, inserted between them, the iron is made to assume the form of the cavities, by means of blows of the trip-hammer, or of the drop. About one hundred and fifty operations upon the various pieces used in the construction of a rifle are performed by these dies. Some of the pieces are struck out by one blow of the trip-hammer. The hammer of the rifle is first forged and then put twice through the drop. This is also the case with the spring cover, mortise cover, breech pin base, carrier lever, and the other thirty odd parts which are used. Some of the pieces are pressed in shape under these steam-hammers when cold, but as a rule the swaging is done while the piece is at a red or white heat. The operations of the various steam-hammers are exceedingly interesting, and the amount of labor they save is almost incredible.

When the pieces come out of the swaging-room they have more or less surplus metal about them, which is cut off or trimmed by passing through machines designed for this purpose.

The rolling, forging and swaging-rooms are connected, and form as it were, one department. In this are the hundreds of forges, furnaces, trip-hammers, rolling mills, dropping and trimming machines. It is a place of deep shadow and smoke, filled with a wearying roar and shifting fires, and hurried through by grimy-faced, bare-armed workmen, whose world of day this is. You will understand, if you disobey, why your guide is insistent in requesting that you touch nothing. The floors are warm, the piles of iron and casts of forgings are hot. Objects of all shapes heaped in orderly piles and looking cold—block are but slightly cooled masses of iron where a touch will mean a painful burn. The air is thick and choking with the heat, and the smell of iron and the sound of hammers and revolving, grunting machines become unbearable.

I stated that the number of pieces used in the construction of a rifle are forty-nine; but this conveys no idea of the number of separate operations performed upon it. The latter amount to over four hundred, no two of which are by the same hand. Indeed, so distinct are the processes by which the eventual result is obtained, that an artisan employed upon one part, may have no knowledge of the process by which another part is fabricated. This in fact is the case to a very large extent. Many persons employed upon particular parts of the work in this establishment have never even seen other parts manufactured, and in general the workman understands only the process of making the portions upon which he is engaged. Of course only the leading processes have been touched upon here.

The wood from which the stocks are made is the black walnut, and comes more or less from Canada. The original blocks are sawn into a rough semblance of the rifle stock before they come to the armory. It then passes through seventeen different machines, emerging from the last perfectly formed. It has yet to be stained by the painter and ornamented (if a fancy rifle) by the inlayer before it is sent to the assembling-room, to be put together with other parts, into the complete rifle.

A gun stock is, perhaps, as irregular a shape as the ingenuity of man could devise, and as well calculated to bid defiance to every attempt at applying machinery to the work of fashinoning it. The difficulties however, have all been overcome, and every part of the stock is formed, and every perforation, groove, cavity, and socket is cut in it, by machines that do their work with such perfection as to awaken in all who witness this process a feeling of astonishment and admiration. No general idea of the process can be given here, but the department must be noted as one of the largest and most important, employing as it does, hundreds of men.

When the several parts of a rifle are finished they are sent in lots to an apartment in the arsenal to be put together. This operation is called assembling the rifle, and the room, the assembling-room. There is a large number of workmen whose operations are confined to the putting together of these parts into rifles, each one having some distinct part to attend to. Thus, one man puts the various parts of the lock together, while another screws the lock into the stock. Another is occupied in uniting the intricate parts that make the magazine and the automatic feeding apparatus which makes the rifle a repeater. Each workman has the parts upon which lie is employed before him, on his bench, arranged in compartments, in regular order, and puts them together with considerable speed. The component parts of a rifle are all made according to one exact pattern, and thus, when taken up at random, are sure to come properly together. There is no special fitting required in each individual case. Any barrel will fit any stock, and a screw designed for a particular plate or band will enter the proper hole in any plate or band of a hundred thousand. There are many advantages resulting from this interchangeability of parts. Spare screws, firing pins, springs, in fact all parts are easily furnished in quantities, and sent to any part of the country where needed, so that when any part of a soldier's gun becomes injured or broken, its place can be immediately supplied by a new piece, which is as sure to fit as perfectly as the original. Each soldier to whom a rifle is served is provided with a tool, which, though very simple in its construction, enables him to separate his gun into its various parts and to assemble it, with the greatest facility. The breaking of a part does not therefore mean the loss of a rifle, as the Government keeps all the parts in quantity ready to replace.

When guns are assembled, that is, put together ready for use, they are tested carefully for manipulation and accuracy. The test for manipulation consists of working the gun thoroughly with "dummy" cartridges and firing it as a single loader or repeater, slowly and quickly, to detect any possible defect in the action. If a gun is faulty in extracting, in handling the cartridges, or does not work smoothly, easily, and rapidly, it cannot pass this test. Rifles are shot from three to ten shots, and shotguns from eight to fifteen shots, to test their action.

For the purpose of this test there are long shooting alleys or ranges of from one hundred feet up to two hundred yards in length where every gun is shot to test its accuracy, the distance varying according to the calibre. A corps of experts devote their entire time to this work, and before a gun is passed by them it must be capable of shooting seven consecutive bull's eyes on a standard sized target for the distance shot. All guns are shot to line up the sights, an expert changing them until they are properly aligned and given the proper elevation. A gun which does not make a good target is condemned.

The final processes of manufacturing which precede the inspecting, packing and shipping of guns are included in two departments: one known as the department for determining velocity, and the other the department of accuracy and penetration—two sections where the work is cleanly and rather scientific in its nature. It seems almost incredible, even in these days of miracles, that it is possible to tell how fast a bullet travels through the air when fired from a gun, yet by the aid of a wonderful instrument known as the "Le Boulange Chronograph," or "Velocimeter," it is done with absolute accuracy.[2] The department for this purpose contains a number of these instruments, operated by two men. Each instrument is connected with a separate shooting alley, or range, where the gun is placed, and where there is a helper who loads and sets the gun in order for the test. The other workman is at a desk which supports the Velocimeter, ready to calculate the distance it shall record when the gun is fired. The Chronograph is connected with the gun from which the cartridge is fired, and with the target which its shot strikes by two electrical circuits. When the apparatus is adjusted, the signal is given and the gun is fired. The moment the cartridge explodes it breaks the circuit connecting the gun with the Chronograph, and the latter instantly begins to record the time of the bullet's flight. When the bullet strikes the target shot at it breaks the circuit connecting the target with the Chronograph, and the instrument stops registering. The register shows the time taken by the bullet in traveling from the gun to the target, and as this distance is known, it is a simple process to calculate the velocity of the bullet in feet per second.

The second of these final manufacturing tests is in this department devoted to discovering the accuracy and penetration of rifle shots. Here is another series of shooting alleys, with targets at the end. Before them are ranged in a tow a number of men who have a gun rest before them, and a telescope at their right hand, through which they can study the distant target. A rack containing rifles is at their left hand. These they take, one by one, place in the rest before them, load, and after carefully sighting, fire. They then look through the telescope to see how near the centre the shot has struck. This sighting and firing is repeated over and over until the gun is known to be accurate or defective. If the latter it is returned for examination.

Penetration is also determined here by shooting into fine boards of a given thickness. The number of boards that a rifle shot should penetrate at the standard testing distance of fifteen feet depends upon the size and character of the cartridge as much as it does upon the quality of the gun. Certain makes must send lead into wood a given depth or they are defective and are returned for general correction. The new navy rifle drives its bullet six feet into ordinary pine wood at a distance of fifteen feet, and each rifle must equal this. Men are constantly engaged in firing to ascertain penetration, and a troop of boys are employed to bring in the wood shot at to the inspector, who notes whether the proper penetrative force has been attained.

Guns passing the tests for manipulation, accuracy and so forth are given a final inspection for exterior finish, etc., and are then ready for the storeroom, packing-room, and subsequent market.

Over this vast organization where thousands of guns are daily turned out complete, the most careful watch is maintained. Nothing could be more admirably planned, or more completely and precisely executed than the system of accounts kept at the offices, by which not only every pecuniary transaction, but also, as would seem, almost every mechanical operation or act that takes place throughout the establishment is made a matter of record. Thus everything is checked and regulated. No piece, large or small, can be lost from among its hundreds of fellows without being missed somewhere in some one of the hundreds of columns of figures. Indeed the whole history of every workman's doings, and of every piece of work done, is to be found recorded. Ask the master armorer any questions whatever about the workings of the establishment, whether relating to the minutest detail, or to most comprehensive and general results, and he will take down a book, in which some figure or column of figures will make answer to you.

And yet, when one comes away, out into the simple world, where there is no roar of countless machinery, no hurry of thousands of hands, no evidence of a careful and exact system, the memory of the great plant with its floors and dark shop and thousand noises becomes a strange evil, making for war. Its motive force is destruction. Its product weapons. It exists because men slay and will not be at peace, and so the mind carries the thought as a burden. And yet this is sometimes modified by the higher thought that it is the enemy of war, in that the motive is to make implements wherewith to compel peace. In such a light the endless procession of guns is not so bad, nay, it is even satisfying in that war by them is made so swift and decisive, that after a while there may be no longer need of war.

NOTES

"The Making of Small Arms," *Ainslee's* 1 (July 1898): 540–49.

1. The company was well known for Winchester rifles, which were prominent in the winning of the West and have been favored by many collectors.

2. Chronograph or velocimeter is a device used to measure and produce visual records with respect to the duration of events lasting fractions of a second up to twelve hours.

4

Scenes in a Cartridge Factory

MAN'S INGENUITY FINDS MANY CONTRADICTORY CHANNELS FOR ITS EX-
pression. The labor to perfect those sciences which tend to save human life
goes on side by side with the labor to create new and more potent methods
for its destruction.

Machines for Lengthening the shells.

This is significantly apparent in the dual operations of governments,
which on the one hand expend vast sums in the development of plans more
or less humanitarian in purpose, while at the same time even greater sums
go toward the improving of those devices which shall be most effective
when applied to the sinister processes of warfare.

This is as true of the United States as it is of any other nation. We have
been foremost in the making of what are called small arms, and their
ammunitions. We maintain numerous arsenals where at all times this work
has been carried on, and now, with war actually upon us, the productive
capacity of these arsenals is taxed to the utmost, while contracts involving
hundreds of thousands of dollars have been placed in outside hands.

122

The concern carrying the largest of these contracts is the Union Metallic Cartridge Company, of Bridgeport, Conn. This single contract calls for many millions of that peculiar type of cartridge known as the "U. S. Army and Navy copper-jacketed," a cartridge differing much from that used in the ordinary rifle.[1]

One of its differences is that its cap or head is twice the size of its mouth—its general shape being not unlike that of a gourd. The large amount of powder—the new smokeless variety—exploding, and its force being required to pass out through a small aperture, results in a tremendous pressure on the bullet.

This bullet is incased in a copper cover plated with tin, as it must be capable of withstanding a velocity of two thousand five hundred and fifty feet per second, a velocity creating friction sufficient to melt lead. The penetrating power of one of these projectiles is so great that after the first five feet of its flight are covered it will cut through fifty-four pine boards, each having a thickness of seven-eighths of an inch, or it will pass through half an inch of solid steel, and it will kill at a distance of over one mile.

The great works at Bridgeport where these cartridges are made are barrack-like structures, with rooms three and four hundred feet long and fifty feet wide, filled with rows upon rows of machines, and the rattle and din of a ceaseless activity.

Save for the forge-rooms where the metals are heated, or annealed, and the chambers where are stored the different kinds of black, or smokeless, powders, there is hardly a spot without its machine of some sort, operated in most cases by girls or women. Thousands of wheels and cogs are revolving, busy with the many separate processes the completed cartridge cases represent. They are being produced at the rate of from fifty to one hundred and fifty per minute. Even the great brass shells for cannon are turned out thirty-five to the minute by the ponderous machines employed in the work.

It is the purpose of this article to describe the manufacture of those cartridges used in the new army and navy guns.

The sheet copper for the shells of these cartridges comes to the operator in strips three inches wide and thirty-five inches in length, and having a thickness of three one-hundredths of an inch. They are selected by a number of men who throw aside all those that are imperfect or are not of an even thickness throughout. The edges of the sheets are first made smooth and their surfaces oiled. After this has been done they are ready to be fed to the presses; a small stop on the die regulates the length of the "feed." The shape given the future cartridge case is that of a flat disk rather larger than a twenty-five-cent piece. Forty like this are cut one at a time from each strip by the double punches of the press. This double punch is a punch within a punch, and as the outer one cuts the disk clear from the strip the inner one passes the piece through a tapering hole in the die, giving it a cup-like shape an inch in diameter and five-tenths of an inch deep. These disks are cut and fashioned at the rate of sixty-five a minute.

In order to "draw" the cup to the size required for the finished shell, the disks are subjected to the action of four additional punches which lengthen them, while reducing them to the proper diameter.

The shells are next taken to the annealing rooms, where they are placed in perforated iron cylinders and brought to a white heat over charcoal fires; a slow process, because if allowed to heat too rapidly the metal becomes brittle.

From the cylinders they are plunged while hot into a mixture of sulphuric acid and water, which frees them from any scale or oxide that the annealing may have occasioned. Afterward they are thoroughly washed to remove the acid.

The shells are now in need of being "trimmed," the last drawing having left them with ragged edges.

The trimming is done in a long room with triple lines of machines. In front of these machines sit the girls whose duty it is to feed the shells to a revolving mandrel which brings them to a circular cutter where the edges are made clean and even.

The next step is the "rimming." At the rate of seventy a minute the shells are caught up from a trough and treated by this process, which leaves them finished and ready for the loading—after they have been put through an alkali bath to remove the oil that has been used in all the various stages of preparation. From the bath they are taken to the drying-rooms to be dried.

The loading begins with the adjustment of the cup-annil, which contains the priming.

The making of the cup-annils is a process by itself. Copper sheets one forty-fifth of an inch thick are cut by small punches into one hundred and seventy-six cups each, and at a speed of forty-five to the minute.

The next machine does for them exactly what the larger machines did for the ragged edges of the cartridge cases—smooths and finishes them.

They are passed on to venting machines, where they are punched with two holes. They are now ready to receive the impression which is to serve as a receptacle for the priming.

This high explosive is manufactured at the Bridgeport works, but visitors are not allowed in the department. It can be seen, however, when it is brought into the room where the cup-annils are charged. It has the appearance of a thick paste, and it is deposited in the cup-annil by what is known as a priming machine, a very ingenious device which performs its delicate work with the greatest nicety.

While the explosive is still moist the cup-annils are carried to the tapering machine and are fitted to the shells and secured in place by "crimping," and the shells themselves drawn or reduced at the mouth to fit the long, slim bullet.

An entire building is devoted to the casting of the bullets, the work being done entirely by men.

Huge pots placed over furnaces hold the molten metal, and as the lead is run off to supply the bullet machines fresh pigs of it are thrown into the pots that they may be kept constantly replenished.

The lead is first cast in bars; these when cool are passed through rolls where they are reduced to thirty one-hundredths of an inch in diameter with a length of forty inches. In this form they are fed to the bullet machine through a vertical tube which rises above a horizontal cutter. Each cut takes only sufficient material for a single bullet. Another machine forces these bits of lead into the desired shape. A single machine can make twenty-seven thousand bullets in a day.

The bullets are next trimmed and then incased in their copper jackets. They are now ready to be fitted to the shells.

The loading is done in the "assembling room." The shells are placed in holes or receivers, on a circular plate. Each one of these holes is so arranged as to pass directly beneath the powder hopper, where the shells are charged automatically.

The machine is provided with a bell which gives notice to the operator of any failure in this particular. The shells are next brought under the bullet feed. The bullet descends through a chute and enters the shell, which is tightly crimped about it. The cartridge is now complete.

During the whole process of manufacture accidents are possible in the loading-room only. As the machines are now made and arranged, the explosion of one cartridge may communicate fire to the few charged cases near it without danger, or the powder in the hopper may explode, it is said, and do no injury either to the operative or to the machine.

As the explosive is the most important factor in the effectiveness of a projectile of any sort, that used in the making of cartridges is subjected to various tests. One of these is the heat test, where the temperature at which it will explode is determined, as this indicates whether or not the proper ingredients were used in the compounding.

The primers are also carefully examined. From each scpaiate lot a number are taken. These are snapped off in a gun. Should a single one miss fire, the entire lot to which it belongs is destroyed. In this way the quality of each cartridge is kept as near the required standard as possible.

The cartridges are tested as to accuracy, penetration and velocity. The accuracy test is made by a number of expert marksmen who are kept busy all day long shooting at the targets in the ranges of the works. By the aid of a wonderful instrument called the chronograph the actual speed of a bullet through the air can be ascertained.[2] The chronograph is connected with the gun from which the bullet is discharged, and with the target, by means of two electrical circuits. When the apparatus is adjusted, the signal is given and the cartridge to be tested, fired. The moment the cartridge explodes it breaks the circuit connecting the gun with the chronograph and the latter instantly commences to register the time of the bullet's flight. When the bullet strikes the target it breaks the circuit connecting the target with the chronograph and the instrument stops registering. The register shows the time taken by the bullet in traveling from the gun to the target, and as this distance is known, it is a simple process to calculate the velocity in feet per second.

In the whole vast factory, covering acres of ground and with its hundreds of employees, such a perfect system is maintained that not a handful of material could be either wasted or abstracted without the knowledge of some one of the many superintendents, whose vigilance is never suffered to relax.

While wars and rumors of wars continue to be factors in our civilization, so long will nations support great armies and so long will the manufacture of arms and ammunition be a matter of vital interest and importance to the governments of the world.

NOTES

"Scenes in a Cartridge Factory," *Cosmopolitan* 25 (July 1898): 321–24.

1. For small-arms ammunition, the term "cartridge" means the completely assembled cartridge case, primer, propellant powder charge, and bullet.

2. For the term "chronograph," see note 2 in the previous article "The Making of Small Arms," included in this volume.

5

Our Government and Our Food

Important Investigations Now Making by the Department of Agriculture Concerning Food

It is not generally known that our Government, through that very important office, the United States Department of Agriculture, has been looking into the subject of the food we consume. It first did so in order to round out certain experiments which had been made in the line of proper foods for animals. For a number of years it had been trying to find out what would best fatten hogs and strengthen horses, and as a result a great system of food investigation has been evolved.

These investigations are based on the following facts: Certain foods when eaten do certain things for the body. One kind builds up the muscles and tendons; another kind aids in forming bone; a third does little more than assist the stomach to digest, a fourth builds up fatty tissue. All really serve as fuel, and yield energy in the form of heat and activity. Now the thing in all foods that goes to build up the muscles and tendons is known as protein. It is abundant in the white of eggs, the curd of milk, the gluten of wheat, and in lean meat. On the other hand, the things that aid in forming bone and assist digestion are called mineral matter. These are usually phosphates of lime, potash and soda. All fruits contain them in abundance, and that is why fruits are so good for the digestion. The things that make the body simply fat—not strong—and add heat and some energy to it, are called fats. Of these the fat of meat, butter, olive oils, oil of corn, wheat and nuts are examples. In the last place there are certain things, such as sugar and starch, which, when taken into the body, are transformed by the digestive fluids into fat. There are called carbohydrates.

As said before, these fats, carbohydrates and protein, furnish fuel to the body. One pound of protein will furnish so much fuel or heat in the body that, if it were applied like fire to a teakettle, it would raise 1860 pounds of water, zero cold, up to 4 degrees above zero. One pound of fat taken into the body will furnish heat equal to what would raise 4220 pounds of zero water up to 4 degrees Fahrenheit. One pound of carbohydrates furnishes

127

heat the equal of what would raise 1860 pounds of zero water up to 4 degrees above zero.

With this knowledge the Government has started out to experiment and learn just how much of these things the food eaten by Americans contains. It wants to find out just how much protein, fats, carbohydrates and minerals a man needs to eat every day in order to be strong and healthy. It wants to know just how much of these things each particular fruit and grain and vegetable contains, and whether some of these things, because of the greater quantity of nutrients which they hold in solution, are not better than others. It wants to find out whether men are not mistaken as regards certain things which they eat; whether, indeed, certain foods do not lack so much of these healthful properties, and contain so much injurious matter, that they are useless, or even injurious, as food.

To this end a great system of laboratories and experiment stations have been established all over the country, equipped with the most modern scientific paraphernalia. Their purpose and value will best be understood when the manner in which they came into existence is related.

In 1886 the Hon. Carroll D. Wright, then Chief of the Massachusetts Bureau of Statistics of Labor, began to investigate how much food factory operatives, mechanics, and other people with moderate incomes consume.[1] When the investigation was over, he sent the mixed mass of statistics to Prof. W. O. Atwater, at Wesleyan University, who put them in such form that they could be understood and compared with any other statistics that might be gathered upon the subject. Professor Atwater had for years previous been much interested in this subject, and was at that very time engaged upon similar work in the vicinity of Middletown, Conn., with a number of students of the university. Mr. Wright afterward lent Professor Atwater the whole machinery of the Massachusetts Bureau of Statistics of Labor to help him in his studies. When Mr. Wright, owing to his fame as an investigator, was called to the United States Department of Labor, he got the Government to interest itself in Professor Atwater's work, so that eventually that scientist was called to take charge of the Storrs Agricultural Experiment Station, where the investigations concerning animal nourishment spoken of were already under way. Under his direction the facts developed by experiments there became so interesting, and the outlook for a great food reformation so clear that the Secretary of Agriculture was interested. He in turn applied to Congress for an appropriation "to be applied to the study of the food and nutrition of man," which was granted, and so the great work began. Its supervision was assigned to the Office of Experiment Stations, a part of the Bureau of Agriculture, and Professor Atwater was made the agent in charge.

The moment Prof. Atwater gained control, he pushed the work rapidly. Through his assistants he got in correspondence with colleges, sanitariums and social settlements of the country, to whom he made clear his object. He wanted, he said, men's food investigated. He wanted to know how much they ate, what they paid for it, what they wasted, what part of that they ate was good and what part bad; how much tissue-building and fuel value, or, in other words, health and strength, each kind of food contained. There were already twenty-six experiment stations, which the Agricultural Department had established years before, to help it in its work of finding out new facts for the farmer. These were all pressed into service, and men were stationed in them to conduct the experiments.

There was a fine response. Wesleyan University immediately decided to help. The University of Tennessee, the University of Missouri, Purdue University, the Pennsylvania College for Women, Rutgers College (New Jersey), the Iowa State College of Agriculture and Mechanic Arts, Maine State College, Hull House, Chicago, and numerous other colleges and settlements responded with cordial assurances of hearty coöperation. Laboratories were established in all of these places, suitable instruments introduced, and a quiet investigation was begun, which has resulted in the important truths now collected and given forth.

The instruments with which the Government equipped its experiment stations are, with one exception, like those to be found in every chemical laboratory. The one exception is the respiration calorimeter, an instrument for testing the fuel value of foods. This consists of an air-tight chamber large enough to contain a man without discomfort, fitted with certain appliances for measuring the amount of heat given off by his body. By it the man is entirely cut off from the world without. The air that goes to him is measured, and that which returns in the form of waste product is analyzed and tested. The same is true of all the food he eats. Even his very energy is gauged, and the facts used in the extremely accurate calculations.

In external appearance the calorimeter is a big box or rough wooden cage. In its essentials it is simply a little house with five separate walls, one outside another, so built as to prevent heat from passing out of or into the inner chamber. So the temperature inside is made stable, and the only heat comes from the body of the subject. That is carried out by a system of water-filled pipes, and is accurately gauged and measured. The water conveys the heat exactly as it does in heating or cooling the rooms of a house.

The only passages leading to the chamber are the pipes which supply the subject of the experiment with air and food, and a window, which is air-tight when closed. The pipe which admits the food is six inches long and fitted with a cap at each end. When it is desired to pass anything into or out of the chamber the cap on one end is removed and the articles are laid inside the pipe, and after the first cap has been again adjusted, the other is removed by the man in the calorimeter.

Once a subject is placed in this machine he is absolutely dependent on the scientists for both food and air. Light comes to him through the window. He can communicate over a telephone. He has a folding cot to sleep on, a folding chair and a folding table at which to sit. If the experiment is designed to determine the muscular energy resulting from certain foods, he has tools to work with.

Everything that goes to the occupant is carefully measured and analyzed. It is known exactly what proportion of protein, carbon and carbohydrates are in his food. The amount passed off from the body, even to the moisture absorbed by the clothes each day is noted with scrupulous care. The man weighs himself several times a day to learn whether the supply of bodily tissue is maintained, increased or diminished. The degrees or *calories* of heat that come from the body are written down in the record book at regular intervals.

Air is supplied by a meter pump. Every stroke of the pump rotates a toothed wheel one notch. At every hundred notches an electric valve is opened, which permits the air from one movement of the pump to flow into the box, from which it is drawn for analysis. Similarly the air that has been used in the chamber is drawn off through pipes and passed through an ammonia freezing apparatus. After it has been frozen it is analyzed to discover what change it has undergone in passing through the lungs. Thus everything connected with relation of food to life is discovered.

This is the most accurate way the Government has of finding out the facts about food. There is another, most commonly followed at those experiment stations where a calorimeter has not yet been installed. It consists of just plain observation of what families eat, and examining into the value of each food product. At each station a family is found which will allow the investigators to make a study of the food consumed by it for one month. An inventory of the amounts and kinds of food material on hand is then taken. Everything that can be eaten is weighed, including coffee, tea, salt, vinegar and the spices, and the value at current prices is estimated.

As the regular meals occur the actual weight of all the material prepared is taken. Methods of cooking are noted, the cost estimated, and samples taken to be analyzed. At the end of the month everything left over is weighed, and the amount is subtracted from the general amount purchased during the month. Even the table and kitchen waste is recorded, and the amount of nourishing material thus lost is carefully computed and deducted from the amount of nourishing material which the whole amount of food purchased contained.

It was found that a pound of food did not by any means represent a stable amount of nourishment. A pound of peanuts for instance would yield as much nourishment as a pound and a half of the best steak. So they had to resort to different words to describe the food as bought and the nourishment gotten out of the food as disgested. Food as purchased they called "food material." The ingredients in the eaten food which serve to nourish the body they called "nutrients."

Another difficulty was nicely obviated. They had to tell how much energy a pound of any given food material furnished when eaten. This they decided to do by describing it in terms of heat. So if the entire amount of food eaten at one meal by a man contained one pound of protein, it could be announced that it had yielded him 7440 degrees of heat or energy.

The total of dietary studies made in this way amounts to many hundreds, and certain general conclusions have been reached. One of these is that Americans eat just about thirty per cent. too much. Another is that families in about the same financial condition and performing the equivalent amount of work do not, on the average, differ in their consumption of food.

The Government now issues a little pamphlet entitled "Foods for Man," which lists several hundred kinds of edibles, and shows exactly how much protein, fat, carbohydrates, ash, refuse, and water each contains; so that a person can judge by the work he does how much he needs, and figure out a diet to suit himself.

The vast discoveries as to what constitutes true food are another and broader subject. In this article only the methods of investigation and scope of the work are set forth. The whole import of the work done so far points to a great reform in eating, which is soon to come. The actual value of the investigations that have been made can be best set forth in another article entitled the *New Knowledge of Food,* which we will publish before long.[2]

NOTES

"Our Government and Our Food," *Demorest's* 36 (December 1899): 68–70.

1. Carroll D. Wright (1840–1909), American statistician and sociologist, was Chief of the Massachusetts Bureau of Statistics. His works include *The Industrial Evolution of the United States* (1895).

2. There was no such article published by the *Demorest's*. Most likely Dreiser was thinking of another magazine article, "Atkinson on National Food Reform," *Success* 3 (January 1900): 4; reprinted in this collection.

6

Atkinson on National Food Reform

The Startling Need of Studying the Impurities of the Food We Eat Graphically Set Forth by the Originator of the Movement—Laborers Often Spend Sixty Per Cent. of Their Entire Incomes for Food

"WITH RESPECT TO NINETY PER CENT. OF THE POPULATION OF THIS country, it has already been conclusively proved," said Edward Atkinson, of Boston, recently, "that from forty to sixty per cent. of the average income of each family is expended in the purchase of food material. In the eastern part of the United States, the average expenditure of income for food of working people, or people in receipt of moderate incomes, is one-half. In the West, where food is more abundant, it is somewhat less. The proportion expended by common laborers for their families supply often reaches sixty per cent. of their entire earnings. To them, the food question ought to be a very interesting subject."

PURE FOOD'S FIRST CHAMPION

Mr. Atkinson is the father of the national movement for the study of the food we eat. He was the first man of any country to begin the investigation of heat in its relation to the right preparation of food. The only scientific oven ever invented is his, and the very first restaurant to prepare food upon a scientific basis was established by him,—the Boston "Kitchen,"—with an equipment of utensils costing over $7,000. It was his advice which first caused W. O. Atwater, now at the head of the government food investigation, to begin his experiments on the subject of nutrition at Wellesley College.[1] A paper by him upon the subject, written in 1893, and submitted to J. Sterling Morton, then secretary of agriculture, so interested that

132

official that he not only published it as a government report, but also started the official canvass which resulted in an appropriation of money by congress for an investigation of what constitutes proper food.[2] Mr. Atkinson is still an investigator along this line, though not nearly so active as others who have since taken up the work.

BAD FEEDING THE RULE

"As a nation, we spend entirely too much money for food," he said, when I called upon him. "It is the one thing concerning which we are densely ignorant. We convert the most abundant supply of the best food material into bad feeding, through our general ignorance. We know nothing about right combinations of food, except what we have learned by hearsay from our ancestors. We know nothing about the science of heat or its regulation. I am not talking now about scientists, but about the people,—the men and women in the streets."

"What is the matter with our food as we now eat it?" I asked.

"A great deal," he answered. "It is not the best. It is not the cheapest. It is not cooked right. The people in this country are the most wasteful in the world. They are not conscious of the fact, but neither is the savage conscious of his savagery.

"You might say to me, 'But the world has done well enough on what it has eaten.' So it has. Had the human race waited for the development of a science of nutrition, mankind would have starved. Men had to use a spoken language long before they had any rules of grammar, but they need grammar, nevertheless. We need a science of food, and men need to conform to it a great deal more than they need to know their grammar."

"Are all nations dangerously far from the truth in their ways of eating?"

WHY THE REFORM IS NEEDED

"Yes, and they are getting more so. People put into their stomachs stuff that should never go there; and the foods that are necessary, like bread, they eat wrongly cooked. All the vast array of delicacies which you find in a modern cook-book are more or less half-cooked or baked concoctions, filled with absolute refuse which the body has to throw off untouched,— food poor in the very elements that go to build up bone and muscle and brain. I tell you, people do not know the use of fire. They have never grasped its import."

"No one would believe that all we eat is wrong," I said.

"No one needs to believe," he answered. "Each race, each country, and almost each section of each country, through a process of natural selection, appears to have reached a unit of food, simple or compound, in which the 'nutrients,' so-called, are to be found in the right proportion. I mean, by this, that they have some favorite combination which supplies them the right elements, like protein, starch, fat, etc., which give them health and strength. How they came to get it is one of the mysteries of the world,—one of the facts of evolution. Now, the English like wheat-bread with cheese. Well, that is a pretty good combination. It serves to supply protein, sugar, and starch,—three of the things necessary to make blood and bone.

ELEMENTS OF A PROPER FOOD RATION

"The Scotch like oatmeal with milk and salt. This is a natural, healthful food combination. It also supplies the three things I spoke of. In France, they eat soup and stews rich in peas and beans, which are very good. Peas and beans and lentils supply the body with all of the elements that meat does. When you eat them, you do not need to eat meat. You also get rid of the need of killing animals if you do that, and you escape the poisons which meat is apt to contain. The blacks of the South like bacon, corn meal and molasses. Many of them live largely on that. In that they have a natural combination, which science will more or less approve of. There is nothing better than corn meal. It supplies the body with more nourishment, pound for pound, than meat, although meat is five or six times as expensive. Molasses is good; it gives the body the necessary sugar. Bacon is not so good, but the three in combination come nearer the true idea of food than the fine combination you would get at the Waldorf-Astoria and pay ten times as much for. They do more for the body.

"Here in New England we like baked beans and brown bread, or salt pork and potatoes. Well, the former is a combination which science will approve of, after urging a slight change in the manner of cooking. Italy, with her macaroni and cheese, India and China, using rice and beans or peas mixed, Japan, loving miso, (compounded of rice, barley, beans and peas,) and Canada, with its porridge made of dry peas, coarse wheat crackers, herbs, and very little pork,—each has something which is good, which contains the nourishment nature intended food should contain. Why, if it wasn't for these things, the world would be worse off in body than it is. We eat masses of other things that we should not, because we don't know their worthless character. We have corrupted tastes, and it is only because we do like some one natural combination which is good, and eat it occasionally, that we retain our health at all."

"Have you discovered what the correct things to eat are?"

What Are the Correct Things?

"I have done my share. I was the first to take up the question of food and nutrition and make a study of it. It was upon my advice that Professor Atwater began his researches, and it was my paper of suggestions which caused Hon. J. Sterling Morton, then secretary of agriculture, to cause the government to begin the important investigation of food, which is now under way. Of course, no one has reached final conclusions, but it is not difficult for the average person to-day, after all the vast amount of investigating that has been done, to find out what he ought to eat and how he ought to eat it."

"What do you advise in that line?"

"The use of grains, fruits, vegetables, nuts, and some meat. It has been demonstrated by the government and others, that we use entirely too much meat. I can only refer you to my cook-book, if you wish a natural plan of eating for a year. I have demonstrated that the best food is the cheapest, and that a man can live and be strong, here in Boston, at least, on ninety-seven and three-tenths cents a week."

"On what would he live?"

"On grains, vegetables, and some meat. He could live for a whole month, for instance, on four dollars and sixteen cents, if he bought twenty-two pounds of flour, three pounds of oatmeal, three pounds of corn meal, and six pounds of hominy,—for grains. Two pounds of butter, two pounds of suet, ten pounds of potatoes, three pounds of cabbage, two pounds of carrots, two pounds of onions, and two pounds of sugar would furnish the vegetable food. For variety, he ought to have, in addition, ten pounds of beef or mutton, two pounds of eggs, (about one and one-half dozen,) eight pounds of beans and peas, fifteen pounds or pints of skim milk, and two extra pounds of suet. The total cost of that here in Boston would be four dollars and sixteen cents."

Mr. Atkinson stopped and figured.

The Raw Material Is Not Expensive

"Twenty-two pounds of flour can be had," he said, "at, let me see,—two and one-half cents a pound,—that's fifty-five cents. Three pounds of oatmeal can be bought for twelve cents. Oatmeal is four cents a pound. We can get the corn meal for three cents a pound,—that's nine,"—and so he went on until the actual cost,—four dollars and sixteen cents,—had been figured out at current market rates.

"Now that," he continued, "if properly divided up, will feed a strong man for thirty days. It will give him three and one-tenth pounds of the very best, most nourishing kind of food every day,—a pound of splendid food at every meal, and it would cost him only a cent and a half (a cent and thirty-nine hundredths of a cent, to be exact,) for the day."

"You would need to know how to cook it, though. Ordinary cooking would not do here."

Cooking Not Understood

"No, it would not. And just here is where the average man is handicapped. His food is cheap, his cooking is extravagant. As I have said, there is, as yet, no popular science of cooking. Further, there is no popular art of cooking. Instead, there is wide-spread ignorance on the whole subject, resulting in a waste which is not only unprofitable, but bad in its influence on the general health of the community."

"What do you mean by right cooking?"

"The science of cooking consists in the right application of heat at the right temperature or degree of heat for the right time, to the various elements of food. That sounds complicated, doesn't it? Well, take coffee. Everyone likes coffee. Here is how the use of heat affects that. If you take the green berry, and, without first roasting it, grind it up and boil it, it is worthless,—that everybody knows. If you take the same berry and roast it too much, so that it is nearly carbonized, and then grind it up and boil it, it is also worthless. If, however, you subject the green berry to a uniform heat at the right degree for the right time, and then boil the ground grains right, you have coffee. Everyone makes it slightly different from any other, because slightly different degrees of heat have been applied. It is very easy to discover the right degree of heat. Scientists have found out the combination. If you roast the grains for an exact length of time, every time, and use an exact, unvarying degree of heat every time, and if you let the ground coffee come to a slow boil by using an exact degree of heat every time, you have the perfect coffee."

The Importance of Exact Heat

"Why shouldn't it be so?" he exclaimed. "If a little too much heat will spoil it, and not enough heat will make it useless, why shouldn't there be a medium heat,—a right heat, which everybody can discover and always know? There is no reason why the world should not always have perfect coffee, if it wants to drink that sort of thing.

"It is the same with potatoes. If they are subject to a little less than boiling heat, they are cooked, but not in an appetizing or digestible manner. If cooked by boiling or by baking at a higher heat, the starch cells of which they are composed burst and they become mealy and digestible. Now, we have all delighted in nice, mealy potatoes. Why aren't we all familiar with the exact degree of heat which will give us this thing? Why haven't many stoves been invented the heat of which could be regulated and observed by a thermometer? As it is, we prepare these things by guesswork. If we hit it right, we are glad; if not, we eat it anyhow, and suffer the consequences, which are more serious than we think. A nation, whose average individual length of life is only forty years, ought to think this thing over.

"If an egg is subjected to boiling heat ten minutes, the yolk becomes mealy and the white becomes horny and indigestible. If subjected to heat at about one hundred and eighty degrees Fahrenheit, for ten minutes, both yolk and white become of the consistency of jelly, and are exceedingly nutritious and digestible. Why shouldn't the world concern itself about that? It pays a high price for eggs. Why shouldn't it get the full value in nourishment of what it pays for, instead of getting something that, for want of this knowledge of heat, wears out the stomach, and helps pull life down to a length of forty years?"

"Have you discovered the proper heat at which all things should be cooked?"

"No, but it can be ascertained easily. I am acquainted with the proper way to cook all the things which I eat. Other men are working out this thing. Bless you, the government has fifty-six experiment stations, one or more in every state in the Union, which are engaged in investigating the food question. The facts are coming out. The perfect science of eating is being rapidly built up now. The great sanitariums of the country are doing this work. I am simply an individual investigator. Anyone can find out by applying to the department of agriculture, how to cook any one thing and all about it."

∞

*This paper, the first of a series, has been especially prepared for this issue of the new and enlarged *Success*. The subject is attracting such attention that the government of the United States has ordered an investigation.

NOTES

"Atkinson on National Food Reform," *Success* 3 (January 1900): 4. Signed "Edward Al."

1. In the previous article, "Our Government and Our Food," Dreiser notes the contribution W. O. Atwater, a professor at Wesleyan University, made to the governmental food investigation. In this article Dreiser notes that Professor Atwater taught at Wellesley College, not Wesleyan University.

2. Julius Sterling Morton (1832–1902), American agriculturalist and public official. His services to agriculture and the Democratic Party were recognized when President Grover Cleveland appointed him Secretary of Agriculture (1893–97).

7

New York's Underground Railroad

THERE ARE ONLY TWENTY TUNNELS IN ALL THE WORLD WORTHY THE name, and only three of these are used by underground railways such as New York now proposes to construct. These three are in London. The construction of each and every one of the twenty has been rightly heralded as a great engineering feat, but this twenty-first promises to take rank as the greatest, largely because of the singularity of the contract and the brevity of time. London's 105 miles of underground railway cost more—something like two hundred millions of dollars—but they were the work of many years and more contractors. This New York Rapid Transit contract is the largest single contract ever let, and Mr. John B. McDonald is the first man to step forward and shoulder so enormous a responsibility. It is picturesque, in that it is an attempt to solve in three years the transportation question for the most crowded city on earth; to dig twenty-one miles under streets which are alive with traffic and threaded with conduits, sewers, and gas mains. It is novel in that one man's plans will be carried out by one contractor, and that a distance which before required an hour to traverse, will now be cut down to fifteen minutes, if we wish to believe newspapers; twenty-one, if we wish to accept the word of the chief engineer. Lastly it will be an electric road, with the motor power fitted to the individual cars, which is something entirely new for underground railroads, few as they are.

The task is not so herculean as one would think when examined clearly. It is like Æsop's bundle of sticks which could not be broken unitedly, but was very simply disposed of when separated. Mr. McDonald may build the tunnel without the aid of other contractors or he may call them in, but in any case it will be a matter of construction corps with one corps to every section. Then Mr. McDonald may, for the better part, sit in his office chair and hear reports.

The prosecution of so great a task is certainly an enormous thing to those who know nothing about engineering, but there are a thousand contractors in the United States who could successfully undertake and complete it if they had the money. So many tunnels have been built, so many machines have been perfected, that the contractor has much to go by. He can see

every detail worked out on paper before a pick is struck to earth, and in this case, paper counts for much.

The Rapid Transit Commission's chief engineer, Mr. William Barclay Parsons, has already surveyed the entire right of way and prepared every detail of construction. The contractor knows from plans furnished him that he is to build a tunnel fifty feet wide and seventeen feet high, from the Post Office to Ninety-sixth Street, which shall accommodate four tracks—two express and two local. The express tracks are to occupy the centre and the local the outer sides of the tunnel. The southern terminus is to be a loop around the Post Office, about which all trains will go. He also knows that this tunnel, where it runs near the surface, as in Elm Street, and Fourth Avenue to Twelfth Street, is to be flat on top, and sustained by three rows of pillars between the tracks (Fig. 1). From there he is to build it quite the same, but much less near the surface, and without disturbing the condition of the street until Thirty-third Street is reached. There the plans furnished show him that he must divide the heretofore single fifty-foot tunnel into two two-track, arched tunnels running under the present Fourth Avenue street-car tunnel (Fig. 2). At Forty-second Street he must abandon the double, arched tunnel for the single, fifty-foot tunnel again, until Ninety-sixth Street is reached, from which point the line branches out in two directions northwards. Here the outside or local track must rise, in order to allow the inside or express tracks to pass under them, thus allowing the branches to separate without interference. The viaducts, wherever specified, must be built as the drawings show, and the two tracks of the east branch, which pass under the Harlem River, must do so in two single, one-track, cast-iron cylinders of a kind specified (Fig. 3). In the whole matter, the contractor has little or no leeway, except in the case of obstacles hitherto unforeseen. Of such there are thought to be none.

So thorough is this preliminary planning, that not a bolt is thought to have been neglected. The details of the stations have all been mathematically arranged.

The underground stations will be entered from the sidewalks of the side streets. The entrances will be covered with ornamental hoods. There will be separate staircases for entrance and exit. The ticket office will be in the centre of the station entrance, under the side street. The platforms will be constructed of cement, and will be 200 feet long, ten feet wide at the ends, and twenty feet wide toward the centres. There will be no square corners in

Rapid Transit in New York—a View in one of the new stations.

the station walls, which will be faced with enamelled brick of some light, warm tint. The stations will be lighted with electric lights in niches in the walls. These will be covered with opalescent glass globes, to give the appearance of daylight. Wherever the station platforms come under a sidewalk, the roofs will be made of glass. The roofs of stations otherwise will be made of jack arches and concrete, and the ceilings will be panelled in wood or plaster.

Such details are the work of students of construction under the chief engineer, and are given to the contractor along with a mass of other details. Thus, the nature of, and the variations in, the soil all along the route have been plotted, and accompany the plans of construction. A year ago borings were made in Elm Street to discover what kind of material the contractor would encounter in his tunnelling. Before causing a pick to be struck, Mr. McDonald knows from his plans that the soil under Elm Street is slightly variable, but nevertheless excellent material in which to conduct such construction as is proposed. It is made up for the most part of a sharp silica sand, ranging in quality from what might be called a good, fine sand to coarse sand and gravel mixed. As far down as it may be necessary to dig he knows, from these reports, that he will find nothing which will slide or give difficulty in handling. Much of the sand here is of such excellent quality that it will pay the contractor to store and use it in the mixing of the mortar and concrete required on the work.

The plans furnished also show him that rock is first met with a Twelfth Street, but at such a depth that it will make an excellent foundation for the four tracks and the pillars which support the roof. Above Thirty-third Street, under the present Fourth Avenue tunnel, there is a bed of undulating rock which he will have to hew out in part. For the rest of the way west across Forty-second Street and north along the Boulevard, or what is now Broadway, he knows that his men will encounter rock, and will for the greater part need to bore and blast their way along. Still his plans show that no part of the route contemplated is a main thoroughfare for water and gas pipes or electrical subways. Elm Street, where the first stretch of work opens, being but newly cut through as a thoroughfare, contains no pipe of large size, and what pipes are there now are to one side and out of the way; although the existence of pipes may be discovered where least expected.

The contractor knows beforehand that at Fifth Avenue and Forty-second Street there occurs the most serious pipe crossing along the route, as the large Croton water main runs down the avenue. Fifth Avenue, however, at that point forms a decided ridge, the surface of Forty-second Street sloping rapidly both to the east and west. His plans, therefore, instruct him that to maintain an even grade he must cause the tunnel to be dug sufficiently below the level of Fifth Avenue to leave all water and gas mains undisturbed overhead. This and the knowledge that he is nowhere infringing

**How the tunnel will be constructed down Elm Street,
where it will run just below the surface.**

upon a house line or undermining house foundations of any sort is made perfectly clear to him. All he has to do to know the nature of the work before him, the character of the next foot of ground, is to consult his plans.

If the reader will ask himself how he would go about it to build this tunnel, supposing the contract were now suddenly awarded him, the remainder of this article will probably have considerable interest, as it will endeavor to solve his problem.

It is taken for granted that, long before bidding for the contract, the contractor has arranged to secure his supply of steel, brick, plaster, and all necessary supplies. He knows also how fast tunnels can be built. It all depends upon how many men can work side by side against the face of a wall. The Hoosac tunnel, for instance, nine feet high and twenty-four feet wide, presented a working area of 216 square feet. Here ten men worked with boring machines, and managed to advance the work seven and one-half feet a day. In the case of the recently constructed tunnel under the East River, four men, working side by side in one place, managed to progress four feet a day; but this was in soft rock, and the tunnel was only 8 feet 6 inches by 10 feet 6 inches. Later, in hard rock, where the walls did not need to be shored up, six men made an average progress of sixty-nine feet a week. The record week was one in which ninety-five feet was driven by one gang coming toward New York, and 101 feet by the other gang making for Long Island—a total of 196 feet for the two gangs working toward one another. The rock they were working in was gneiss, similar to that which the present contractor will encounter. He can, therefore, figure out about how many feet one drill gang can make a week, and so how many drill gangs will be required to do twenty-one miles of underground work in three years.

This matter has already been figured out as requiring forty corps of construction—that is, the route will be divided into forty sections. Shafts will be sunk in all these places, and tunnelling machinery installed. Then the various corps will work toward one another, and the excavated sections will eventually be united.

It is a popular fancy to imagine that increased depth underground means increased difficulty. This is not true. It is just as easy to dig a tunnel under a mountain with thousands of feet overhead, as it is to dig ten feet under Broadway and avoid the surface, supposing Broadway to be resting on stone. It is all a question of drilling machinery and dynamite, and not much of the latter.

Thus, in digging the loop in Park Place and about the Post Office, perhaps two shafts twenty feet square will be sunk to a depth of thirty or thirty-five feet. From these shafts the tunnels will start. There will be no great show of material overhead. The earth as it is dug out will be hauled away, and no unsightly mounds left standing about, for a very few carts will suffice to haul away all the *débris* that can be taken out of one excavation or shaft a day. If the tunnellers should strike stone, they could not progress more than ten feet a day at the utmost, and probably not more than five feet. This amount can easily be disposed of by a half-dozen carts as it is sent to the surface. So there will be apparently little doing about any of the various openings.

This primary tunnelling is always the most interesting to the lay public, although it is not nearly so complicated as the after work of building the masonry, laying the tracks, and constructing the stations. The method of doing the latter seems commonplace, however, because similar work can be seen above ground. In the present case, the direct tunnelling will not be any different from that employed in almost every other tunnel throughout the world. After the shafts have been sunk, and the hoisting engines with derricks placed over each, to lift the excavated material, the Beach hydraulic shield, an apparatus designed to protect the workingmen while excavating the earth, will be introduced. The shield consists of a strong cylinder, somewhat resembling a huge barrel with both heads removed. The front end of the cylinder is sharpened so as to have a cutting edge to enter the earth. This cylinder is driven forward two feet at a time, by means of hydraulic rams. In it the men work, and when they have cleared away two feet more, it is again moved forward. This protects them from immediate danger of falling earth. The arch builders follow after, erecting the tunnel walls and roof either of brick, stone, or cast-iron plate.

When stone is struck, and pick and shovel no longer avail, small machine drills, such as are used in digging out foundations, are introduced—four, six, eight, or even ten, according to the size of the tunnel, and the confronting rock is drilled full of holes, say, three feet deep. When the wall is thus completely honeycombed, a small charge of dynamite is put into several of the holes and exploded. As may be imagined, the honeycombed rock readily crumbles, and is dug out and loaded on little cars, which haul it back to the main shaft, where it is lifted out. The little track on which the small cars haul away the earth is daily extended, as is the incandescent lighting system, so that the men always have light and a little earth-hauling railroad at their back. It is plain that no great masses of material are ever handled at one time. Rapidity of building is due solely to the number of shafts sunk along the proposed route.

Perhaps the most difficult work will be where the tunnel runs near the surface, as in the first section along Elm Street. Here the whole street will have to be torn up and the four tracks laid at the proper depth, after which the street will be covered by a roof of iron beams, resting upon supporting columns of iron, which will thereafter support the overhead traffic. That and the place at Ninety-sixth Street where two tracks rise and cross over the remaining two will probably give the contractor the most trouble.

Those who imagine that a busy street like Fourth Avenue or Forty-second Street cannot be tunnelled under without disturbing the street-car lines and heavy traffic overhead, should remember that it has been done before, and that right in the heart of the metropolis, under Broadway. For instance, in 1868, Mr. Alfred E. Beach, the inventor of the hydraulic shield to be used in the present tunnel, constructed a tunnel extending under Broadway from Warren Street to Park Place, large enough to receive a small street railway car.[1] This tunnel was between three and four hundred feet long, and was built to show that underground transit was feasible. At that early period the need of rapid city transit for passengers was strongly felt, but there was great opposition on the part of property owners along the line of the proposed railway, through fear that the buildings would be injured if a tunnel were carried on a lower level than the foundations. Also every one objected to the serious loss of business which would result from the closing and tearing up of the streets. Mr. Beach, however, built his tunnel by the method described, and now invariably followed, and few persons, except those directly interested, had any knowledge that a tunnel was in progress until after it was completed. This tunnel was nine feet four inches in exterior diameter, and its floor was twenty-one and a half feet below the pavement. It ran under sewers and Croton water mains without disturbing either, and was built during hours when the street was thronged with omnibuses and heavy teams. It was duly opened to the public, and many thousands of people enjoyed the privilege of riding in the car, which was worked back and forth by the pneumatic, or air-pressure system. Long ago, however, the tunnel was neglected, then forgotten, and now the fact that it is there in working order to-day will strike the average New Yorker as remarkable.

Indeed, the building of the present tunnel is going to be comparatively easy, for the right of way runs directly under the main streets, without invading private property. In London, owing to the formation of the city, the underground roads pass athwart the streets and cut through private property in all directions. There the cost of $5,000,000 per mile (quite three times as much as a mile will cost here) was due to damage done real estate, caused by cutting through blocks of buildings and tunnelling under houses quite near the surface. In some places the roads ran under grave-yards without disturbing the graves and vaults above.

Of course the building of so vast a work cannot be accomplished without many petty irritations. In many places sewers will have to be taken up and relaid, but not fifteen miles of them, as has been loudly proclaims. The chief engineer states that very few pipes and wires will be encountered, as the tunnel runs too deep. Still, the case of Philadelphia may be repeated. There, after beginning the immense railway subway and tunnel, it was found that Philadelphia had a considerably large number of mains for water and gas, conduits for electricity, and sewers than were known to exist at the different bureaus. They were all in active operation, and on many occasions offered serious menace, and several times damage to the building of the new sewers. Still the contractor is supposed to figure such chances in his $35,000,000 bid.

He has the experience of others to go by. He will hardly be caught by people who claim that their house walls have been damaged, for trickery of this sort is notorious and the remedy known. In London, many house-holders having learned, when it was all over, that a tunnel had been con-structed under their ground, discovered cracks in their buildings and hoped for compensation. Mr. Greathead, the contractor, made himself the model of all contractors by producing for these complainants photos of their buildings before the tunnel had been begun, with cracks very much in evidence. He had, indeed, possessed himself of photos of every wall and building in the least likely to be within the limits of the tunnelling effects. Mr. McDonald will unquestionably do as much in New York.

Beyond question, the building of this rapid-transit tunnel will be a world feat in engineering. The contractor himself admits that he will need 10,000 men, and a State law requires that he shall not pay them less than $2 a day. Two million cartloads of material will be taken out, and perhaps 500,000 wagon loads of brick, mortar, steel, and so forth taken in. Engineer Parsons estimates the weight of steel beams required at 65,000 tons, and the number of cubic yards of enamelled facing at 20,000. These, with 500,000 lineal feet of underground track and 60,000 feet of elevated track make imposing figures. One statistician figures that the 10,000 men employed would make, if rolled into one, a single giant 150 feet tall, and that the $35,000,000, if cast into one, would make a silver dollar 732 feet in diameter. The 79,960,423 cubic feet of rock and earth to be removed would make a shovelful of earth and stone 432 feet across at the base. All this is beside the mark, however, except for lovers of comparison.

What is more to the point, is the fact that the tunnel is under way, and its beginning marks a new era in the matter of individual responsibility. The next contractor will not hesitate to step forward and undertake a $50,000,000 contract. The giant contractor is the wonderful thing.

Commercially and socially there is nothing New York stands more in need of than this and many other tunnels. Owing to the peculiar shape of Manhattan Island, and the impossibility of increasing the number of the surface and elevated roads that now exist, the conditions of travel in the city are such that they are not to be equalled in any other capital of the world for the discomfort that comes of overcrowding. This state of affairs having seemed inevitable has been borne with good grace, and so strong is the influence of habit that people have grown to accept the inconvenience of travelling while standing and holding on to a strap as if it were the most natural thing in the world. The remedy has not come too soon. Moreover, Manhattan Island is already overcrowded—in some quarters a thousand souls to the acre—and property values have reached astonishing heights. A thousand dollars a front foot is demanded for property on any part of the island, and the rates increase as the centres of wealth and trade are approached. This is due to the fact that it is inconvenient to live outside of the island, where ferry-boats delay and railroads keep not their schedules. More, there is no speed attainable in reaching the suburbs by present methods. The moneyed classes, therefore, pay more and live on the island, where they can reach their business quickly. Flats have increased in price until to-day the majority of residents on the island pay from $900 to $1,500 a year for shelter alone. Living has become so expensive that the average citizen is compelled to accept the inconvenience of the suburbs in order to be able to maintain his position at all.

This the new underground railway will in part obviate. Large as it is, it is only the beginning of a system which will tunnel both rivers in various directions and make Brooklyn and Jersey City as near to the heart of business as Harlem. It will cut the time of entering the city to such an extent, that the residents of the island will have no advantage over those who live in Yonkers, Flushing, Orange, or Mount Vernon, now removed nearly two hours from the city. It will immediately make 100 square miles of new suburban territory available for residential purposes. Rents and prices in

New York will not be lowered, but a halt will be called on the present rapid increase, and the man with a small position will not be taxed with the misery of early rising and train chasing in order to earn his daily bread.

As a proof of this, a study of the new time schedule will not be amiss. To-day a man cannot go from the Battery to the Harlem River in less than sixty minutes by the "L" train. If he takes any of the surface cars, it will require something like an hour and thirty minutes. The man who lives in Yonkers or Bronxville, fifteen or twenty miles north of the Battery, cannot reach his home in less than an hour and a quarter or an hour and a half, and he is dependent upon infrequent trains. He must be at the depot at certain fixed times. The "L" and surface trains carry no man to Harlem in less than forty-five minutes from such points as Eighth, Fourteenth, Twenty-third, and Thirty-fourth streets. The new tunnel train will carry passengers to Ninety-sixth Street (Harlem) in fourteen minutes on the express trains, twenty-one on the local trains, stopping at all stations. It will carry them to Kingsbridge or Bronx Park—230th Street—in forty-seven minutes. Yonkers and Mount Vernon will be sixty minutes away on trains which start every three or four minutes.

William Barclay Parsons, the man who has schemed out the system which Mr. McDonald will construct, is a very interesting figure. Whatever rapid transit plans have in the past twenty years been devised for New York have been his. His career is most closely associated with the solving of this one gigantic problem. So early as 1886, 1887, and 1888, Mr. Parsons was engineer for the New York District Railway and the City Railway, two proposed underground railways in New York—the former under Broadway, the latter having a route through and under private property. In 1894 he was made chief engineer of the present Rapid Transit Commission, which position he still holds.

Mr. McDonald is one of the most prominent contractors in this country. Among other work, he has constructed many hundreds of miles of railway; the tunnel built by him in Baltimore, on the Baltimore & Ohio Railroad, being considered the finest example of masonry work in the world. Born fifty-six years ago in Cork, Ireland, Mr. McDonald was educated in New York, and has lived since then in this country.

NOTES

"New York's Underground Railroad," *Pearson's* 9 (April 1900): 375–84.

1. Alfred Ely Beach (1826–96), American publisher and inventor, in 1868 invented the so-called Beach shield, which was propelled slowly forward through the earth by several hydraulic rams. After the shield was forced forward, a new section of tunnel was constructed. In 1870, a car was driven back and forth on tracks in the tunnel by means of pneumatic power. This event inaugurated the underground transit in New York.

8

The Descent of the Horse:
Tracing the Horse's History 2,000,000 Years

AMONG THE STORIES OF EVOLUTION THERE IS NONE MORE INTERESTING than that of the horse—the animal concerning whose descent Huxley preached, and the facts concerning which stirred the world a score of years ago.[1] Huxley did not have all the data wherewith to prove that the horse of to-day has come to us through many changes, and that his ancestors were once no larger than foxes, but with the few details he had he was able to convince the open-minded and gain for himself, among the unscientific, a large measure of fame by this one paper alone. Since Huxley's day, however, the proofs have been coming in fast, so that to-day there is no longer doubt about the matter.

In the American Museum of Natural History, in New York, are several cases of fossil bones which tell the horse's natural history much better than any scientific paper could.[2] The casual observer may see there a series of skulls of horses which ascend in size from the first, which is no larger than that of a fox, to the last, which is that of the present-day horse. In the same place may be seen a series of skeleton feet, the smallest being about as large as would carry a fair-sized fox, the largest the hoof of the present-day horse, between which there is no break in the matter of ascent or evolution. Each one is only slightly different from the other, and yet, as the series progresses, one sees that toes disappear and bones become larger, until, at last, instead of having a horse's foot with four toes on the fore feet and three on the hind, we have a horse's foot with only one toe so enlarged that it is now called a hoof, but with traces of the other now nearly vanished toes still in evidence. There is also a case containing the skeleton of one of the very earliest known horses—an animal that must have lived several million years ago at the least, and probably a great many more. Yet a student of anatomy could take this same small skeleton and trace with its aid every bone in the body of the horse of to-day. All are there, either entire or in part, and the skeleton, if enlarged, could readily be mistaken for a present-day horse's skeleton, with, of course, the exception of the feet.

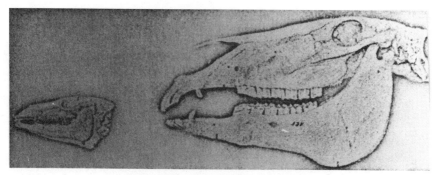

**Skeleton of the head of the first horse
(the size of a fox) and of the modern horse**

This remarkable assemblage of the facts of the case represents one of the most interesting portions of the scientific labor of the day. It involves the discovery of the large prehistoric lake beds of the Rocky Mountains, and the arduous working of the same by scientists of the widest experience and ability. The collection has only recently been completed, and it is but now that the evolution of the horse may be said to be proved. The story as a whole is exceedingly novel, and may be told as follows:

There were no horses in this country when America was discovered, and yet the horse had its origin here. This fact has been recently established by American scientists, who have unearthed a complete skeleton from the Bad Lands of Wyoming, of one of the earliest ancestors known. This early horse has been named Orohippus, and must have lived not less than two million years ago. He has four toes on his fore feet, and three on his hind feet. There must have been still earlier horses than those yet discovered, having five toes on each foot, for this was the original form of all mammal feet. At the present day there are traces of these vanished toes in every horse.

At the time when the horse was a small animal the size of a fox or less, this country was largely a marshy tropical region, covered in part by many lakes and great rivers, and dominated by animals of gigantic form. The vegetation was much the same as it is to-day in the South. Many of our exotic plants were common. The little horse fed upon tender grass and leaves. He inhabited the plain rather than the jungle, but the plains in those days were soft, and more or less marshy. Our Sierra and Rocky Mountain ranges and our wide stretches of dry prairie were not in existence. The great hoof of the horse is proof of how gradually the earth became hard. In those days of soft earth he needed the five toes which nature had given him. All the mammals of that time had these five toes, which served, among other things, to prevent their sinking in the mud.

The food the horse ate did not require grinders, so he did not have them. He needed teeth more for grazing and defence than for chewing. In those days the two canine teeth, which are now commonly absent in mares and are undeveloped in all horses, were then long and formidable. His back teeth were then imbedded in his jaws by long roots. They had short crowns with comparatively smooth surfaces, and were without any trace of cement.

From this time on the evolution of the horse has been marked principally by his growth in size, the elongation of his head and neck, changes in his teeth and in his legs and feet. Aside from these, the anatomy of the horse of to-day could be very well illustrated by the skeleton of the Orohippus, small as it is.

The reasons for the horse's growth in size are not difficult to trace. It is thought that being subject to pursuit by larger animals and attack from all sides, it was compelled to run fast and often. This was its principal means of defence in that day of ponderous beasts. Such exercise naturally enlarged the muscles of the limbs and body. Their enlargement and use required the eating of more food, and gave the appetite for it. There followed a natural expansion of the digestive organs. The veins, arteries, and every channel by which the nourishment is supplied to the system grew to meet the increasing requirements. Thus through millions of years the body enlarged. The direction which motion takes in the legs of the horse, coupled with the use and growth just described, is the supposed reason for their extension. As the body was lifted higher from the ground by the growing legs, the horse was compelled to reach constantly in grazing and in the cropping of overhanging branches, and its neck was developed by the process.

In the matter of the teeth, the evolution is also apparent. The horse of to-day needs grinders with rough surfaces in the eating of hard food. The first horses ate the very tender vegetation which then formed their only food supply. But as grains appeared, and changed climatic conditions produced more rugged vegetation, the crowns of the teeth became broader and longer, and developed a rough surface. Many ages after the Orohippus, a coating of cement appeared upon the crowns of the teeth. In the process of chewing, this covering of cement was wrinkled, and gave to the horse its present form of grinding surface.

There is a difference in the formation of a horse's fore leg to-day and that of its earlier ancestors. In the fore leg of the earliest known horse there were two bones, the radius and ulna. These were as distinct and separate as they are in a man's forearm to-day. At a later period the ulna is smaller and the radius larger. At a still later period skeletons discovered show that the radius had become the chief bone and the ulna hung like a pendant. The lower half of it had entirely disappeared. To-day the fore leg of the horse seems to possess but one bone. Examination, however, will disclose the upper end of the ulna still united to the radius. Traces of the lower end of the ulna can be found in the foot of the modern colt. A like change occurred in the hind legs. The tibia remained and now forms the lower portion of the leg, while the fibula, which was in early ages a complete bone, has almost disappeared.

Many causes worked together to effect the evolution of the horse's feet. In the first place, as the mountains lifted up and the lakes were drained from certain portions of the earth, the ground became harder. Wider and drier plains appeared, over which these little horses could range. There-fore, finding food and safety on higher and harder ground, they avoided marshy places. This affected their feet. In travel, the exercises of their limbs threw their weight largely upon the third toe, which developed at the expense of the others. Accordingly, the latter became smaller and smaller, through the ages, until they eventually disappeared. The present foot of the horse is the old third toe. Its hoof is the enlarged and hardened nail.

It is impossible to tell why the horse should have vanished from the country where it originated and thrived, and how it happened to reappear in Europe to return to its first home with the arrival of the Spaniards with Cortez.[3] It may have found its way into Europe across the land which was once where Bering Strait is now.

If this is true, the horses, left to themselves, evolved to their present stage and vanished as most other animals have done when the perfection of the type had been reached. Those that crossed into Europe were preserved by the uses to which man has put them.

For hundreds of years horses have been found with what were con-sidered strange deformities, for which no explanation could be given. It was the fact that these freaks existed that first called the attention of Professor Marsh, of Yale, to the structure of the horse's foot.[4] He found upon examination that in every case there were evidences of toe forma-tions common to earlier forms of mammals. His knowledge of evolution led him to suspect that the horse of to-day could by this means be shown to have descended from some earlier forms possessing toed feet. It was about this time that efforts were made by a few scientists to open the fossil beds in the Bad Lands of Wyoming.

In the fall of 1874 Professor Marsh started West with a small expedition. He was escorted into the wilderness by a few soldiers, until they were stopped by a band of Indian chiefs, who opposed their progress. All efforts to cajole or influence them were futile. Professor Marsh was advised to abandon his expedition. At midnight, however, when the braves were sleeping, he stole from the tents with his little band, knowing that death would result in his detection. It was necessary to work rapidly, not only for fear of massacre, but because of the intense cold. They were obliged to cut holes in their frozen beards for the passage of food, and the water froze in the cups as they ate. A rich deposit of fossils was found, and the bones as they were unearthed were placed in heaps.

On the second morning Indian sentinels appeared on the surrounding hills. Outposts of the expedition brought reports of threatening preparations for attack. Professor Marsh was undaunted, however, and remained another day, in order to pack the bones collected so that it would be impossible to injure them in transportation. When this had been satisfactorily accomplished, he stole back through the threatening wilderness, and arrived safely in New Haven at last, with what proved to be the most important prehistoric remains. Among the fossils secured in face of such danger and hardship were the remains of certain of the four-toed ancestors of the horse, and it was these that created the conviction that the horse had its origin in America.

NOTES

"The Descent of the Horse," *Everybody's* 2 (June 1900): 543–47.

1. Thomas Henry Huxley (1825–95), English biologist, whose detailed investigations in comparative anatomy, paleontology, and evolution exerted a great influence on nineteenth-century biology. Huxley was also one of the first to accept Charles Darwin's theory of evolution and did much to support and publicize Darwin's views.

2. The American Museum of Natural History, founded in 1869, is an institution in New York City dedicated to scientific research and public education in the fields of natural science and anthropology. The museum also has one of the world's largest and most comprehensive fossil collections including a complete skeleton of a forty-seven-foot-long Tyrannosaurus rex, a meat-eating dinosaur that lived about eighty million years ago.

3. Between 1834 and 1921 the Cortez had two houses, the upper house being a senate. The composition of the senate reflected the successive changes in government; a conservative government restricted its membership and encouraged life tenure for senators, while a liberal government favored making it a democratic, elective body.

4. Othniel Charles Marsh (1831–99), archaeologist at Yale University, discovered over one thousand fossil vertebrates, mainly dinosaurs, during his many scientific explorations of the Western United States. His collections of fossils, now in the Peabody Museum affiliated with Yale, was unparalleled. The first vertebrate paleontologist (1882–92) of the U. S. Geological Survey, Marsh was a pioneer in the field in the United States.

9

Apples:

An Account of the Apple Industry in America

One of the most important industries of the country.
210,000,000 barrels of apples are produced annually.

It is an established fact that the United States now holds the record for rapid development of fruit industries, such as the growing of oranges and lemons, peaches and grapes. As a nation we eat more fruit than any other, and grow considerably more than we eat. Eighty millions of dollars a year is the figure for strawberries alone. A hundred millions would scarcely cover the value of all the grapes marketed. Peaches we raise in astonishing quantities, in orchards containing as many as 300,000 trees, but our banner crop, so far as fruit is concerned, is apples. We have produced as many as 210,000,000 barrels in a single season, and have sold as high as 3,000,000 barrels to England alone. We carry in cold storage every winter anywhere from 6,000,000 to 10,000,000 barrels of the crop of the season before, in order to secure better prices. Ships weigh anchor in New York, three at a time, in a single week, bearing apples to Europe. Indeed, it is one of the greatest industries the country has ever witnessed, and promises to take rank as the chief fruit crop of the world.

"Tell me about apples," I inquired of a great apple broker whose dealings in them aggregate millions of barrels in the year.

"I wouldn't know what to tell you," he answered. "I handle only a few million barrels myself."

"Don't you know where the great orchards are?"

"I really don't. Of course there are a good many in every State. I deal with those in Montana and Nebraska, but, of course, they are not the great apple-producing States."

"Montana," I said; "do they raise apples in Montana?"

"There are a good many big orchards there. You've heard of Marcus

153

Daly, haven't you? He has one there with 60,000 trees. I have one in the southern part with 50,000."

Montana an apple State, and mining still credited as its chief industry! How silently the changes of time are accomplished.

"If you want to see apples," said another interested broker, "you want to go to Iowa. They've got the finest apple country there in the world. Why, apples leave Glenwood by the train-load—thirty and forty cars to a train. I saw one man from Lockport, N. Y., contract for a train-load of apples in that town last fall—thirty-eight car-loads."

"And where is Glenwood?"

"In Mills County, the greatest apple county in the world."

Mills County, and, indeed, all the southwestern section of Iowa, is truly a wonderful apple country, but not much more important them one of a score of regions in various parts of the country which produce apples. In that county alone there are over 900,000 trees, averaging at the lowest ten bushels a tree per annum. One hundred and fifty thousand of these trees are in one orchard. The total output is close on to 3,000,000 barrels, or enough to supply the present American sale to England.

New York, however, has two counties, much smaller than Mills, which do even better than this, and as a State it raises three times as many apples as Iowa. The counties referred to are Niagara and Orleans, in the western tier, which together raise 7,000,000 barrels of the best kind of market apples. All through this area are orchards holding 20,000, 30,000, 40,000, and occasionally 100,000 trees, which in blossoming make of the roadsides a paradise. Nowhere is the spring with its blossoms and moonlight more effective. Apple-blossoms seem to show particularly distinct in the dim radiance of the night, and orchards, covering 800 acres, show with a snowy whiteness of incomparable quality in the valleys.

Oregon, Washington, California, and Colorado have only recently come into the market with astonishing quantities of apples, considering the short time they have been raised there. California has never been an apple State, nearly all of the land being given to grapes, oranges, and the more tropical commodities; but one area—that of the Pajaro Valley—is of interest because of its rapid development. Fifteen years ago there were scarcely 1,000 trees in all the region where now 600,000 may be considered a low estimate. Apple orchards have been set out by wholesale, and commission agents deal in apples by train-load lots. One important brokerage firm in Denver, Col., has a standing order for 150 car-loads annually, which are shipped east and distributed in the immediate vicinity of Denver.

In this same respect Colorado also is peculiar. It has been only a little over fifteen years since there was any movement looking to supplying even the local, let alone the outside, demand for apples in this prosperous mining State. Apples were imported and sold at higher rates than oranges or bananas, both of which were exceedingly expensive. To-day there are in Colorado over 100,000 acres planted with apple-trees exclusively, and the value of the crop is estimated variously at from two to three millions of dollars. Fruit culture began here in the spring of 1882, when, to use the words of a local historiographer, "Messrs. E. A. Hotchkiss and Samuel Wade brought in a few fruit-trees and set them out." They were the first trees planted in the most important apple region in Colorado, and included a few peach-pits brought from Wichita, Kan. In the fall of the same year the little sappers which had sprung up from the latter were the wonder of the country for miles around.

The man who planted them innocently proclaimed that he never expected to eat any fruit from them. The same man is to-day the owner and shipper of the product of nearly 50,000 trees of the same variety.

But if Colorado is wonderful in this respect, what must be thought of Missouri and Kansas, two States which twenty years ago produced nothing at all in the way of fruit, and yet which to-day yield the banner apple crops of the world? Separately and individually they produce more apples than any other State in the Union, and together raise more than any foreign nation, not even excepting Russia. In Kansas are 15,000,000 apple-trees, all in bearing, which bring as many million dollars into the State if they produce only a barrel of apples each a year. This is the same State in which, eighteen years before, the first man to plant an apple orchard of any important size was looked upon as a crank. The same individual has since become a millionaire.

Missouri has just as many trees and several of the largest orchards in the world. The chief of these—2,300 acres—is at Westport; the other, containing 300,000 trees, at Olden, Mo. Never before in the history of apple-raising have there been such orchards. Throughout the State are others—800 acres being a common size—which produce their hundreds of carloads of apples as regularly as the seasons.

The marvellous development of apple-raising in these two States has been attended by the rise of another industry which has revolutionized the whole fruit industry, and made possible the enormous orchards so rapidly planted and matured. This is the novel cold-storage system as applied to stationary quantities of fruit. Refrigerator cars and meat-storing plants have long been common, but the storehouse adapted to fruit, with its moderate temperature of 38 degrees throughout the summer and winter, is something new. The first one was built in Missouri in 1892. There was not one in all Kansas until 1896.

The effect that cold-storage facilities have had upon the entire fruit industry is something not easily measured. Before their day the extra-large orchard was a mine of disaster. There never has been a way of disposing of immense quantities of fruit rapidly, except at a sacrifice of profit. The only success has lain in holding crops for a better market. Before cold-storage days there was no method of doing this. Now, however, if the apple yield is so enormous that prices fall to little or nothing, the grower can store his fruit and wait for better prices, which winter and spring always command.

So late as 1896 it took all the persuasion imaginable to induce the chief apple-grower in Kansas to store 2,000 barrels at a local storage company's risk, no one believing that the apples would be good a month or two after their arrival. To-day the average storage company carries from 300,000 to 400,000 barrels for the orchardists of the vicinity which it represents, and there are cold-storage houses in every city of over 10,000 inhabitants in the United States, to say nothing of those in the villages and towns of the various fruit areas throughout the country. The 10,000,000 barrels of apples mentioned as being carried from season to season by these houses is a mere fraction of all the business they do.

One may get a very concise idea of how rapid has been the rise of the apple-orchard farming in these two astonishing States by consulting the ninth biennial report of the Kansas State Board of Agriculture, where is a statement made by Wellhouse & Son, one of the largest apple-growing companies in the world and the pioneers in planting commercial apple-orchards. These figures concerning their own growth demonstrate the success that has attended apple-raising everywhere in the West. The original plantation was an orchard of 120 acres, near Fairmount, Leavenworth County, made in 1876. In 1878 another 160 acres were planted, and in 1879 the growers ventured still another 160 acres, making a total of 440 acres planted in three years, and representing a total investment of perhaps $50,000.

In four years from planting the first orchard produced 1,594 bushels. That was in 1880. In 1881, 3,887 bushels were harvested, and in 1882, 17,037 bushels measured the yield, by which time a few apples were received from the second orchard, set out in 1878. In 1885 the third orchard that was planted started to bear, and continued to increase with the other two, until in 1890 the 440 acres yielded 79,170 bushels, which were sold for exactly $52,000, or $118 per acre. In the ten years following the combined orchards yielded nearly 300,000 bushels, and realized, after all expenses, about $85,000. This was more than 10 per cent. profit for every year since the last 160 acres were planted, although the orchard did not come into full bearing until ten years later, when the present estimate was made. Since then cold storage has been the factor which has made it possible to market the enormous yield of this orchard at profitable prices.

All apple-orchards are equally profitable if carefully attended to. The Hon. John Y. Stone, the leading grower of Iowa, very recently figured out that any twenty acres set to apples should in the course of thirty years of fruitage yield an average income of $4,000 a year. He estimated on planting 200 trees to the acre, and removing half of them after the first ten years, when crowding would become dangerous—a system which would require each tree to yield but a dollar's worth of apples each year in order to make up the fine income desired.

What more this wonderfully productive and valuable fruit means to new regions may be seen in the case of Oklahoma and Arkansas, parts of which have since become known as the Ozark apple-belt. It is much the same story as that of Colorado over again, only in the case of Oklahoma the apple industry is of even more recent origin. Orchards have been set out, 20,000 trees at a planting, all over the territory, and the apple crop is rapidly assuming massive proportions. In northwestern Arkansas, which is a part of this region, one finds what many consider the most important fruit region in America. All things seem to have conspired to perfect a fruit-growing district. Water, soils, height above the sea, mild temperature, all work together to make a perfect orchard land. There were shipped out of this region last year over 2,000 car-loads of green apples and vast quantities of the dried variety. One sees miles upon miles of splendid orchards in passing, from the family garden of a score of trees to the larger tracts of from 1,000 to 2,000 acres, all apples. The whole region is astir on the subject, and those allied industries of packing, barrel-making, drying, and storing are rapidly following in the wake of the splendid development.

With all this there are now only about 2,000,000 people in all the immense Ozark region, which includes Oklahoma, Arkansas, and south-western Missouri. It is a country whose resources, when fully developed, will readily sustain a population of 50,000,000 and more. Alone it could furnish the world with apples if properly gardened, although apples are but one of the host of its resources.

It would be useless, however, to go into many more figures of the same sort, although among the older States the output is something enormous. Every State in the Union raises some apples, usually about half of all it consumes. There are the special States, however, which raise much more than they consume, and upon which the States in which the shortages occur depend. Thus Maine supplies its local demand for apples fresh and dried, to say nothing of cider, and has 3,000,000 barrels over all to ship. New Hampshire does exactly the same, except that her quota for shipment is larger by 200,000 barrels. Vermont ships 1,200,000; Massachusetts, 2,000,000; Connecticut, 1,500,000. These are the smaller sources of supply. New York, Pennsylvania, Michigan, Ohio, Indiana, and Virginia are vast apple producers, supplying all local demands outside of the cities, and having from 6,000,000 to 10,000,000 barrels each to spare for shipment. The national apple reports are invariably full of brief sketches of the condition of the fruit in these regions, because the nation looks to them for its market surplus. Missouri and Kansas are in the lead, but they cannot and never will be able to supply a demand that is yearly becoming greater and more urgent.

Here one reads such items as the following, which might well be duplicated for any of a thousand towns throughout the country where the apple crop is all-important:

"Advices from Hazleton, Pa., say that the apple crop promises to be immense in that section this year. A ride in any direction will disclose tree after tree laden with apples so that the limbs fairly bend beneath their weight, in some cases to the point of breaking. It is a common thing now to see young trees propped up to support the burden of fruit. Even the scraggy, gnarly trees growing by the roadside have the fruit strung upon the branches as thick as onions suspended from a string in a country store. The yield will be upwards of a hundred thousand barrels."

An evaporator plant—drying apples for the market.

A keener suggestion of what the whole subject means can be had by taking a closer view of just one apple county where the commercial significance of the yield can be studied. Mills County, Ia., is as satisfactory as any, being a type of a prosperous apple county throughout the East and West. Here are 900,000 trees. In this county a ten-bushel yield to the tree would be considered rather below the average, and yet such a yield requires 180,000 wagon-loads to remove, and something like 18,000 cars to ship. For the period in which the picking lasts (a trifle over three weeks) this yield gives employment to over 20,000 people, at three and one-half cents per bushel, or between fifty and ninety cents a day. The growers themselves receive forty to fifty cents a bushel, or about $4,000,000. All this in one county, and upon land which represents only a twenty-ninth of all the acreage in the county.

In conclusion, it may be said that the growing of the American apple has but only now begun. For all that we raise 210,000,000 barrels, we have not nearly enough for home consumption, and our foreign trade is nothing. This is due partially to a lack of facilities—the ability to harvest, store, and ship quickly and cheaply. Chief of these is the inability to ship cheaply and at great speed. There is a movement throughout the land looking to a permanent solution of this question, and fast refrigerator lines are being established on every railroad in the country. Private companies are beginning to see that it is their business not only to establish a fast refrigerator line to meet a demand, but to create the demand after furnishing the facility. I have in mind one refrigerator line which was established before there was any profitable call for it, but which induced farmers to grow apples in order that it might have the carrying of them. Not only this, but it taught the farmers to raise and pack them, and afterwards found a suitable market to which to ship, and an honest sale for them. In its second year of business it hauled 500 cars of apples alone. This was in Texas.

We are showing a great array of American apples at Paris—apples than which there is nothing finer in all the world. There will be a demand for these shortly, and when it does come, the United States will have more orchards and greater commercial benefits from this one fruit than will all the rest of the world combined.

The Canadian apple industry also has features of great interest. The entire line of provinces bordering the United States has orchards of great size, and these are encouraged not only by Canadian cities, but by the mother country, England.

The shipments from Halifax for the season of 1899–1900 to all foreign ports aggregated over 2,000,000 barrels. There were shipped to New York and Chicago at the same time over 9,000,000 barrels. Manitoba is one of the most important of the western provinces in this respect, the number of trees looked after in specially farmed orchards aggregating between 500,000 and 600,000.

NOTES

"Apples," *Pearson's* 10 (October 1900): 336–40.

10

Fruit Growing in America

Iт is a tradition among the fruit-dealers of New York city that when it was desired to celebrate the signing of the Treaty of Peace in 1814 by a grand banquet, only a half-barrel of raisins could be found in the city for the making of a plum pudding.[1] Of dried cherries there were none, and apples were scarce. At the present writing California alone holds a record of 103,000,000 pounds of raisins shipped out of the State in one year, and a fair crop of apples in New York State would supply the entire world. The money paid for 103,000,000 pounds of raisins, as the housewives buy them, amounts to something like $26,000,000, and there are other States which grow raisins.

The present condition of the fruit trade in the United States, however, is something which at best can only be shadowed forth to the mind, for statistics appall, and vast figures mean nothing. It is matter of railroads and States, of millions of acres and thousands of packing-factories, of ships and warehouses and trains. Men transact millions of dollars' worth of business a year in some small branch of it, and yet they can tell you nothing. I met a man who handles $200,000 worth of grapes every season, but he could not inform me concerning grapes in the United States. His dealings were with one vineyard alone. I sought another man whose peach-orchard in Georgia contains 212,000 trees, but all he knew about was his own orchard.

"I don't know," he said, "how big the peach crop is in this country. My orchard isn't so very large—there are a good many like this."

"Tell me about apples," I inquired of an apple-broker, who for fifteen years has seen the apple-market grow so that he himself controls two orchards, in different States, as large as Central Park.

"On my life, now," he answered, "I couldn't. I don't know. I might tell you about Montana and Kansas, but I don't know much about the other States. There is an awful lot of apples raised in this country."

"Montana?" I said. "Do they raise apples in Montana?"

"Some of the finest orchards in the world are there," he answered.

"Large ones?"

161

"Oh, sixty to one hundred thousand trees. You've heard of Marcus Daly, haven't you? He has an orchard of sixty thousand trees out there."

"Have you any idea of what the annual yield of apples in the United States amounts to?"

"Well, no. In 1894 it was worth about $150,000,000; but that was six years ago. What it will be this year I couldn't say."

"Does that represent the price to the consumer, or the amount the farmers received?"

"The farmers, of course. It would be three times that if we were talking about consumers."

So it was with oranges, pineapples, strawberries, and melons.

Out and away, however, from the jungle of brokers and commission merchants, who occupy and enliven a goodly section of every American city, some order is to be found. Here and there, in States and capitals, dwell men who keep watch—apple experts, and wiseacres in grapes, who know and can tell how stands the production of these things. Thus it is that one may learn of $80,000,000 worth of strawberries grown and consumed in these United States in a single season.

This seems difficult to believe, even when it is taken into consideration that the strawberry season begins in all the large cities in late November, and ends the following August, and that the prices fall from a dollar to six cents a quart as the season advances, and then gradually rise to a dollar again at the end. One must see the depots and the trains, the flourishing gardens, blooming in January in southern Florida, and the careful picking still going on in August far north in New Brunswick and Nova Scotia. It is berries from these extremes which make the price a dollar for the first and last boxes sent to the cities.

The wonder of it all is, however, the brief period of time in which the growing of strawberries has assumed such enormous proportions. Twenty years ago all the strawberries eaten by the 2,000,000 people included in New York, Brooklyn, and Jersey City were grown in Long Island and New Jersey. Since then the producing area has been gradually extended. Delaware, Maryland, and Virginia began to grow them, not only for New York, but for the Boston market, and fast freight lines were established to transport the product. Then the Carolinas, Georgia, and Florida were added, and now Alabama, Mississippi, Tennessee, and Arkansas raise vast quantities of strawberries, and ship to all large cities.

It costs but two cents to ship a box of strawberries from southern Arkansas to New York; and many are the car-loads that come across the land at express speed to supply the Eastern demand.

The production of blackberries, raspberries, and other such fruit has been estimated, but since the estimates are all large, let the least of them serve for illustration. Huckleberries are not so numerous. They are not even gathered by growers, because they are wild. Mountains and swamps are their strongholds, and men must gather them under difficulties; yet $1,000,000 worth are marketed in New York alone.

But the proportion which the fruit trade has reached is most significant in the larger fields of oranges, lemons, grapes, and apples. Two years hence, if not next year, the California orange crop will supply every market in the country, and, it is asserted, at prices that will exclude all foreign competition, without the aid of a protective tariff. Last year 12,000 carloads of oranges and lemons were shipped from that State, and this season the crop is estimated at from 15,000 to 18,000 cars. Yet there are 200,000 trees which have not yet come into bearing.

In Florida the yield for the present year will be 1,000,000 boxes, or 3300 cars. Arizona has developed this industry to the extent of shipping 100 cars a week, and yet, previous to 1873, oranges were not commercially grown in the United States. All we ate were imported.

A nearer view heightens the meaning of these figures. Thus fifty cities east of California receive one car-load or more of oranges per week from the coast. This is not large when thought of in connection with New York, but when spoken of in connection with Dayton, Utica, Indianapolis, Grand Rapids, and the like, it becomes more interesting. Lots of five cars are frequently cut out of through trains at Detroit and distributed up the east coast of Michigan—thus Mt. Clemens, one car; Saginaw, one car; Kalamazoo, one car, and so on.

No one need be advised of the extent of the orange-orchards in California, but of Florida a word may not be amiss. In a small portion of Manatee County, near the towns of Manatee and Palmetto, are twelve orange-groves, aggregating 33,000 trees, and in the entire county are 300 other groves, with a total of more than 300,000 trees, planted in the last twelve years.

Near the town of Winter Haven, in the middle section of the State, there are 1000 acres of trees which produce 75,000 boxes of oranges. Around every village convenient to a railroad in the lower half of the State are orange-groves, a score or more, containing anywhere from 500 to 5000 trees, so loaded with golden fruit that the branches must be propped to sustain the weight. This is the second-rate orange section of the Union. In the true orange country—California—the marvels of this industry are numerous. From groves and storehouses in Riverside County 999,120 boxes of oranges and lemons were shipped during the first three months of the present year.

It took nearly 3000 refrigerator-cars to remove them, and at one time there was a glut of railroad cars, a veritable tangle of orders concerning

Harvesting Georgia peaches

cars, which threatened to cost thousands of dollars in loss by delay. The annual crop is worth fully $4,000,000 to the growers on $40,000,000 invested.

These things concerning oranges are not more remarkable than that which may be told of peaches. We have long had great peach areas in Delaware and Michigan—areas which, because of the annual wail about frost, have become more or less generally known; but the great strides in this field are as yet the secret of the growers. Perhaps most residents of Indiana are not aware of the fact that there are peach-orchards aggregating 500,000 trees in the southern quarter of their State. There are peach-trees all through that favored common-wealth, but the number referred to are scientifically grouped and gardened, with a view to marketing the fruit the world over.

In northern Alabama the past decade has seen 300 distinct orchards of peaches planted, and yet this State has scarcely been heard of in the peach-market. Only last spring an orchard of 100 acres was set out on high ground near Midland City, and the owner will now patiently wait for returns. Thousands of crates are already shipped out of the State, but the million or more trees have their entire future before them. Texas, Missouri, and Tennessee are also in this field, emulating Georgia, which is the wonder and the envy of all who would raise peaches.

No more significant sign of the growth of our fruit industry is to be had than the great change in the State last mentioned, where, only recently, cotton was king. Since the civil war the old order has been changing, and planting interests have become diversified, large farms have been cut up, and, among other things, the fruit interest has been steadily growing. In middle and southwest Georgia, where extensive cotton plantations once abounded, choice orchards have been planted, and packing-houses, canning-factories, and crate-factories have followed the extensive growing of fruit. There is a section of the State, traversed by one of the large east-coast roads, which is full of the new-found riches of fruit. This part of the State is singularly productive, and during the dull summer months, when cotton and grain crops are laid by, there are busy scenes among the peach-pickers and peach-packers. The whole section of the State, from Griffin to Smithville, thence to Albany, Cuthbert, and Fort Gaines, is one unbroken stretch of fruiting trees and perfect-bearing species. There is one man at Marshallville who individually controls 120,000 trees. Possibly this is one of the largest peach-orchards in Georgia. One combination of men in Fort Valley controls 300,000 trees. In the neighborhood of this town are 700,000 trees in full fruitage this year. And yet the peach industry is known to be in its infancy here. In spite of tons of fruit shipped to Eastern and Western markets, the industry has just begun. The railroad traversing this one section handled 1786 refrigerator-cars last season, loaded and iced at the various points of shipment. In the past ten years the same road has built twenty-five miles of spur tracks to accommodate growers whose orchards were coming into fruitage. To give some further idea of the extent and the importance of this one fruit crop here, it may be stated that in the neighborhood of Albany there are (in round numbers) 55,000 peach-trees; Barnesville has nearly as many; the little town of Buena Vista has 12,000; Cuthbert, over 40,000; Marshallville, 500,000; Smithville, 50,000; and new orchards are planting every season.

What this means to the State where once the old pine barrens grew up in waste, and the rugged clay hills seemed given over to desolation, may be better imagined than told. Those allied industries of storing, packing, canning, which follow the march of nature's bounty, have come here. Money has flowed in streams of a hundred thousand and more to the smallest of towns. Far and away stretch these ministers of nature, soldiers of a well-trained army, tents of a well-regulated camp, bearing their gifts of goodness and beauty. In season the broad roadways, lined on either side for miles upon miles with the green branches of these trees, are filled with covered wagons bearing the rich yield to store. In packing-houses, at intervals, are hundreds of workers, selecting, wrapping, crating. It is almost a carnival season, in which men, women, and children turn out to honor with their labor the ripening of Georgia's new-found wealth. And yet it must not be forgotten that this is the peach crop in but one section of Georgia. Elsewhere in the State are large orchards, and outside of it in the rest of the country. The Delaware crop, spread over many sections of that small State, was estimated at 4,000,000 baskets for the season just past. Connecticut furnishes the same number, and boasts one orchard of 112,000 trees. Maryland equals Delaware, and Michigan surpasses both. Near Cumberland, Maryland, is one orchard of 200,000 trees, controlled by the Allegheny Orhcard Company. At Benton Harbor, Michigan, resides one gentleman whose extensive orchards thereabouts yield him $80,000 a year. One county in New Jersey—Sussex—raised 500,000 baskets at a dollar a basket, received by the growers, and one village of this county—Glenwood—shipped 80,000 baskets at the same price. There are five counties in New Jersey equally noted for peach crops.

Dealing thus with separate fruits, one might come to imagine that the growing of one kind or another monopolized certain States or sections. As a matter of fact, it is just the reverse. Thus New Jersey, so rich in peaches, produces a great many more grapes and vegetables. New York, so prolific of apples, is astonishingly productive of grapes, and Pennsylvania grows a dozen fruits in enormous quantities. California produces more of almost every common fruit than any other State in the Union.

It is in the recently introduced fruits, and in those States and regions which have gone into growing for the markets, that the best examples of rapid increase are to be noted. In 1875 what fruit was to be had in Colorado came from California, and was sold by the pound at fabulous prices. With slight modifications of price this condition continued until 1882, when better railroad facilities were inaugurated, but no perceptible change was effected until three years later, by which time Denver, a city of 35,000, with innumerable dependent mining-camps, was using per week only eight cars of all sorts of fruits. At that time bananas were not to be had before June, and the first car-load ever received in May netted the importers a profit of $1400. Then began the local growing of fruits, since which time 130,000 acres have been planted with fruit trees alone, 99,000 given to apple-orchards.

In 1896 a few crates of Rockyford melons—a species of cantaloupe—were shipped out of the State on speculation. They had previously been grown for home consumption in what is known as the Arkansas Valley of Colorado—a strip of land 120 miles long and five miles wide, which begins at Pueblo, in the northwest, and ends at Holly, in the southeast. Some New York commission merchants, seeing the great merit of the first samples which came East, hastened to Colorado and began a campaign of organization which resulted in 133 car-loads being raised and sent East the very next season. These being sold at a profit, there was a grand rush throughout the valley to plant melons, with the result that 1500 car-loads were produced in 1898. Now, then, behold the marvel of this rapidly growing fruit industry. In Florida, Georgia, the Carolinas, Alabama, Arkansas, and Texas, growers heard of the wonderful success of this melon, and having an eye to business, planted a few acres. To-day 23,000 acres, scattered throughout nineteen States, are devoted to the raising of Rockyford melons, and more are being constantly added. In some places the introduction has been due to the efforts of the agents of large commission houses; in others to representatives of great refrigerator lines, seeking to build up a business for their cars. Seven hundred car-loads were raised in Texas alone three years after the melon had been introduced to the world outside of Colorado!

Equally rapid, but far more suggestive as indicating the new order when fruits will no longer be brought to this country from abroad, has been the growing of prunes, the commercial rise of which can be traced to a package of scions brought to San Francisco from France in 1856 by Pierre Pellier, and by him sent to his brother Louis, at San José, California. Not until 1870 was a large orchard planted; and it was 1881 before there were a dozen fair-sized orchards in the United States. The output of the largest growers in California at that time did not exceed five or six tons of cured fruit per annum, while to-day the prune-producing capacity of the orchards of the United States exceeds 100,000,000 pounds of cured fruit a year. With this remarkable rise comes a falling off in another direction, namely, that of prune-importing. Ten years ago we imported nearly 60,000,000 pounds from abroad, whereas to-day the total imports are exactly 650,000 pounds. The other fifty-nine and some odd millions that we used yearly to import we now grow ourselves, and have a surplus to sell.

A similar change has been effected by the growing of raisins in this country, the immense yield of which has been cited. There is no record of any raisins grown for market previous to 1863. Only 6000 boxes, mostly from two vineyards in Solano and Yolo counties, California, were produced in 1873. Since that time has taken place all the immense growth, requiring 3500 cars each year to haul that which California has to spare of this one fruit. We have cut the imports from abroad from 41,817,016 pounds in 1890, to a bare 10,000,000 this year, and have begun exporting. Little transactions like that which took place last March, in which thirty-five car-loads were sold to one Chicago commission house for $155,000, are becoming common. The local demand in several of our large cities frequently calls for much larger quantities.

But raisins are only a fraction of our grape-growing industry—an affair which includes all our American wines and fine brandies, as well as the fresh fruit retailed in baskets. One commission merchant in New York informed me recently that he has frequently sold as many as seventy-three car-loads of grapes in a day to residents of the German, French, and Italian quarters of the city, who make their own table wines.

"It is cheaper for them to make their wines than to buy the American bottled goods," he explained.

At Vineland, New Jersey, are 10,000 acres devoted to grapes, from which hundreds of thousands of gallons of unfermented grape juice are bottled, as well as car-loads of the fresh fruit shipped. Ten villages in Pennsylvania are equally notable for their wine and fresh grape product. The great grape section of the East, however, is that portion of western New York and northern Ohio which borders about Lake Erie. Here grapes are raised by the hundred thousand tons—thirty to forty thousand car-loads in a season.

In the West the extent of the grape product is almost beyond belief. Michigan is an important grape-growing State, and so is Wisconsin, but nearly every State has one or two important orchards and wine-cellars. California, of course, leads all others in this, as in so many fruits, producing five times as many grapes as the New York and Ohio vineyards mentioned. The largest vineyard in the world is there, not long ago the property of the late Leland Stanford, and now managed by his estate.[2] It lies in the heart of the Sacramento Valley, about 200 miles north of San Francisco, and embraces an area of six square miles, every acre of which contains 680 separate vines. Here, indeed, is a city of grapes—laid off in blocks of 1400 vines, and traversed by streets and alleys of geometric regularity. In late June, when the fruit begins to ripen, and throughout July, when in a wash of golden sunlight and silvery moonlight that purple perfection is reached which marks the vintage, earth holds no more impressive scene. Now come the harvesters, a thousand and more, working from vine to vine and singing in the sunlight. Wagons patrol the long roads, gathering the boxed product, and wine-presses creak throughout the day and night, draining this secret blood of the soil, red with essence of sun and moon. Thousands upon thousands of tons are thus brought to press—250,000 in all—and car-loads are packed and sent away. So great is the production of wine and brandy that the government has found it necessary to build a warehouse upon the grounds—a warehouse two acres in extent, where the casks are stored and the taxes estimated.

The most interesting phase of the entire development is the matter of organization. The apparent jumble of growers' associations, commission merchants' leagues, refrigerator lines, and cold-storage companies merely means that we have reached that point where it is possible to see the coming day when the products of a single garden can be profitably distributed over the entire Union. The day is near when there will be no inconvenient spot in the land where a barrel of apples will rot because there is no profitable way of marketing them. The improvement is, in a very large measure, due to the profit which all could plainly see was being made thirty years ago out of fruit imported from abroad.

"If they can bring oranges from Italy," thought the man in California, "and make so much money, why cannot I raise them here and thrive?"

In that very thought lay embodied the billions of dollars' worth of facilities which in thirty years have sprung up to answer the nation's appetite for fruits. To-day the owner of an acre of land, anywhere near a railroad in the fruit-growing section, commands more facilities by which to market his product than did the owner of a thousand acres twenty years ago. He is the beneficiary of services which growers' associations and commission merchants' leagues have compelled. He can get a rate for his half-dozen crates of fruit which is nearly as low as the large grower pays who charters a car, because the railroads have been taught to see the wisdom of running "pick-up" cars which stop at every station, picking up one kind of product until there is a car-load of it. Then it is auctioned as a car-load lot in one of the many cities, and the profits divided *pro rata.* The steady insistence of commission merchants, who lose when fruit is delayed or rots on the way, has caused the establishment of refrigerator lines with express privileges, so that it costs only $120 to ice a car from San Francisco to New York, because it comes across the continent in a little over five days. The complaints of organized farmers have brought about the development of the science of storage, and the building of immense store-houses for the preservation of everything perishable which may lack a profitable market at the time it arrives.

I have in my hand a card showing the temperature at which various fruits keep, and for how long. This tells me that at from 32 degrees to 35 degrees F. apples keep for eight months. Every apple-grower knows this. It is a part of the great trade development. In May of the present year there were 500,000 barrels of apples of the crop of 1899 in storage throughout the United States, held thus through a long winter for better prices, because there was no profitable demand in the fall. Some of the apples were in every city east of Denver, because every city now has a cold-storage warehouse, designed to aid in the distribution and marketing of fruits.

This progress, which is the order of the day, is serving to bring *supply* and *demand* into closer touch, and to make accumulation and distribution flow through smoother and swifter channels. It has made possible the fact that figs, apricots, and olives, now grown in California and Arizona, have cut the once immense foreign importation of those things squarely in two. And further facilities along the same line will end in destroying entirely the business of importing foreign fruits. The great truck-gardens of the South furnish their luscious products to half the homes of the country within thirty hours after being gathered; and the products of California are handed to the consumer more quickly this year than they were last. Men are awake at night—hundreds of them in New York—tramping down to the long piers where the cars are ferried in, to inspect and calculate by the dim morning light, in order that goods so perishable may not be delayed a moment in reaching the consumer. If forty cars of oranges arrived in the railroad yards in Chicago at three o'clock this morning, depend upon it they were duly met by commission agents, and by noon of this very day were auctioned, paid for, and delivered to those who sell oranges by the dozen. These short-lived products must be hastily gathered, rapidly trans-ported, quickly sold—and they are.

Turning to the whole field again, it is plain that any attempt to offer a reasonable estimate for the whole volume of this astonishing business would be impossible. The government has never secured an adequate nor certain census. It is well known that a billion dollars would be a modest estimate, but how much it actually amounts to will possibly never be truly known. An effort was made to have the subject adequately covered by the present census, but the result is not yet certain.

In a larger sense the importance of these astonishing figures is much clearer. One sees clearly the potent fact standing as the meaning of it all—the resources of the nation. If a ten-thousandth part of the land given us shall, by moderate cultivation, supply the fruit of 70,000,000 people, crowd the warehouses, glut the rails with trains, how shall all the land respond when appealed to by labor? Clearly a hundred million, and yet a hundred million more, may come, blossoming into life, and the land shall offer them the welcome of food. A thousand million, dwelling side by side, could not embarrass the bounty of nature, which yields a hundred favors for every blessing asked. For every crop growing, ten thousand times its need of chemicals in the soil! For every ray of sunshine used in perfecting bloom and fruitage, ten thousand left to pass! Man shall perfect himself in the wisdom of these things, and there shall no longer be a cry for food. He shall prepare the estimate of that which is his need, and that which is asked shall be given.

NOTES

"Fruit Growing in America," *Harper's Monthly* 101 (November 1900): 859–68.

1. The Treaty of Peace in 1814 refers to the Treaty of Ghent, Belgium, signed by the United States and Great Britain on 24 December 1814. A conflict between the two nations began with a declaration of war by the American Congress on 18 June 1812, in retaliation for British interference with American trade and shipping on the high seas and, to a lesser degree, for alleged British complicity in Native Indian hostilities on the frontier.

2. Leland Stanford (1824–93), American businessman, politician, and philanthropist, aided in the completion of the transcontinental railroad. He was governor of California (1861–63). In 1885, as a memorial to his son, he founded and financed the Leland Stanford Junior University, generally known as Stanford University.

11

The New Knowledge of Weeds

Uses of the So-called Pests of the Soil

VAST SUMS OF MONEY AND AN ARMY OF MEN ARE BEING EMPLOYED BY the government to locate, understand and put to their proper uses the weeds of the country. From every town and hamlet and country wayside this great government gathers reports concerning these vegetable outlaws. The impudent dock that surreptitiously slips his seed on to the coat of a passerby in Nebraska is recorded in the annals of the Agricultural Department, and the line of the dock's progress is marked on the maps which show the areas of distribution in the United States. It is now known what and where the weeds are, and a constant surveillance is kept over them. Those that threaten to become pests are headed off by all the forces of government. It is a fact that an order to kill some lone specimen of a pernicious Canada thistle has been sent by telegraph from Washington.

There is, however, little need of encouraging the destruction of weeds. The thing important now is to utilize those that have been found indispensable. There are weeds that are soil renewers, weeds that are food for man and beast, and weeds without which thousands of acres of our most fertile lands would be wastes to-day. These weeds the government is endeavoring to preserve. It is surprising in the light of these discoveries to consider man's attitude toward weeds in general. That he should have sworn at them, sought measures of extermination, plowed them toilsomely under year after year, and yet himself remained really handicapped in the battle for subsistence because he lacked the aid which one or more of these would have readily given him seems incongruous. One kind if properly used would have supplied deficient soil with potash, another would have brought it the needed lime, a third the nitrogen or phosphorus, taking it out of the atmosphere and depositing it where his crops of cereals and vegetables would readily draw upon it and wax strong. In one he could have found a better food for his cattle than he ever had before, in another a hardy worker capable of thriving with scarcely any rain and yet making returns in food or fertilizer far beyond the petty achievements of the most pampered and cultivated of domestic plants. The outlaws of husbandry have for ages

171

held the secret of binding the sands of the sea so as to fix the shore; of digging deeper than any plow and searching for the minerals which make deficient land arable, and of drawing upon the atmosphere and taking from it the valuable chemicals which no farmer is rich enough to buy in sufficient quantities to make his poor holding profitable. These bandits of the garden have turned out for the most part to be saviors and man's best friends, and so clear have their distinguished merits become that scientists are even apologizing for the need of calling any of the remaining, and as yet little understood vegetation, *weeds*. So we have all unused plants now divided into poisonous and non-poisonous, with the reservation that all may be and probably are extremely useful. If poisonous, the new attitude is to find out why. Where the poison comes from—out of the air or the earth? How is it distilled? What is its nature? Whether it is a known or unknown poison? What its effect may be on one and every other object, particularly upon life and growth? These and others are the questions scientists seek to answer by investigating the weeds.

The result is a new world of information of immediate or ultimate usefulness. So far the investigations have served to show that we are in our infancy as regards a proper knowledge of food. The available supply has already been increased a thousand-fold. The possibilities of increasing the strength of the soil have never been so numerous. The time is already in sight when the ability to examine a stretch of land and prescribe the proper weed to nourish and cure it will be realized. The time also is not far distant when the poisonous weed will have been mastered and applied, and the most useless weed put in its place and made to do serviceable work.

Already from the kingdom of weeds has come the host now recognized as serviceable grasses. We have sixty native species of clover, seventy blue grasses, twenty-five grammas and curly mosquite grasses, all wild and all abundant.[1] They have flourished on the great plains, and though not understood have produced more beef and mutton than all the cultivated hay grasses put together. The cattle of the ranchers have been wiser in their selection of them for food than men. Besides, there are ninety lupines, twenty wild beans, forty vetches, forty beggar weeds, twenty kinds of wild rye, thirty kinds of brome grasses, and meadow, pasture, woodland and swamp grasses without number.[2] Each of these has always been considered a weed and a nuisance, and yet each is especially adapted to a soil or climate and to some particular use. There is a wild millet, common to the South Atlantic coast, which grows from six to ten feet high, and is a splendid cattle food. There is a wild brome grass now approved of which was never thought to have any value until one almost identically like it was imported from Russia as a cattle food. There are wild perennial beans in the southwestern mountains of the United States which grow luxuriantly with only twenty inches of rainfall annually, and yet many of them far surpass in productiveness and forage value those which have come to us from foreign lands and require good soil and a normal rainfall. There are free seeding wheat grasses in the Northwest still generally looked upon as weeds, which equal the best of our hay grasses. In the mountain parks the government agents have found a wild green turf which rivals in fineness and beauty the best artificial lawns.

This order of grasses is in part claiming commercial attention. Already some are used as fibre in the manufacture of twine or paper. Some are used in making hats and many other articles of woven work. They are planted to subdue or bind the drifting sand of the seashore, to hold the soil of railway embankments, and to prevent the washing out of dikes and levees. Others are used to aid in reclaiming fields denuded of their soil by rain. It has been shown by the government that through their growth and decay the fertile prairie loams have been formed.[3] They were and still are the forerunners which nature sends to cover the bare surfaces and to lessen the steriliz-ing effect of heat and drought. Not all have value as food for either man or beast, but it has been found that all of the number described serve some purpose in the economy of nature, and they are not yet completely understood.

The weeds of the cities and villages which are best known to us all have unquestionably the worst reputation and are looked upon as the most useless and harmful. They are some twenty-five in all—the good classed with the poisonous, and all misunderstood and considered evil. In New York, Philadelphia and Washington the residents see vacant lots growing with wild onion in winter, dandelion and bulbous buttercup in spring, then wild carrot, prickly lettuce and sweet clover, and after them the horseweed, ragweed, cocklebur, Mexican tea, slender pigweed and jimsonweed of the late summer and autumn. Chicory, horse-nettle, burdock and gum-succory are in abundant evidence throughout the season.[4]

Some of the most prominent weeds of Boston are burdock, rough pig-weed, chicory and fall dandelion. In Chicago rough pigweed, tall ragweed and cocklebur are abundant, while there are hundreds of acres within the city limits covered almost completely with Canada thistle and Russian thistle. In Denver false ragweed, squirreltail grass and Russian thistle are among the most noticeable weeds, and in San José, California, the vacant lots are chiefly occupied by wild licorice, spiny cocklebur, wild heliotrope, milk thistle and tarweeds. In Atlanta, Augusta, Auburn, Mobile, New Orleans and most other cities of the Gulf States tarweed is looked upon as the pest of early summer and sneezeweed of the late summer and autumn; the latter is a yellow flowered composite, which has been introduced during the past fifty years from west of the Mississippi.

It is known now that the presence of these weeds, collectively and uncared for, is not all bad. When young and growing, besides giving a more sightly appearance to utterly vacant ground, they purify the air, and herein lies the chief benefit conferred by their presence in cities. Numerous fires in dwellings, factories and locomotives, and the breathing of the people continually rob the air of its oxygen and charge it with carbonic acid gas. Growing plants of whatsoever kind, and weeds in particular, reverie this condition by drawing off into themselves the carbonic acid gas, and often other injurious gases, and giving out oxygen in return. So a vacant lot covered with healthy growing weeds is much better for the public health, and certainly is more pleasing to the eye than the bare ground.

They have another effect not so good. When they stop growing they cease purifying the air, although it is not certain, as some suppose, that they rob it of its oxygen. They harbor injurious insects and fungus and bacterial diseases, which later they communicate to cultivated plants. When they become rank and begin to decay they shade the soil from the purifying and drying effects of the sun and wind, and, it is thought, keep it damp and sour—a fit breeding place for malaria. The ragweeds produce a pollen which is extremely irritating to persons afflicted with asthma or hay fever. The mayweed, tarweed and stinkweed produce disagreeable odors. The wild garlic is eaten by the cows, which gives the city residents reason to complain of the bitter flavor of garlic in the milk delivered them. Henbane or deadly nightshade, jimson weed and purple thorn are deadly poison and give cause for more opposition to weeds in cities.

Notwithstanding all this, the charge is not against the individual weeds, but their collective neglect and misuse. They are not understood. Every one knows that dandelion is an excellent pot-herb when taken by itself and cultivated. It is not so generally known that this is true of chicory, milk-weed and pigweed, although the government is now calling attention to their value as food. Prickly lettuce, while not thoroughly understood, is known to be liked by sheep and is therefore thought to have some quality which will eventually make it useful. The same is exactly true of the wild carrot. The other weeds—wild onion, horseweed, ragweed, cocklebur, jimson weed, burdock, tarweed and sneezeweed—have done the service to humanity of exciting interest in the weed question. Their size and strength, the manner in which they multiply and the use which they make of what they find in the soil and atmosphere has stirred up investigation of a most profitable order. Part of the knowledge acquired has been how to kill them cheaply and effectively where they are a nuisance, but this knowledge is not now considered so important. Later a study was made of their growth and distribution until the whole vast scientific knowledge of how so-called weeds grow, multiply and distribute themselves was gathered. The investigation as to what it is that these weeds take from the soil and the air is under way, and the investigation will not end until it is known what they do and what is their place in nature. In 1898 an interesting pamphlet covering the character of thirty poisonous plants and the cure for injury by them was issued by the government. Since then several poisonous plants have been especially investigated by individual scientists. One of these, the common poison ivy, has been thoroughly analyzed by Dr. Frank Pfaff of the Harvard University Medical School. He discovered that the poison in the ivy which does the damage is a non-volatile oil to which he has given the name of the plant. It is an oil that has not hitherto been known to science, and is found in all parts of the plant, even in the wood. Why it should poison the skin when touched is not yet known, but the fact that it will poison only the spot which it touches and will not spread has been found out. Dr. Pfaff also discovered that it is readily removed by alcohol, and that old poisons by this plant are readily cured by two or three applications of a mixture of equal parts of alcohol and sugar of lead.

As much is now being done for corncockle, jimson weed, sneezeweed and others, remedies for which are already known, although the character of the poison is not.

Out of this branch of weed-study is certain to come remarkable information, for the poisonous plants are the most strangely constituted and given to astounding variations. For instance, the common poke berry presents a spectacle of contradictory qualities. Birds eat the berries which to men are poisonous. Cattle may eat the leaves when green and fresh, but if, perchance, they should eat a wilted leaf it would poison them. The roots are deadly poison, yet the shoots which grow up six inches high in the spring are an excellent food for man—the rival of asparagus and equally healthful. Science has at last paused to inquire why this should be so, and some day the chemical action which can make a deadly poison by wilting a leaf when the fresh one is harmless will be discovered.

Similarly it has been observed of American false hellebore or itchweed that the seeds are poisonous to chickens, and that the leaves and roots are poisonous to men and horses, but that sheep and elk, which chew the cud, seem to relish the plant.[5] In all, the poison, when in the system, acts alike, paralyzing the heart and spinal cord. The poisonous element of corncockle has not yet been explained, but its curious action has already been observed. When extracted it mixes freely with water, froths like soap and, though odorless, will, when inhaled, produce violent sneezing. Caper spurge, the common gopher plant or spring wort, is curious in that the mere handling of it will poison to the extent of producing pimples and often gangrene. It is a thing that cattle can eat without harm, and goats eat freely, but the milk of the latter will then be deadly poison. In men a moderate dose will produce a general collapse and death in a few hours. The poison of the sneezeweed develops mostly in the showy yellow flowers, and is violent. The young plants are comparatively harmless, and even in the mature ones the poison varies greatly—some having scarcely any at all.

In the case of this plant and the woolly and stemless loco weeds some effort has been made to find out where they get their deadly poisons. That of the loco weeds is a most subtle thing. The poison of the woolly loco produces strange hallucinations in its victims. It effects the eyesight and silently reaches one after another of the vital functions, killing the victim in two years' time.

Some animals after eating it refuse every other kind of food and seek only this. They endure a lingering period of emaciation, characterized by sunken eyeballs, lusterless hair and feeble movements, and eventually die of starvation. So mystic an element gathered from the earth and the air naturally causes wonder and the desire to know what such things may be and why they are.

Weed investigation has also resulted in a great addition to the known foods for cattle, and the discovery of a number of plants that will fertilize the soil. During this century and within recent years a score or more of valuable leguminous plants have been discovered in what were considered weeds, and hardly a year passes that new ones are not added to the list. They are plants which make food for cattle and which, when planted in poor soil, improve it by taking from the atmosphere and the deep subsoil things which the surface soil needs.

The manner in which they are known to improve poor soil forms a remarkable scientific discovery. Their roots extend into the stiffer and more compact subsoil, where no ordinary plant can reach, and after loosening and opening it up so that air and water can have action upon it, suck up from below great quantities of potash salts and phosphoric acid. When these weeds are plowed under or die, these salts and acids are left near the surface where they can be utilized by the cereals and root crops which live upon them. For instance, wheat and potatoes flourish well where these weeds have gone before and done the work of getting the necessary food for them from the subsoil and the air.

Much land is of no value until these weeds come in and make it so. This is particularly true of sandy soils and reclaimed marsh lands, which are deficient in potash, a thing necessary in all farming land. On these the deeper rooted legumes, such as gorse, broom, alfalfa, lupines, sulla and the perennial beans are of great value. Their roots not only reach down very deep and bring up potash from the subsoil in the manner described, but their leaves take great quantities of nitrogen from the air. Now, when a soil is rich in potash and nitrogen it is good soil, and as these plants die and leave their gathered potash and nitrogen on the surface, the sandy and marshy soils become good land. All the farmer has to do is plow these rotting weeds under and he has land on which he can raise cereals, root crop and tobacco—that hardiest, most wearing plant upon soil.

The government has induced farmers to try the Florida beggar weed. One experimenter reported that by planting it in his field and plowing under the annual crops for two successive years, the soil had been completely changed in texture and color. Another farmer discovered that a crop of beggar weed turned under, will, when decomposed, retain near the surface in ready reach of the roots of succeeding crops not only all the nitrogen that it took out of the atmosphere, but also whatever fertilizers were subsequently applied. A third reported that all his field produced more luxurious crops after having been given over one season to a rank growth of this weed.

To find out how much chemical value this weed really takes from the air and the subsoil, the government planted a sandy field (bare of any of the qualities on which ordinary cereals and vegetables can thrive) with beggar weed, and when the crop was at its height harvested it, root and all. The crop was then reduced to ashes and the result analyzed. It was found that every ton of beggar weed ashes contained 508 pounds of lime, 230 pounds of phosphoric acid, and 482 pounds of potash. Twenty to twenty-five tons of beggar weed hay were required to made one ton of ashes, but every acre yielded four tons of beggar weed. It was figured out that at a four ton yield per acre, which is an average, one acre of beggar weed would yield 150 pounds of nitrogen, worth fifteen cents a pound, or $22.50 worth of nitrogen, and potash and phosphoric acid worth $5.25, making a total of $27.75 worth of fertilizing chemicals taken from an acre of soil worth nothing at all.

As good a report can be made of red clover, alfalfa, cowpeas, the soy bean, crimson clover, Dakota vetch, Texas pea, the Stolley vetch and others, though some, as, for instance, the Texas pea are being allowed to die out. Crimson clover, particularly, is an excellent soil feeder, but will not do well north of a line drawn through New Jersey, East Tennessee and Central Texas, for it cannot withstand severe winters. It requires, also, a great deal of moisture, and so is better adapted to the needs of the Southern farmers. It has been proved an excellent preparatory crop for Indian corn, being sowed in the corn rows in late summer and turned under in time for the spring planting. It may be used in the same way for cotton or tobacco.

Incidentally, the habits of growth and distribution which characterize weeds have been thoroughly studied and a splendid picture of the intricate working of nature in these things has been evolved. There are maps in the Agricultural Department showing the present distribution in the United States of the Canada thistle, Russian thistle, nut grass, wild carrot, prickly lettuce and a score more, which show at a glance just where these weeds are to be found and the extent of their range. There are separate documents and papers for each one of over three hundred weeds, giving their life history, merits, demerits and present location and distribution.

What has been discovered about the migration of weeds shows how wonderfully life prevails even in the face of great hardship. It has been found that a weed no less than a man struggles to live and to propagate its kind, and that it will make thorough use of the poorest opportunity. Wind, water, the tides, the migration of birds, the moving of cattle, all furnish the average weed an opportunity to distribute its seed into new regions. These now common to the United States have for the most part migrated from Europe and Asia. Of a list of 200 so-called injurious weeds, published in 1895, it was found that 108 were of foreign origin, while ninety-two were native. Of the former, twelve or fifteen had migrated only a short time before from Central and South America.

How they migrate has been accurately shown in the case of every kind of weed extant in the United States. Some travel exceeding slow by means of runners or slender radiating branches, which reach out anywhere from ten inches to ten feet along the ground and produce plantlets at the ends, which take root and grow. Others progress by spreading underground, working too deep to be disturbed either by grazing animals or mowing machines. Still others, finding the battle for life difficult, develop strange qualities. Professor A. N. Prentiss, of Cornell University, has demonstrated by experiment that a Canada thistle root, cut into pieces one-forth of an inch long, can produce shoots from nearly every piece. So when the share of the plow digs down to cut and tear this inhabitant from its home it more often aids in its further distribution.

One of the most interesting yet least known methods by which plants travel short distances is by throwing their seeds. When the pods of the common tare are mature they dry in such a manner as to produce a strong oblique tension on the two sides of the pod. These finally split apart and curl spirally, with such a sudden movement upward as to hurl the peas several feet. Many others progress in the same way, the common spurge and wood sorrel in particular.

Many weed seeds have special adaptives that enable them to take advantage of the wind or to float lightly on water. Dandelion, prickly lettuce, Canada thistle, horseweed, milkweed and many others equip their seeds with some feathery or winglike apparatus that enables them to sail. Ordinarily the distance this equipment can carry is two miles, but a high wind or hurricane would bear them ten or fifteen. Yet with two exceptions, the most rapidly migrating weeds have not traveled in this way. Frozen ground or snow is another great aid to the hardy migraitng weed because seeds are blown along for great distances. Buttonweed, giant ragweed and barnyard grass all progress in this way, because their seeds are produced late in the season, and many of them are held with such tenacity that they are dislodged only by the strongest winds, when the conditions are favorable for distant journeys. By that time the ground is usually frozen or covered with snow, and the seeds skip merrily along before every stray gust. This method of seed dispersion is now known to account in part for the general presence of ragweed, mayweed and others along our country roads. It also shows that weeds are distributed much more rapidly over fields left bare during the winter than over those covered with some crop that will catch the rolling seeds. Professor Bolley, of the Fargo (N. D.) Agricultural College, found by experiment that wheat grains drifted over snow on a level field at the rate of 500 feet a minute, with the wind blowing twenty-five miles an hour. Lighter or angular grains were found to drift more rapidly.

Some weeds migrate by tumbling, the whole plant, seed and all, withering into a sort of ball and rolling before the wind. Such are best developed in the prairie region, where there is little to impede their progress, and where there are strong winds to drive them, but they are found also in the Eastern states, where they may be seen in ditches, gullies and fence corners, swept bare of their seeds before the winter is out.

Some weeds depend for their widest distribution upon the hooked character of their seeds, which stick to the hide of cattle or the clothing of men. They have been known to travel hundreds of miles this way, and the ground about the great stock yards in Chicago and other cities is rich in weeds not common to that territory. Migrating birds sweep seeds through space for thousands of miles, and it is thought that some of the weed importations from Central and South America have come this way.

Railways are highways no less for the progressive weed than for man. Seeds drop from cars and from the clothes of passengers all along the line. The most prolific weeds, particularly the Russian thistle, have been introduced at widely separated points throughout the United States almost simultaneously by this means. They come in straw used for packing, and in grain not perfectly cleaned. The country towns that receive the freight are breeding places and the men who handle it are carriers. The weeds get everywhere, because the seeds survive long and are equipped to cling and travel. By centuries of struggle they have acquired the ability to adapt themselves to almost any quality of soil or to any kind of atmosphere. They earn their right to live by the most hardy efforts. No plant of culture could ever endure the knocks which they receive and survive. Heat, cold, drouth, frost, soggy rains, unnatural soils, all afflict the traveling seed by turns. Yet it will face the situation, dig deep, reach high, even change its diet and its very nature before it will give up the struggle. That it should be of some use is a long-delayed but just conclusion of science. The outlaw of the fruitful fields is to-day most often the helper and savior of the arid way. Equiped with a powerful constitution and giant energy, the worst of the weeds may readily become the best of the plants.

NOTES

"The New Knowledge of Weeds," *Ainslee's* 8 (January 1902): 533–38.

1. Grammas, or gramas, is a pasture grass of the Western United States belonging to the genus *Bouteloua* (as blue grama and black grama).

2. Lupins, or lupines, is a wild vegetable, a plant of the genus *Lupinus,* a genus of herbs with digitate or unifoliolate leaves.

3. Loam is topsoil, a usually fertile and humus-rich soil consisting of a friable mixture containing 7 to 27 percent clay, 28 to 50 percent silt, and less than 52 percent sand.

4. Burdock is a hardy wild vegetable plant that grows in the northern and middle Atlantic regions of North America. Burdock roots are considered delicacies in Japanese cuisine. Japanese farmers settled in the northern West Coast around the turn of the century cultivated burdock roots and used them as common vegetables like carrots.

5. Hellebore is a plant of the genus *Helleborus* with digitate leaves, an acrid taste, an offensive odor, and irritant qualities when taken internally.

Part III
American Landscapes

1
New York's Art Colony
The Literary and Art Retreat at Bronxville

MOST OF US HAVE FIXED IN OUR MINDS HOW THE RICH LIVE, AND HOW, also, the exceeding poor—the newspapers keep this knowledge fresh by constant comparison—but not all are familiar with that third class, neither rich nor poor, but talented, who sometimes live in colonies and are to a certain extent exclusive. There are literary and art colonies, outside of

The entrance proper to "Lawrence Park."

London and Paris, where artists dwell in a sort of æsthetic community and work out their ideals with such aid as harmonious surroundings and intellectual companionship afford. New York has many colonies of the wealthy, but only one extensive art and literary colony, and that is at Bronxville. It is true that there are a number of painters living at Nutley, New Jersey, and some writers, artists, and actors who dwell at New Rochelle; but those places are not colonies by any means, and the non-literary, non-artistic individual has as much right to move in and acclimate himself as any one. This is not possible, however, at Lawrence Park, where to enter the colony requires the consent of the residents and the good-will and special desire of some one already a resident of the colony.

This colony is really the outcome of a desire on the part of Mr. Lawrence, whose observations of art colonies near London and Paris awakened in him a desire to bring together a similar colony upon the outskirts of the American metropolis. To this he gave much of his attention after returning to New York, and finally selected the present beautiful grounds, in which he constructed his own residence, and, after laying out the plan of the colony, invited one or two American masters of the brush to take up their residence within its precincts. Since then the colony has gradually grown, until to-day it is one of the most desirable residential spots about New York and the centre of an exclusive neighborhood.

There is something plausible and appropriate about people of a literary and artistic turn dwelling together, and the Bronxville colony is of interest on this account. The Lawrence Park colony consists of six painters, seven writers, and two architects, together with several residents whose artistic tastes qualify them for agreeable companionship with the select company. The painters are Will H. Low, the decorator; William H. Howe, the famous cattle painter; Otto H. Bacher, artist in black and white; H. T. Schladermundt, whose decorative work is also widely known; Milne Ramsey, painter of still life; and Lorenzo Hatch, an artist of wide repute.[1] Among the writers, Edmund Clarence Stedman, the banker-poet, has his resi-

**The retreat at which Will H. Low wields his brush
far from the turmoil of the outside world.**

dence there; Tudor Jenks, editor of *St. Nicholas,* has a pretty cottage; and Ruth McEnery Stuart dwells at the colony inn.[2] Mrs. Alice W. Rollins, the author; Mrs. General Custer, the contributor, and widow of famous Indian fighter; Dorothy Quigley, and Mrs. Homes all have homes within the grounds.[3]

Among the remaining company are Will W. Kent, the architect, who with John La Farge drew up the plans for the new cathedral of St. John the Divine; and William A. Bates, another architect, to whose art all of the well-arranged cottages of the Park are due.

This village of the elect is twenty-six minutes from the heart of New York, and comprises ninety acres on the banks of the Bronx in Westchester County. Although it contains many houses of the most pleasing and varied type of architecture, and is set on a hill, it is astonishing how perfectly it manages sometimes to hide itself. You drive into it past a little colonial lodge, with a fine bluff of massive rock on your left, and on your right a screen of old apple trees with a meadow stretching out at their feet; past the club-house, or Casino, a most attractive rendezvous for the denizens of the Park, buried amidst vines and flowers and rocks and pine trees; past the manor house of gray stone, where you can put a friend up for a day or a month, and in household emergencies have meals for yourself; in and out of the trees and the picturesque houses perched about on the rocks or hidden away among the great oaks.

There are no fences; every one appears to own everything. You will find the lawn of one resident winding curiously into that of another, whose grounds, in turn, merge into still another occupant's. There are no flat lawns or regular gardens, but the slopes are dotted with trees, ribbed with fine rock, and starred with wild flowers. Every turn reveals a glimpse of graceful stone and modest gable where some chosen worker has his abode. A single winding road runs in and out around the Park under the arching trees, gathering up the little houses on the way, so that though they are in half-circles from each other, they are all on the same winding street.

In this place apart the colony of artists live and work. They all know each other, and no one can come to the Park unless some of those already within knows, likes, and vouches for him. One must either have talent or a *savoir-faire,* according to the literary and artistic code prevailing, to be eligible at all for such privileges as the colony extends.

Some may smile at the idea of Genius suffocating under mountain peaks, but a member of the colony merely points to a cottage near at hand and exclaims: "There is a studio whence have emanated pictures that have taken many a medal at the Salon and our own expositions." He will tell you that stories, verses, and essays have been written there, and that all the colonists knew them by heart, having heard the manuscript read by fire-light long before they appeared in print. When the colonists want a house they build it for themselves, for the architect of all their charming homes is one of them. They write plays for themselves, and act them themselves, that make their evenings cheerful at the club-house, where in the morning the children of the Park have their lessons, and where on holidays cotillions and charades are given.

  The colony post-office is tiny, but it subserves its uses, and it brings the colony greetings from famous people the world over; and many shelves in the cottage libraries have their books made valuable by the compliments of the author. They are really a clever company, these Bronxville colonists. For a while Kate Douglas Wiggin was a resident of "Gray Arches."[4] Some of the stories which have added to her fame were written there, as well as several of the songs in her "Kindergarten Chimes."

NOTES

"New York's Art Colony," *Metropolitan* 6 (November 1897): 321–26. Signed "Theodore Dresser."

  1. Will Hicok Low (1853–1932), American painter, illustrator, teacher, writer, and lecturer. He was pupil of Ecole des Beaux-Arts, under Gérôme, and of Carolus Duran in Paris. Low's works were exhibited in major museums in the United States. He received medals for his drawings at the Paris Expo (1889), at the Chicago World's Fair (1893), and at the Pan-Am Expo (Buffalo 1901).

  William H. Howe (1846–1929), American painter. Born at Ravenna, Ohio, he began the study of art in Germany in 1880 and later went to Paris. He received many medals from the Pennsylvania Academy of Fine Arts, the Chicago World's Fair (1893), and other exhibitions. His permanent collections are in the St. Louis Museum of Fine Arts and the Cleveland Museum.

  Otto H. Bacher (1856–1909), American painter, etcher, and illustrator. Born in Cleveland, he became a pupil of Duveneck in Cincinnati and of Duran, Boulanger, and Lefebvre in Paris. He spent some time with Whistler in Venice. He died in New York, having received many honors and medals.

  Herman T. Schladermundt (1863–1937), American mural painter. Born in Milwaukee, he worked and exhibited most of his work in the United States. He received awards from the Architectural League and the Chicago World's Fair (1893).

  Lorenzo J. Hatch, American artist of considerable reputation, was a bank-note engraver in the employ of the Treasury Department at Washington, D.C., about 1875.

  2. Edmund Clarence Stedman (1833–1908), American poet and critic, best known for criticism and anthologies of American and Victorian literature. Born in Hartford, Connecticut, he attended Yale and in 1855 went to New York City, where his early career was divided between business activities and work on the New York *World,* for which he covered the Civil War. Dreiser wrote a magazine article, "Edmund Clarence Stedman at Home," *Munsey's* 20 (March 1899): 931–38; reprinted in *Selected Magazine Articles,* 1:84–91.

  Tudor Jenks (1857–1922), American lawyer and writer of books for children, was editor of *St. Nicholas.* He was born in Brooklyn and died in Bronxville, New York.

  Ruth McEnery Stuart (1849–1917), American writer, was born in Marksville, Louisiana, and died in New York, New York.

  3. Alice Wellington Rollins (1847–97), American poet and novelist, was born in Boston and died in Bronxville, New York.

Elizabeth Bacon Custer (1844–1933), was born in Bacon, Missouri, and died in New York, New York.

4. Kate Douglas Wiggin (1856–1923), American author of children's books and educator, began her literary career as a writer of stories for children. Her early works, including the enormously popular *The Birds' Christmas Carol* (1887), were intended to raise funds for kindergarten work. Among the later ones was *Rebecca of Sunnybrook Farm* (1903).

2

On the Field of Brandywine

Peaceful and Picturesque Aspect of the Scene of the Great Battle of the American Revolution

BRANDYWINE, THE HISTORIC FIELD OF THE FAMOUS REVOLUTIONARY battle, the valley across which Lord Cornwallis and Lord Howe marched the English Redcoats and the hired Hessians, along the old road from Baltimore to Philadelphia; the scene from which General Washington reluctantly retreated with his fifteen thousand hard-worn troops in command of his generals, Sullivan and Greene—Brandywine is now simply picturesque, and the memory of the great battle is as a tale that is told.[1]

There is no more lovely vale in all Pennsylvania than this historic ground through which the Brandywine river wends its peaceful way. It comes from a spring but a little way inland, and flowing with a generally southeasterly course through green meadows and gently sloping hills, leaves Pennsylvania—and the beautiful soil of Chester County, to enter Delaware and empty into the Christiana river at Wilmington. Its course has always been one of sylvan quiet with but one exception, where for a day, at Chaddsford, September 11, 1777, its shallow waters were stained with the blood of contesting men, and murderous bullets raked its banks and toppled over its invaders with a fierceness that still excites in the pages of American history.

To-day the Brandywine at Chaddsford and the old battle ground is an artist's retreat. The clover on those gently rolling hills where thirty thousand men struggled with musket and cannon is now a veritable tangle of velvety softness. Its valleys are given over to the picturesque stone cottages of the dairymen, for the valley of Brandywine is the Wessex of America. The banks of the stream are graced by the presence of loveliest cattle, whose spotted coats of brown and black, and red and white, shine in the warm light of a summer's day. They stand in pools under the trees, wade the historic stream from bank to bank, and forever remain the delight of the painters of nature whose easels are often set down in these green fields, where all nature combines to delight and inspire. Dairies and cream-

188

eries have sprung up everywhere, and the waters of the river are used to keep clean and cool the buildings of this simple industry. Instead of stage coaches careening along the old Baltimore road, from Philadelphia to that city, crossing the Brandywine at the spot where the battle began, trains now rush along iron rails, and the product of the dairyman offers the principal excuse for their stopping.

For all that the great cities are near at hand, the field of Brandywine is still a secluded nook. It has not changed in stick or stone since Bayard Taylor dwelt within the circle of its loveliness.[2] The poet's birthplace, Kennett, is but a few miles from its banks, and Cedarcroft, the home of his later years is even closer by. All the quaint architecture with which he was familiar still stands as it stood before him. The old colonial home in which Washington made his headquarters during the battle, is as it was, unchanged. The stone house at which Lord Howe rested, in the rear of his army, shows its sloping roof over the branches of green orchard trees. In one place, on a knoll overlooking the stream at this point the remains of an earthen breastworks is dimly in evidence, a long curving mould over which nature has spread her kindly mantle of green. Four miles from the ford the old Birmingham meeting-house of the Friends of colonial days still stands, and looking away from this woodland hill-top to other hills, and down into long, house-dotted valleys between, the mind cannot grasp that such loveliness could ever have been desecrated by war, and that this simple House of God was once a hospital for the wounded. And yet, around it the battle raged, bullets riddled its very doors, and men fell back from it, urging horses and guns as the great forces moved toward the goal of contention, Philadelphia. The native recounts how Lafayette was wounded nearby and how he was carried into the meeting-house for medical treatment, and a little column, of poor design, proclaims the actual place and quotes some patriotic utterance of Lafayette, made on his return to the scene twenty-five years after.[3] It is a pleasant valley, but there are those to whom all its history is even now a sealed or unknown book.

Nature makes pictures for the eye at Brandywine, and her vagaries make a gallery of masterpieces, whose exhibits are removed and redistributed with each succeeding day. No artist can accurately represent the filmy beauty of the mists that hang over the little river at morning. At high noon there are pools, such as painters endeavor to portray, in which great-eyed cattle stand knee deep, disturbing the drowsy hour with the tinkle of their bells. At evening silvery mists move like friendly wraiths along the valley, and the far hills are as a hem of purple at the edge of a cloth of green.

The idler who follows the willful windings of the stream cannot but feel the soothing sense of beauty that everywhere prevails. Here an old stone mill dips its gray walls into the cool, bright water and extends its wheel that the river's kindly strength may aid it in its labors. At another a farmer's lawn extends to the grassy brink, and a convoy of ducks sails proudly past like some merchant fleet bound for a foreign shore. Little gray stone houses of colonial date, whose chimneys send up spiral curls of smoke into the thin air, grace the middle distance and flocks of pigeons make their circling journeys from hill to barnyard and barnyard to hill, to and fro across the water. There are little boats moored at every turn and within some small bay can be seen the minnows, their senseless journeyings in schools forever the despair of the well-ordered mind.

In some such meadow here ten years ago Bayard Taylor formed his Bacchic procession, with Edmund Clarence Stedman astride a peaceful ox, and all the merry company following in the wake of the wandering cattle.[4] It was on the occasion of a visit paid by the banker-poet to Taylor at Cedarcroft, and the two with their wives and friends had come out to the riverside to spend the day. It was late afternoon when some cattle came loitering near to the merry company, ranging, as cattle will, in soldierly order before them, forming an even line. It was then that the inspired thought came to Taylor and, seizing the leader of the cattle, he called for honeysuckle, which he twined about the horns of the stolid ox. Then Stedman was persuaded to mount and a procession of the company was formed for a march about the field. All the cattle followed, the delightful poet leading the Arcadian company, with many peals of laughter.

Such tales do not sound unnatural when related of the valley of the Brandywine. It is ground consecrated by nature, by history and by art. On its hillsides, so lovely at morning, have sounded the drums and guns of war. Where its limpid waters flow slow and still over gleaming pebbles men fought for liberty; and ducks now float through the idle hours where soldiers crossed. On these green hills Taylor and Stedman have dreamed poetic dreams, and here equally rest soldiers whose names and homes are as little remembered as the clouds that graced their day. Where Washington trod and Lafayette bled, where soldiers fell, are now the walks of the farmer and the dairyman, the haunt of the painter and the occasional resort of the historian. No spot is more beautiful, none richer in that which time has consecrated, none more redolent of that peace which abides in nature and, when sought in sympathy, makes at rest the weary heart.

NOTES

"On the Field of Brandywine," *Truth* 16 (6 November 1897): 7–10. Reprinted, with minor changes, in "Brandywine, the Picturesque, after One Hundred and Twenty Years," *Demorest's* 34 (September 1898): 274–75. The *Demorest's* version is reprinted in *Selected Magazine Articles,* 2:77–83.

1. Charles Cornwallis (1738–1805), First Marquis, was a British general and statesman. Richard Howe (1726–99), Earl, was an English admiral.

2. Bayard Taylor (1825–78), American travel writer and poet. He was born in Kennett Square, Pennsylvania, and died in Berlin. Taylor's many books about his travels to Africa, Europe, and Asia made him known as "The American Marco Polo." Dreiser wrote a magazine article, "The Haunts of Bayard Taylor," *Munsey's* 18 (January 1898): 594–601; reprinted in *Selected Magazine Articles,* 1:43–49.

3. Marquis de Lafayette (1757–1834), French general and statesman.

4. Edmund Clarence Stedman (1833–1908), American writer. See a note on Stedman in Dreiser's "New York's Art Colony," reprinted in this volume.

3

A Notable Colony

Artistic and Literary People on the Picturesque Bronx— Who They Are and How They Live

Most of us have a fixed idea in our minds as to how the rich live, and how also the exceeding poor—the journals keep this knowledge fresh by constant comparisons—but not all are familiar with a third class, the middle artistic and literary, who occasionally live in colonies after the fashion of the millionaires at Newport, and are, to a certain extent, exclusive. Sometimes they gather for the summer in rural places of striking beauty—writers, poets and painters—and pass the time in agreeable social companionship. At others they colonize, as in this instance at Lawrence Park on the Bronx, and abide together winter and summer, the year round.

There is something appropriate about people of a literary and artistic turn dwelling together, and the art and literary colony at Bronxville is interesting because of this appropriateness. The people in it have a common feeling with respect to outdoor surroundings. They enjoy the quiet of a woodland retreat, the satisfaction of a modest house done in quaintly distinct architecture, and the pleasure of intellectual association and companionship.

The Lawrence Park colony consists of seven painters—Will H. Low, William H. Howe, Otto H. Bacher, Lorenzo J. Hatch, H. T. Schladermundt, W. T. Smedley and Milne Ramsey; six literary lights—Edmund Clarence Stedman, Ruth McEnery Stuart, Tudor Jenks, Mrs. Custer, Dorothy Quigley and Mrs. Howes; two architects—Will W. Kent, who with John La Farge drew up the plans for the new cathedral of St. John the Divine, and William A. Bates, to whose exquisite taste the delightfully arranged cottages of the park are largely due; and about six others.[1]

Their homes are gathered in this Park at Bronxville, once the beautiful upland forest of an old estate, which in summer is rich with foliage, soft with green mosses and lovely with delicate ferns. They are within half an hour of the heart of New York City, and yet are where dainty little brooks trip in and out among the wild flowers, and great ledges of magnificent

192

rock are bright with nodding columbines. Even in winter, fir and larch and hemlock keep the Park green, while in spring the sun shines through the great boughs and lightens a scene that is rural in the extreme.

The colony is really the outcome of the observation of its founder, Mr. Lawrence, whose knowledge of art colonies in the vicinity of London and Paris awakened in him a desire to bring together a similar colony upon the outskirts of the American metropolis. To this he gave much of his time after returning to New York, and soon found that artists and writers generally welcomed the thought and were in good mood to take advantage of any such opportunity. At that time there were a few painters living at Nutley, N.J., the result of an attempt at colonization, and there were also a few writers, artists, and actors dwelling at New Rochelle; but those places were not colonies by any means, and the non-literary, non-artistic individual had and still has as much privilege to move in and acclimate himself as the most elect. The Lawrence Park colony was the first satisfactory attempt at exclusion of all but writers and artists; and it is not possible to enter there, but with the consent of all the residents and the good will and special desire of some one already a resident.

To the selecting of the site the founder gave much study, finally securing the present beautiful grounds. He looked to it that it was convenient to the city and yet wholly devoid of metropolitan characteristics, and that it was, in summer or winter, all that the lover of landscape would desire. The ideal site was discovered at Bronxville. It was a wide stretch of hill and dale, hidden from the railroad by a wooded bluff. Within it were several brooks, one or two fresh-water ponds and a thick growth of trees and foliage covering the major portion of the soil.

The first thing Mr. Lawrence did was to select a convenient site for himself, where he built a rural mansion. He had a winding roadway hewn and dug quite around the grounds in the direction of the least resistance. This he supplemented with paths to the ponds and brooks, and then introduced a few oil-lamps and some benches. Next an artesian well was drilled, and lastly, some board walks were laid down for comfort in foul weather. The improvement of the Park was then left to others as they should arrive.

One of the very first to come was Will H. Low, whose house and studio were built for him according to his own specifications. It was not long thereafter until Edmund Clarence Stedman decided to take up his residence there. The founder then looked to the introduction of water, fenced in the entire area, built a lodge-house and gate, and erected a casino where those who joined the little company might meet in friendly concourse. As other notables began to move in, a small manor-house, partaking of the nature of an inn, was built, and finally, in 1898, a great inn was erected.

This last was constructed with a view to accommodating a more transient class of literary and artistic souls, visitors and friends of those resident in the Park, and others who might desire a place of resort of so
reserved a nature. Guests, however, must accord, in respect to character
and attainment, with the idea that it is a literary and artistic colony. Either
the management knows of them beforehand, or they come recommended
from some source or other. Money is not a consideration outside the mere
expense. It is the mental attitude which is considered important.

In this connection it is interesting to note that with this restriction the inn
has proved a success. It is well filled the season round with artists, writers,
and those who are more or less in touch with the forms of culture, and a
number of artists maintain studios there.

The inn was built from plans and specifications of the colony architect,
Mr. W. W. Kent, and was decorated by the resident artists. Mr. Low did the
ceilings and walls of a music room, and Mr. Wm. H. Howe decorated
portions of the lobby and the dining-rooms. Others of the artists executed
portions of the general ornamentation. The building in its entirety is considered an excellent example of modern skill and taste.

This village of the elect comprises ninety acres on the banks of the
Bronx, in Westchester County. Although it contains many large houses of
the most pleasing and varied types of architecture, and is set on a hill, it is
astonishing how perfectly it manages sometimes to hide itself. You drive
into it past a little colonial lodge, with a fine bluff of massive rock on your
left, and on your right a screen of old apple-trees with a meadow stretching
out at their feet; past the club-house, or casino, a most attractive rendezvous for the denizens of the Park, buried amidst vines and flowers and
rocks and pine-trees. It is at the casino that the road branches, and here is
set what one might call the lamp of knowledge, for it lights an attached
bulletin board set in a glass case and locked with a key. Here are posted all
warnings concerning approaching teas, dances, parties, games of whist and
other nefarious engagements concocted by the more pleasure-loving of the
local company.

> *There will be a bicycle party to*
> *Mamaroneck, Saturday.*
> *All going post their names in the*
> *Casino.*

is a common announcement of the summer-time which the board displays.

The main road leads on past the manor-house of gray stone, where you
can put a friend up for a day or a month, and in household emergencies
have meals for yourself. It winds in and out among the trees, past all the
picturesque houses perched about on the rocks or hidden away among the

Residence of Edmund Clarence Stedman.

great oaks. They all look as though they had always been there and meant to stay; an effect not so much owing to the creosote staining of their shingles as to a certain fitness in the adaptation to their surroundings.

There are no fences; everyone appears to own everything. You will find the lawn of one resident winding curiously into that of another, whose grounds in turn merge unmarked into those of a third, and so on. There are no flat lawns or regular gardens, but the slopes are dotted with trees, ribbed with fine rocks and starred with wild flowers. Common grounds have been set aside, however, for tennis and other outdoor sports, and there are little concealed paths for those who care to stroll, and a tiny lake where rustic benches have been placed, and where the evening hours in warm weather can be passed in quiet and meditation.

Every turn reveals a glimpse of graceful stone and modest gable where some chosen worker has his abode. The main road encircles the Park, gathering up the cottages on its way, so that though they are in half circles from each other they are all on the same winding street.

On the other hand, this is no Elysium without watermains, no lightless paradise. The more earthy needs seem to be looked after very circum-spectly to say the least. The houses are equipped after the fashion of flats in town—"furnace, bath, hot and cold water," and all that is usually involved in the mundane agent's glittering panoramic description.

The sea is a little way off at Larchmont and New Rochelle, and trolley cars run from Bronxville to Yonkers, where the company may embark on the Hudson if they choose. They are within three minutes of the railway, which would be a rather disturbing fact, were it not for the hill or bluff which rises as a barrier between the tracks and the charms of the Park. Market wagons are admitted into the sacred precincts under protest, and express wagons gain entrance on the plea of utility alone.

The merits of the colony as a theory and a fact have been amusingly argued by the residents from time to time, not all literary and artistic souls being able to agree upon them, or upon Lawrence Park as the ideal spot for their illustration. The late Mrs. H. W. Rollins exchanged a number of letters with city-bound geniuses who warily refrained from tasting the delights of the colony life; and one of those wrote a most amusing letter of inquiry, after receiving a glowing description.

"This may all be very well," wrote the doubter, "but I know you, and I do not believe in you. You are an optimist of the first water, an enthusiast of the deepest dye, and your name represents the first syllable of the most unreliable adjective in the English language. It is all very well to have a view from your west window, but where do you set the baby's bath-tub? No doubt it is nice to have a piazza and a loggia, but have you a butler's pantry? Of course there are picturesque open fire-places (which also, of course, smoke), but where is the furnace?

"You exult in not having to cross a ferry when you enter the city, and on being landed, not on a network of docks, but just comfortably between the shopping district and your friends' houses up-town; but you have forgotten that you have to go through a tunnel. It is very fine to have beautiful drives in every direction; but suppose you cannot afford to keep a horse? And you do not miss the sea? If you do not happen to be especially addicted to the society of mountain pinks, where do you get human beings? You say you are within three minutes of the railway. Horrible thought! especially when you aggravate the situation by mentioning thirty-six trains a day. I do not know which I envy you the less: the silence of your mountain pinks or the shrieks of your locomotives. I understand where you find your anemones, but where do you get your beef-steak? No doubt you have strawberries, but do you not experience difficulty in getting real city cream on them? You mention birds, but I fear they are mosquitoes, and that you omitted the 't' when you mentioned how they 'sing.' That you say nothing whatever about malaria excites, rather than allays, surprise. You have a generous landlord; but I do not want a landlord; I want to own my own house. And what is your rent, anyway?

"P.S.—Do not forget to include in it the prices you have to pay extra men for shoveling off your snow, planting your mountain pinks (oh! excuse me, I really did not mean to doubt your word to that extent), and raking off your dead leaves?"

The replies made to these gibes were entertaining to a degree, and in a way they serve to illustrate some of the social details of the colony.

"You bathe your baby in the Bronx, of course," wrote Mrs. Rollins under caption I in the categorical reply. "Though on very cold days, if you prefer, you need not 'set' your tub, because it is already set. We have the cosiest little bath-room imaginable, with hot and cold water, and an eastern window flooding the room with such sunlight as your baby never yet saw, much less felt.

"Of course we have a butler's pantry. May I turn the tables and ask whether you, madam, have a butler? We have everything except gas, and electric light glimmers in the distance for us.

"The furnace is in the cellar, where it ought to be.

"Of course, there is a tunnel. You cannot leave New York except by ferry, or tunnel, or balloon. We think three minutes of tunnel to be the least of these. Besides, do you not remember that Dean Hole wanted the approach to his Rosary to be obscure and narrow, that the visitor might come with sudden gladness and wonder upon the glowing scene, as the traveler by rail emerges from the dark tunnel into the brightness of—let us say Bronxville?

"You do not keep a horse because everybody else does, and if you did, too, they would have nobody to invite, for in our Altruria one half of us does know precisely how the other half lives, and takes pains to supply what is lacking.

"Miss the sea? How can I, when half our drives end at New Rochelle, or Larchmont, or Mamaroneck, where we hire a boat for the rest of the day, or go in bathing? And when trolley cars will carry us to Yonkers to embark on the Hudson at any moment?

"Society? Why, my dear, we are within twenty minutes (by express) of all the society there is in the city of New York. Besides, we find that society is not altogether averse to spending Sunday in a park, and taking tea on a piazza when the dogwood is in bloom. Then, too, we are ourselves a society. We all know each other, and you cannot come to our Park anyway, unless some of us know and like you. You must either be a genius or a delightful person to be eligible at all for such privileges as we extend. You need not smile at the idea of genius suffocating under mountain pinks. In yonder red cottage there is a studio whence have emanated pictures that have taken many a medal at the *Salon* and our own expositions. Stories, verses and essays have been written here that we knew by heart, hearing the MSS. read by firelight, long before you saw them in the great magazines. The young architect who has such a pretty house here had a hand in the plans for the great Cathedral of St. John and in building the most beautiful mausoleum at Woodlawn, and his house is a museum of endless drawings, and pictures and books. When we want a house we build it ourselves, for the architect of all our charming houses is one of us. We write the plays ourselves and act them ourselves, that make our evenings cheerful at the club-house, and there in the morning the children of the Park have their lessons.

"On holidays we give cotillons or charades there. We hire music for the cotillons, because everybody there wants to dance; but when we want music alone, we have one who plays charmingly on the violin, another who entrances us with the piano, and two who sing unique and fascinating Spanish songs to their guitars, and who, indeed, have composed songs that you may have heard in the outside world. Our post-office is tiny, but it brings to the Park many delightful greetings from famous people across the seas or in many other states; and many shelves in our libraries have their books made valuable by the compliments of the author, so that we know, long before you do, what Elihu Vedder and Lafcadio Hearn and the author of 'The Light that Failed,' are doing.[2] When simplicity in our entertainments is unavoidable, we make a virtue of necessity, and some of our finest feasts have been made festive by the wit of authors and artists, lending themselves as cooks or waiters for the occasion. Society, indeed!

"Within three minutes of the railway, yes; but a wonderful hill, clothed with pines and embroidered with wild flowers, rises close to the gates, hiding every bit of steel rail and iron engine, and absorbing all the echo of the dreadful locomotive. Market wagons come to the door with every known edible, or you can order your box from town and have it delivered by express at your door. As for cream, you are far behind the times, my dear. Nobody eats cream on strawberries nowadays. We dip them in sugar and eat daintily from the stems.

"If you wish to own your home, you can buy as much or little as you choose, and build to suit yourself, with only such restrictions as you yourself would wish to have made. There are certain things that you cannot do in the Park, but they are the things which you would not wish anybody else to be allowed to do. Or you can hire one of the houses already built, and by paying a little extra rent every year, gradually buy it. The Park is also an apartment house, with its apartments side by side, instead of on top of each other, and with space and air and foliage between, and with a janitor who shovels and rakes (I ignore the suggestion of planting) without extra charge."

However one may smile at the "banter and brag" of these arguments, they nevertheless about describe the conditions of the colony. The residents are really a clever company, and more or less public interest justifiably attaches to their labors.

NOTES

"A Notable Colony," *Demorest's* 35 (August 1899): 240–41. Reconstructed with substantial changes in content from "New York's Art Colony," *Metropolitan* 6 (November 1897): 321–26.

1. For Will H. Low, William H. Howe, Otto H. Bacher, Lorenzo J. Hatch, and Herman T. Schladermundt, see note 1 in Dreiser's "New York's Art Colony," included in this volume.

William Thomas Smedley (1858–1920), American painter, was born in Chester County, Pennsylvania, and died in Bronxville, New York. He studied engraving in Philadelphia and art in the Pennsylvania Academy of Fine Arts. He went to New York and to Paris, where he studied under Jean Paul Laurens. In the 1880s he worked as illustrator for the *Harper's* and exhibited at the Paris Salon.

For Edmund Clarence Stedman (1833–1908), American poet and critic, see note 2 in Dreiser's "New York's Art Colony," included in this volume.

Ruth McEnery Stuart (1849–1917), American writer, was born in Marksville, Louisianna, and died in New York, New York. See note 2 in Dreiser's "New York's Art Colony," included in this collection.

For Tudor Jenks (1857–1922), American lawyer and writer, see note 2 in Dreiser's "New York's Art Colony," included in this volume.

Elizabeth Bacon Custer (1844–1933), was born in Bacon, Missouri, and died in New York, New York. See note 3 in Dreiser's "New York's Art Colony," included in this collection.

John La Farge (1835–1910), American sculptor, landscape and figure painter, and decorator. He was born in New York, became a pupil of Couture in Paris and William M. Hunt, received many awards and honors, and died in Providence, Rhode Island.

2. Elihu Vedder (1836–1923), American painter, was born in New York City and studied painting with Henry Ellis Mattson. After becoming a pupil of Picot in Paris in 1856, he worked both in Europe and in America: his reputation was enhanced by his illustrations of Edward Fitzgerald's *Omar Khayyám* (1884). He died in Rome.

Lafcadio Hearn (1850–1904), American writer, known in Japan as Koizumi Yakumo, was born on an Ionian island as the son of an Irish father and a Greek mother. He grew up in Greece, Ireland, England, and France, emigrated to America, and went to Japan, where he became a Japanese subject and a Buddhist. He wrote many books of fiction, nonfiction, and criticism, based on his experience in America and Japan.

4

Good Roads for Bad

An Account of the Marvellous Enterprise that is now being Shown by the United States in the Matter of Good Roads

IN MANY MATTERS OF ENTERPRISE THE UNITED STATES LEAD THE WORLD, but in one respect no American can deny that his country is years behind all other civilised lands—in respect, that is, to the condition of the roads.

American roads are often described in a general way as "the worst in the world." Certainly there is no other great nation that possesses such disgraceful highways. The magnificent roads of England—such roads as were made for us by the Romans and have borne the traffic of 2000 years—have no parallel in the States, and although the land is covered with a network of crude roads, these are hardly worthy the name, and for the most part are periodically impassable.

Not only are American roads bad, but the streets of many of the largest towns are disgracefully paved. This would probably be excused on the ground that so much of the traffic is overhead. It is, however, more particularly with the country roads, and with the extraordinary efforts that are now being made to improve them, that we are here concerned.

The good-road question has latterly become the subject of vast agitation. The United States Government, impelled by cyclists, has gone into the whole matter in the most energetic manner conceivable, acting through the Department of Agriculture. It has studied the question of what constitutes a good road, and has set about spreading the information gained. Experimental road-making stations have been established in every State in the Union. Hundreds of pamphlets have been published, showing just how a good road is made. Object lessons in road-building are given annually in all the States, when a section of excellent roadway is constructed, so that the people may see exactly how the work should be done. These lessons, first organised in 1894, have done more than anything else to help forward the great movement for perfect roads the land over.

The Government, in its exhibitions, usually constructs three specimen roads—which will cost something like £1200—a modern macadam road, by way of showing the ideal, and a "sand," and a "dirt" road, by way of contrast. Now, incredible as it may seem, sand and dirt roads, so-called, are very common in the States. The various types of "roads" in England, as we understand the word, include nothing of the kind. To us a sand road means a road with a surface of hard lime or sandstone—and an excellent and pleasant-looking road it is. To Americans a sand road means a road with a surface of about 6 in. of *river sand* on a clay bed. Nor would an English surveyor ever dream of drawing up plans for what Americans understand as a "dirt" road. Ruts and bogs are its chief characteristics.

The specimen macadam road is made first when the object lessons are in progress. This is built to a width of 12 ft. and is carefully paved with the best quality of stone that can be obtained at a practicable distance. The pavement is laid 6 in. thick, consisting of 4 in. of stones broken to a length of not more than 2 in., and a 2 in. layer of smaller stones on top. The natural soil of the country is first properly prepared as a foundation.

Given a good rocky foundation, this model macadam road precisely meets the usual requirements of a country place, although, of course, it would hardly compare with the typical 18 in. thick English macadam road, with its 6 in. of best granite on top, and 12 in. of brick or similar material beneath. It is, however, a hundred-fold improvement on the typical American road.

Having constructed the macadam road, the sand road is next built. This is a simple matter—it does not require much engineering to cover a clay bed with 6 in. of river sand. Neither the bed nor the surface of the road is rolled, for the aim of the Government officials is to make it resemble, as nearly as possible, the ordinary country sand road.

The dirt road is soon cut out. It is then thoroughly drenched with water, and a narrow-tyred waggon, heavily loaded, is drawn over it until deep ruts are made, and the surface exactly resembles that of most American roads during a large part of the year.

The three roads are now ready for the experiments that are to prove their respective worth. A heavy farm waggon is loaded up, and is drawn over each, and the amount of force required to haul it is determined by the use of a little machine called "trackometer." This instrument accurately registers every pound the horses pull at each stage of the haul, displaying the figures in clear view of the onlookers. It is demonstrated by these experiments that under the best conditions a team harnessed to a heavy waggon is submitted to a series of continuous jerks, which become, on a bad road, a succession of heavy blows, transmitted by the collar. They are cruelly painful, bruising the shoulders, harassing and torturing the animals, and soon wearing them out.

During one of these experiments a team of small mules readily drew twelve bales of cotton on a heavy waggon up a grade of 1 in 10 of the macadam road the trackometer indicating a pull of 1000 lbs. The same team came to a deadlock in going *down* a six per cent. grade of the sand road, after pulling the indicator to 1900 lbs. Nine bales of cotton were removed before the load could be put in motion again. The driver refused to venture at all upon the dirt road with the twelve bale load.

The United States Government has recently been strongly advocating an entirely new scheme in road making. This is a system of laying parallel lines of steel plates, about 8 in. wide, on the highways, at a sufficient distance apart to receive the wheels of all vehicles of average size. The tracks each have a projecting flange on the inner edge, to prevent the wheels of carriages from slipping, but as the flange is only one half-inch in height it is not too high to prevent vehicles from leaving the track whenever the driver so desires. The steel plates of the track are built solidly into the roadway, having flanges which project both downwards and outwards, and are imbedded in the concrete of the road-bed.

In several States the Government has built sample roads with these novel tracks. At Omaha, a road 800 ft. long was built as a test of cost and value, and was the scene of a number of interesting experiments. In one of these a load of eleven tons was first drawn by twenty horses over a common road, which lay alongside the steel track, and then the same load was drawn by *one* horse along the steel track road. This load was twenty-two times the weight of the animal.

Another interesting experiment made before the large crowds that assembled was that of running a motor-car up and down the steel track. It was proved that it moved with such ease that it required but a fraction of the motor power ordinarily used. A bicycle was also employed by the Government, to show how useful these steel roads would be to the cyclist who could keep straight on an eight-inch track.

The cost of constructing a steel track was £700 a mile in the case of poor roads, and £300 a mile where a fair road was already in existence. Whether it would ever be worth while to lay down extensive lines of these tracks is a question which one may well doubt. They could be built to great advantage on hills—the stone tracks for carriage wheels that exist on many English hills have long ago proved this. For motor-cars and cyclists they would be an inestimable boon—but whether their cost would be repaid by the possible advantages they would give to ordinary carts or carriages on level roads is very doubtful.

It is evident that a bad road cannot be made into a good road merely by laying down steel tracks, for it is a fact that more wear and tear is given to a road by the action of a horse's hoof than by the wheels of a cart or carriage. Whereas the wheels run smoothly and easily, the horse, if he weighs a ton, brings about a quarter of a ton pounding down on the road with every stride. To lay down steel tracks for the wheels, therefore, and to make no provision at the same time for the part of the road where the horses trot, is absurd. Moreover, for the £700 that it would cost to lay down a mile of steel tracks a splendid road, with a surface almost equally good, could be built.

A third branch of the United States Government work lies in advocating wide tyres for waggons and carriages. Never was a cause more ardently taken up than this. Leaflets have been issued by the Agricultural Department and distributed over the country, making it clear to farmers what an advantage it is to have wide tyres on bad roads.

When an American talks of "wide" tyres, he does not mean, however, a tyre of the enormous breadth that one sees on English farm waggons. A tyre of 3 in. width is considered wide, and it is this width that the Government advocates. Experiments made in every part of the country show that a team can draw on a waggon with 3 in. tyres just twice as heavy a load as upon a waggon with the extremely narrow tyres that are general in the States.

The United States Government is evidently sparing no effort to bring the "good road" question to a satisfactory conclusion. Ten of the States had exhibits at the Paris Exhibition illustrating how good roads ought to be made.[1] This was rather daring; but the ten States in question know their business. They have the worst roads, but they are determined to have the best.

NOTES

"Good Roads for Bad," *Pearson's* 9 (May 1900): 387–95.

1. The Paris Exhibition (1889), also known as the Paris Exposition, inspired the building of the Eiffel Tower, then the world's tallest structure, designed by the French architect A. J. Eiffel (1832–1923). This achievement stimulated the planners of subsequent expositions to have some structure—a massive building, a town, or a shore—serve as the physical center and symbol of the exposition.

5

The Story of the States No. III.—Illinois

IN SOME OF THE PUBLIC BUILDINGS OF CHICAGO — THE THEATRES, THE halls, the office buildings, hotels, and depots—one finds evidence to-day of something which, for want of a better definition, may be called an historic art exposition. You can see it in several office buildings in the down-town portions, where, over elevator entrances and lobby exits, are sculptured heads and bas-reliefs of Marquette and Joliet, of De Soto, La Salle, and Tonti.[1] You can see it in the theatres, where by paintings and reliefs are illustrated those magnificent incidents of early exploration—the lone Marquette sailing down the Mississippi, the indomitable La Salle guiding his hardy company over the ice and snow of the prairie south of Chicago to the open waters of the Illinois. All the early incidents, from the building of the Fort of the Broken Heart, at the extremity of what is now Peoria Lake, to the erection and massacre of Fort Dearborn, at the entrance of the Chicago River, are here illustrated in one form or another. The parks contain monuments, the public institutions paintings, the walls of several theatres reliefs of the most delicate modelling, detailing in a feeling way the story of these early adventures, which will yet form the basis for a world of American romance.

The early story of the State is involved with that of Ohio and Indiana, of which it was successively a part. All of these date their beginning from the arrival of the French missionaries and traders. In the adventures, the explorations, and the battles with the Indians, which form so large a portion of the early account, all shared alike. In a special sense only can Illinois claim that which actually occurred on her soil.

"Who are you?" called out Marquette in Algonquin dialect to the Indians whom he discovered at the mouth of the Des Moines River.[2]

"We are Illini,"* replied one of their chiefs, and because of the sweetness and tenderness of this earliest of Western missionaries a pleasant

---

*"We are *men*." The Algonquins thus proudly distinguished themselves from the Iroquois, whom they regarded as beasts on account of their cruelty. From this time the Indians of this district became known among the French as Illinese or Illinois, whence the State name.

interview followed, at which fish, hominy, and buffalo meat were served and eaten. This was June 24, 1673.

On the long journey back, after going nearly to the Gulf of Mexico, Marquette and Joliet, with their five service men, entered the Illinois River, rowing upward to its source until the present sites of Kaskaskia and Utica were reached. There they found that there was no way back to the great Michigan which the Indians knew, except by foot, and so, guided by red men who volunteered to accompany them, they were led to the Chicagou† portage. Here was a broad waste of grass and prairie flowers, channelled by two lazy streams that met from opposite directions, and flowed united into the lake. This was Chicago as nature made it, and as these men, who were its first discoverers, saw it. Here it was that the Indians and Frenchmen parted company, and in their frail canoes the latter skirted the western shore of Lake Michigan on the long northward journey to Canada. Such was the discovery of Illinois.

On the banks of this same Chicagou River was built only a few months later the lonely cabin which was to shelter a dying priest. It was unquestionably the first house in the new territory, and the one home of the noble Marquette in what was later to be Illinois. He came to it because, sincerely loving the Indians, he wanted to get back to them, and, having come so far, was taken ill. This wretched shelter was built on the South Branch, and here, through months of rain and snow and open winds from the lake, a dreary winter was spent. Joliet had already returned to Canada, falling in on his way with Robert de la Salle, who was afterwards to carry on the exploration of the Mississippi. Bands of roving Indians visited Marquette to bring him food, and several companions staying by him saw that he did not die of neglect. He kept a journal, and from it we learn that soon a trader came and established a post there, and that this trader sometimes brought such food to the missionary as the open prairie provided. The short visit to his beloved at Kaskaskia, his last desire to reach Canada before he died, the long march in return, and the death and burial at Sleeping Bear, on Lake Michigan, May 18, 1675—these things are historic.

The work of Marquette was taken up by La Salle. It was at the Fort of the Broken Heart, near Peoria, that some of the incidents most dramatic in the life of La Salle were enacted. Here had come, through what hardships Heaven only knows, he and his band, prepared, as he thought, to build a vessel which would carry him and his down the Mississippi, and allow for material being taken along which would aid in the building of a village. Forges, ship carpenter's tools, and iron work he had brought here, and

†The old spelling of Chicago. It is believed to be an Indian word meaning *onion, garlic, leek, or skunk*. Skunk weed is the Indian name for the onion, which used to grow abundantly on the banks of the Chicago River.

"We are Illini."

men, thirty-four of them; and here, when the keel was already laid, came desertion. Partly from want of pay, partly through a disposition to cut loose from restraint, his men interfered with him, and now he had to tramp all the way back to Canada for other men and other supplies. Through streams and forests and open stretches of tenantless country this man, with his five faithful companions, began that march which ought to be famous in history. Winter still hung over the country; the small streams were not yet released from its icy grasp, and when the travellers had reached the upper tributaries of the Illinois, the canoes by which they came had to be abandoned. With shoulders laden, but hearts untrammelled, they marched back, not in retreat, but to get more supplies—to return.

And when, after making all that unrivalled effort, and gaining new supplies and new energy, they returned, it was only to witness what treason and battle and desertion could do. Ashes and desolation, with wolves quarrelling over the spoils of battle, and men departed without a trace of their whereabouts! It is Father Hennepin who has left us the information that from the fact that the many difficulties under which they labored almost broke their hearts springs the peculiar name of the fort.[3]

Yet from here La Salle finally set forth, and it was to this place that he returned after he had been to the mouth of the Mississippi at the Gulf, and had named all the vast southern territory Louisiana in honor of Louis XIV., the king of France.[4] It was the lone trader at the Chicagou portage who saw him go, and the same who saw him eventually return triumphant.

France, however, was not to retain it. When the colonies grew, the boundary question between England and France in America became all important, and eventually resulted in what was subsequently known as the French and Indian war. Lawrence, Augustine, and George Washington, as members of the original Ohio Company, which attempted to build a fort at Pittsburg to protect the grant of territory now included in what is Ohio, but then claimed by the French, were at the bottom of this. Naturally France objected. Soon all the Indian tribes of Canada and the lakes were involved, and the whole of Europe was also up in arms. In the far west, however, which was then Illinois, only the mildest form of hostility developed; and with Wolfe's victory for the English on the Heights of Abraham, September 13, 1759, all the territory east of the Mississippi fell into English hands.[5]

At Kaskaskia, the old seat of empire in this region for fully one hundred and fifty years, still another event of dramatic significance occurred. This was in connection with the final introduction of American rule. When the Revolutionary War broke out, the English seized Detroit, and from that point commanded not only Ohio and Michigan, but all the western territory. Kaskaskia was then a village of one thousand inhabitants, ruled by a Frenchman, Rocheblanc, who, however, was loyal to British interests, and protected by Fort Gage, into which the English shortly intended to throw a garrison. By a strategy suggested by himself, Colonel George Rogers Clark, a true patriot and an ardent lover of independence, succeeded in diverting attention from his movement, and making his way down the Ohio to a point some distance below Louisville, where he struck out through the wilderness and appeared suddenly in the streets of Kaskaskia.[6] It was the evening of the fourth of July, 1778. No British soldiers were present, but a small company of French did garrison duty at the fort. So completely were they taken by surprise, however, that the victory was won before resistance was thought of. The governor, Rocheblanc, and a few leading citizens were seized and put in irons. Every inhabitant was ordered to remain in his house. Meanwhile the conquerors made night hideous by their tumult in order to terrify and prevent retaliation.

Being but a mere handful, and fearing eventual opposition and reprisal, Clark now shut himself in the fort, and had secret reports issued, detailing the terrible things he intended to do. The inhabitants were to be deported and sent in different directions. Families were to be unmercifully divided. When M. Gibault, the aged pastor, and a few of his aged flock came to beg permission to have a last final assemblage in the village chapel, the doughty colonel grumbled a fierce assent. When this was over, the aged curé again appeared, supplicating that each might be allowed to carry away a few provisions with them.

"The wilderness is so wide," he said.

"What for?" exclaimed the colonel, in assumed amazement.

"We are to be driven away from our homes."

"Nonsense," he shouted. "Do you take us for savages?"

The hitherto impenetrable immobility and harsh exterior now blossomed to the natives as something tender and charitable. All the ill reports only served to throw into brighter relief this wonderful generosity. Not only were the Americans blessed and extolled—their rule was counted exceedingly beneficent. Instead of opposition and mutiny, coöperation and assistance were effected, and in a short time the same Frenchmen were marching joyously along under him toward the capture of Vincennes.

When the American Revolution closed, the destiny of the territory, part of which is now Illinois, was settled by placing it under the flag of the United States at the treaty of Paris, signed September 3, 1783, and ratified by Congress at Philadelphia, January 14, 1784.

At Fort Dearborn, which had been built in 1803–4, was enacted the last of that which was remarkable before the rule of the State began. This was the massacre of its garrisons during the war which broke out between England and the United States in 1812. General Hull, who had been sent to hold Detroit, at once attempted to notify his outpost at Fort Dearborn, in order that they might save themselves by marching to Fort Wayne.[7] All the savages were up in arms. The only runner who could reach them was Winnemac, a friendly Pottawottomie chief. Faithful to his trust, he arrived at Fort Dearborn on the 9th of August, 1812, and handed his dispatch to Captain Heald. This was to evacuate if he was not sufficiently powerful to maintain it.

Wolf's Point, Chicago, 1832.—
A trading post conducted by a pioneer named Wolf, located
at the fork of the North and the South Branch of the river,
above the site of Fort Dearborn.

Under the impression that he was not, Heald and his garrison, number-ing sixty-six men, set forth on the 15th of August. They had not gone farther than what is now Eighteenth Street in Chicago, however, before they were attacked by five times their number of Pottawottomies, and half of their number slain. The remainder were taken prisoners, and after endur-ing months of hardships, were eventually exchanged. A monument in West Eighteenth Street, Chicago, which was erected by the late George M. Pullman, marks the place of the massacre.[8]

The history of the State, however, as we understand, is not exactly of these things. Out of stress and strife and great adventure Illinois arose, until finally it got to the place where it was a part of Ohio Territory, and then Indiana Territory, and finally it was Illinois Territory, with all Wisconsin belonging to it, and not enough people throughout the whole area to make up a fair-sized county. And the following was the manner in which it came to be a State:

Up to 1809, the present State, then but a county in Indiana, had been receiving its due share of the Western tide of immigration. Nearly all of those who came settled in what is now the southern half of the State, Alton being quite the northernmost limit of white settlement. It is true there was a fort and trading post at Chicago, but no population other than the half hundred soldiers and traders. Below Alton, in what are now Randolph, Monroe, St. Clair, and Madison counties, quite a number of people had settled. There were villages of a half hundred and more at Cairo, Quincy, and the like, for settlers needed to be upon some avenue of communica-tion, and these the Ohio and Mississippi afforded. When the population grew to be upwards of thirty-five thousand, the local representatives, Messrs. William Biggs and John Messenger, then sitting in the Indiana legislature, which met at Vincennes, decided that it would be a good thing for them if they could obtain a division, and have Illinois erected into a territory. Locally the thing was satisfactory enough, and the idea of having a territorial legislature meeting at Kaskaskia was rather pleasing. So the thing was talked about, and finally made into a semi-public matter, and the Government appealed to for a division.

Whether Indiana Territory could be thus divided or not depended upon the election of a delegate to Congress. The Illinoisians were anxious to elect one favorable to a division. The Indianians were indifferent. When it came to a choice, one Jesse B. Thomas, a member in the legislature from an Indiana county, was selected, but only after he had given actual bond to be in favor of the division. With the aid of the Illinois vote in the legislature and his own, Mr. Thomas was elected, and, true to his pledges, he secured a division. He did even more than this, for he had himself appointed to one of the supreme judgeships of the newly created territory, and, coming home with the appointment in his pocket, removed to Illinois and very comfortably entered upon his duties.

It was not long after this until the politicians, who became rather more numerous with the growth of the State, began to agitate the question of Statehood, and having by 1818 the customary forty-five thousand population which was considered sufficient, it could hardly be prevented.

Nathaniel Pope was Congressional delegate from the Territory of Illinois at this time, and it was to him that the territorial legislature gave instructions, asking that he petition Congress for the enactment of a law under which the territory could form a State government. Naturally he acquiesced, but the conditions under which he did so were peculiar.

By the Ordinance of 1787, fixing the limits of three States to be formed out of the Northwest Territory, it was provided that Congress should have power to form one or more States from the territory set apart for the Western State (which was what is now Illinois and Wisconsin) out of land lying "north of an east and west line, drawn through the southerly bend or extreme of Lake Michigan." This would have given Wisconsin the city of Chicago.

But Pope, when the ordinance which had been drawn in accordance with the above came up in Congress, moved to amend by changing the northern boundary line to the north latitude of 42° 30', where it is now.

"It is," said he, "for the best preservation of the Union."

With rather remarkable foresight, he pointed out that the State, by reason of its geographical location more than the fertility of its soil, was destined to become, at no distant day, both populous and influential. If the northern boundary line were arbitrarily fixed, rather than naturally determined, and the State's commerce confined to the Mississippi and that river's southern tributary, its commercial relations with the South would become so close, that in the event, at some future day, of an attempt at the dismemberment of the Union, Illinois would cast its lot with the Southern States. If the northern boundary was so fixed, he thought, that the State could have jurisdiction over the southwestern shore of Lake Michigan, it would naturally be united with Indiana, Ohio, and Pennsylvania, and the cords of commercial interest would bind it forever to the interest of perpetual union.

Persuaded by this argument, the amendment, as suggested, was adopted, and Illinois received a strip of land fifty-one miles in width, which has been very vital in our national life. Illinois strength to oppose slavery was generated there. The Republican party owes almost its national life to the men of this section who voted for Trumbull, and afterwards Lincoln, and elected them.[9]

In accordance with the privilege which this ordinance conferred, a legislature was called to meet at Kaskaskia, which, having organized the State government and put it in motion, adjourned to meet again in the winter of 1818–19. At this second session the members, being mostly ignorant and unpretending men, enacted the laws of Kentucky and Virginia almost verbatim, as the code for Illinois. A governor, one Shadrack Bond, was put in office, but for a long time there was little or no order in State affairs. It is said that for every session until the first general revision of 1827 all the standard laws were regularly changed. Tastes and whims were constantly consulted. The rage for amending and altering finally became so great that Governor Ford cynically declared that it was a good thing the Holy Scriptures did not have to come before the legislature.

"They'd show the Lord," was his curt conclusion.

Another politician summed it up in a statement in which he said that a session of the legislature was like a great fire in the boundless prairies of the State, in that it consumed everything. Again, it was like the genial breath of spring, making all things new.

One of the most humorous things in connection with this first session was the removal of the State capital from Kaskaskia in 1820, and the manner in which the new capital came to receive its peculiar name. The legislature appointed commissioners to select a new site, and the latter, having made choice of a place then in the midst of a wilderness, they consulted with one another as to what would be a suitable name. An outrageous wag arose among them, it is said, and earnestly suggested that since one of the most famous tribes of Indians in Illinois had been known as the Vandals, he would advise that the new capital be named Vandalia. It would perpetuate an interesting and historic name, and would serve to give the future generation of the State a key to the character and sympathies of the fathers.

This so thoroughly pleased the unlearned commissioners, that the scandalous old desecrators of Rome received a new lease of memory here.

"It would better illustrate," said old Governor Ford afterward, "the modern rather than the ancient inhabitants of the country."

From the very inception the people of Illinois were progressive, as, perhaps, this unrest might indicate. Things were in a very crude shape, however. The law-makers were, as a rule, only newly arrived in the country, and were elected because of their supposed superiority in the matter of learning. Thus one of the first three associate justices of the State Supreme Court was a total stranger, a William P. Foster by name, who had come to the State only three weeks before. This man was no lawyer, never having either studied or practised law, but he had winning and polished manners, and managed to ingratiate himself. When assigned to hold court on the Wabash Circuit, he never went near it, but hid his incompetency by strutting about and pleading other duties as long as he

Lincoln's old mill, near Salem.

could. Finally, when it became absolutely necessary for him to do something, he pocketed his salary and fled the State, leaving a trail of indebtedness in his wake.

Others of the early leaders stayed only so long as there was any chance of receiving rapid political preferment, and on finding that impossible moved away. The majority of them held offices in a dozen new States in the course of their lives, and naturally administered the affairs of all with a single eye to their own profit.

The people, though, were unusually ambitious, and possessed an almost unreasoning desire for progress. This led to a number of serious social complications later. From the very beginning they had taken up an idea, newly broached by Albert Gallatin, a local financier, Alexander M. Jenkins, and others, of having a canal dug from Lake Michigan to the Mississippi. This canal, which was eventually constructed, and was more recently made the basis of the vast drainage system from the Lake, through the Chicago River, into the Illinois, is still the shadow of the very much larger thing which it was meant to be. Ships from the Lake to the Gulf was the earliest Illinoisian idea, and ships from the Lake to the Gulf is the cry of this latter generation. It is the conception of kinds and sizes of ships only that has changed.

The early population of the State which made this distinctive plea for an almost national highway of water was a peculiar people. Fully one-half were descendants of old French settlers, those who had founded Prairie du Rocher and Prairie du Pont, Kaskaskia, Cohokia, and Peoria. These people had fields in common for farming, and farmed, built houses, and lived in the style of the peasantry of old France a hundred and fifty years ago. Many of them had intermarried with the native Indians, and there was a strain of that in their blood. They hunted, fished, raked the prairie for furs and wild fowl, and made long journeys for trading. Nearly all of them wore the Madras cotton handkerchief for a headdress, the cape or blanket garment for a covering.

As for the American population, they were chiefly from Kentucky, Virginia, and Pennsylvania. Trained to a pioneer life, they farmed ardently; raised cotton, wool, and flax for their own clothing; spun, wove, and dyed their own stuffs; and did, in short, everything that was common to the labors of the pioneer.

The south part of the State was originally settled by the poorer class of people from the slave States. It is from this fact, it is supposed, that Illinois came to be called the "Sucker State." These immigrants were people who were not rich enough to own slaves, and who came to Illinois to get away from the imperious domination of their wealthy neighbors. Coming from tobacco-growing countries, they were compared to the useless suckers of the plant, which are stripped off and thrown away. Another origin of the term is, however, given.

The discovery of lead about the Galena district drew to that territory, in the years 1826 and 1827, hundreds and thousands of persons from Illinois and Missouri, who came to work the mines. It was estimated that the number of miners in this section in 1827 was six or seven thousand. The Illinoisians ran up the Mississippi River in the steamboats in the spring season, worked the lead mines during the warm weather, and then ran down the river again to their homes in the fall season. There was thus established, it was supposed, a similitude between the migratory habits of the these people and those of the watery tribe called suckers. It was given to them at the Galena mines by the Missourians.

During the first ten years of their Statehood, the people were confronted with questions considerably more practical than that of the great canal, and one of these was the slave trade.

It seems that in enacting the laws of Virginia and Kentucky as the State laws of Illinois, all the slave restrictions of those States had been included almost without reading. Nobody knew anything about the matter, and, indeed, there was quite a strong opposition in a large portion of the growing population to anything looking toward slave ownership. Still the statutes so stood, and when various incidents were construed upon this law to mean that slavery was permissible, a great disturbance followed. People talked and debated, and it was decided by those who favored slavery that a convention would have to be called to reorganize the State constitution so as to make slavery permanent.

One of the things which helped to form opinion on this matter was the tide of immigrants now pouring into Missouri through Illinois from Virginia and Kentucky. In the fall of the year every great road was crowded and full of them, all bound to Missouri, with their money and long trains of teams and negroes. These were the wealthy and best educated immigrants from the slave States. Many of the people who had land and farms to sell looked upon the good fortune of Missouri with envy. The lordly immigrant, as he passed along, maliciously rejoiced to increase it, and pretended to regret the short-sighted policy of Illinois, which excluded him because of his slaves from settlement amongst them. This stirred the one great flame of opposition to freedom for the negro, and made the fight against revision difficult.

The question was not many years in begging a decision, however. It was made a State issue in 1822, and, after a remarkable campaign for that early day, it was voted down. Though the slave men were temporarily defeated, they still had the written law as borrowed from Virginia in their favor, and naturally this left the question open for a very bitter contest later.

The other difficulty that went hand-in-hand with this concerned money, or rather the lack of it. Every one wanted to see the State grow and flourish, and there was a genuine rush to build houses and lay out towns in anticipation of the approaching immigrant.

There being little gold or silver in the State, and that only in the shape of worn coins of other nations, the people dreamed of creating their own money. Illinois was a State. Why should not the world look upon it as good security? Legislators, the first ever assembled in the State, openly asserted that Illinois could create all the money it wanted. At the second session, which assembled at Vandalia, the new capital, in 1820, the Illinois State bank was created, with a capital of a half million dollars, based on the credit of the State. This bank was allowed to issue paper money; and the legislature, outrivalling the silliness of the people themselves, supposed that by enacting a law they could compel not only the people of the State, but the government of the United States, to accept this issue at its face value. Of course the government could not do this, but that did not hinder the legislature from so ordering, at any rate.

Confederate Prisoners at Fort Douglas, Chicago 1864.

One of the best anecdotes illustrating the whole matter was told of Colonel Menard, a Frenchman by birth, the first lieutenant-governor, and president of the State Senate, who, when the question came up as to whether the scrip of the bank should be made legal tender and received at the land office, a Federal institution, or not, did up the whole business as follows:

"Gentlemen of de Senate. It is moved and seconded dat de notes of dis bank be made land-office money. All in favor of dat motion say aye; all against it, say no. It is decided in de affirmative. And now, gentlemen, I bet you one hundred dollar he never be made land-office money."

That was the upshot of the matter. The money never was made legal tender. Other banks gained permission to circulate paper, which soon became worthless, and in two or three years the money affairs of the people were so complicated that a hard financial crash followed. Governor Coles, and, after him, Governor Edwards, did what they could to obtain sane and conservative legislation, which was finally enforced by the logic of trade itself.

It was at the conclusion of this earliest of Illinois' several money troubles, which lasted until about 1830, that the final Indian war broke out. In this war, which lasted from July 15, 1830, to August 27, 1832, if one reads the story of Black Hawk, the sad hopelessness of the thing is more pitiable than the putting down of the rebellion is interesting.[10] Keokuk, chief of the Sauk and Fox Indians, had ceded to the government the territory lying between the Mississippi and Rock rivers, but Black Hawk, a dissenting leader of those Indians of the tribe who still favored England, had recently returned to hunt upon it, and consequently clashes with settlers followed. War was declared, if a few hundred men scouring the northern country could be called war, and, in the course of four years of more or less guerrilla fighting, the Indians were finally dislodged. This was the last of the red man so far as Illinois was concerned.

This war was still in its beginning, however, when the second and most wonderful of all the historic, financial, and social upheavals of the State occurred, an upheaval whose effects in the matter of taxation were felt for fully half a hundred years later. It might, in a general sense, be called the State and money trouble.

By the sudden evidence of growth in every direction at this time, particularly Chicago, where from a mere village in 1833 a city of several thousand had sprung up, and in 1836 was still growing, the people were most enthusiastically aroused. The story of sudden fortunes made there went all over the State, first exciting wonder and then amazement, and lastly a gambling spirit of adventure, which, like a gold-mining craze, aroused in everybody an all-absorbing desire for sudden and splendid wealth. Towns were laid out, houses erected, and plans of plots shipped far and wide for advertising and sale. It was waggishly remarked by many people that the whole country was like to be laid out in towns, and that there would soon be no room for farming. Be that as it may, the craze took the form of an internal improvement campaign, which ended in large public meetings and the appointment of delegates to an internal improvement convention, which met at the same time the legislature did (1836–37), and drew up a system "commensurate with the wants of the people." This system included railroads, canals, public highways, and buildings galore. I am not quoting a dream book when I say that the legislature of the same winter in question, representing not more than 300,000 people all told, passed a system or bill providing for railroads from Galena to the mouth of the Ohio; from Alton to Shawneetown; from Alton to Mt. Carmel; from Alton to the eastern boundary of the State; from Quincy, on the Mississippi, through Springfield, to the Wabash; from Bloomington to Pekin, and from Peoria to Warsaw—altogether about 1,300 miles of road. It also provided that the Kaskaskia, Illinois, Rock, and Great and Little Wabash rivers should be dredged and deepened, and that $200,000 should be distributed among all those counties through which no roads or improvements were to be made. There were other features in connection with it equally impossible and ridiculous, but these were the most important. Orators declaimed ingeniously that the State could well afford to borrow hundreds of millions of dollars for these things, and people applauded. Yet every time a tax question came up there was strenuous and equally unreasoning opposition. The result of all this was simply a large public debt. One road was built from the Mississippi to Springfield, but it cost a million, and was not worth one hundred thousand when finished. Others were started. A deal was made with the Illinois Central, then a mere corporation on paper, by which the State gave it every other quarter section of land along its route in return for 7 per cent. of all its future annual profits. More work on the Illinois and Michigan Canal, which had been begun on July 4, 1836, and was now lagging, was done, and when the State had 478,000 population, it had an indebtedness of $14,237,348. That led to a scheme of repudiation, and then the whole people learned by some very bitter taxation experiences what it means to be honest.

Along with all this the capital was removed from Vandalia to Springfield, in 1837. That cost $600,000. It was done to get the votes of nine members from the Springfield region for that wonderful improvement idea. When it was all over, the thing was roundly abused by the people, but then it was too late. The new burden had been saddled.

Right in the midst of this improvement folly occurred one of the most magnificent things in the State's history, and one of its gravest errors. Eliah P. Lovejoy died for his faith that the negro should be free.[11] It was all because of that unthinking adoption of the Virginia laws. Although all of those who wanted to call a convention and revise the constitution so as to permit slavery were defeated in 1824, the thing was never thoroughly settled at that. Thousands believed the State was injuring itself by this anti-slavery idea. If they could not have slavery openly voted for, at least they didn't want it talked about. When Lovejoy came with his miserable little printing-press from St. Louis to Alton, and there set up the "Alton Observer"; when he began to attack slavery and say that it was wrong, they threw his type and press into the river, and told him to begone. That, however, the man's divine faith in his cause would not allow. In the old Lower Alton Presbyterian Church, surrounded by men with rifles, and addressing those who were madly divided for or against the one vast problem of the hour, he declared his faith in his divine mission.

"I cannot leave Alton," he said; "I have no intention of leaving. A voice urges me to a higher duty. I may be mobbed, the people may do what they choose to me, but here I remain. And as I remain, so will I exercise my right as a free man to believe and to publish my belicf."

That was at Alton.

When a new press finally came, and abolitionists gathered with rifles to protect it, the mob allowed it to be safely landed, but not much more. In the house where it was placed, Lovejoy and the others who guarded it were attacked, and the patriot shot down. Then the press was thrown into the river again, and the idea that its miserable metal stood for made as powerful as a giant in the land. So freedom of the press was suppressed in Illinois.

In 1840, three years later, came the Mormons. They were already a powerful sect, odious in Missouri and Ohio, but welcomed here for what was thought to be their sufferings. By juggling with both parties and appealing to that spirit of petty intrigue and self-interest in political aspirants so common throughout the country, they managed to get a corporation privilege which is one of the most astonishing documents in all American law annals. The rights vested in Joseph Smith and his council at Nauvoo were those of a Tsar.[12] He could almost hang offenders of his own faith, and those who came to arrest him lost jurisdiction the moment they entered upon his territory. Indeed, an autocratic cancer had been engrafted upon the State by the desire of petty politicians for office and the wish to conciliate the Mormon vote.

A man cannot worship God and mammon, however, and neither can a religious organization of this sort be all in all to two political parties. Sides had to be taken at one time or another, and finally the Democrats became offended, and then there was set up the cry that the Mormons were doing everything that was unconstitutional and dangerous, and that if they were not curbed evil would follow. This aroused the attention of the people to the matter, the fiercest of political battles was waged for a period of six years, and finally the remarkable expulsion came, thousands of Mormons packing bag and baggage and making off for Salt Lake. The growing State of Illinois was too much for them. Its political corpus was becoming too large and too healthy for them to handle.

Through all of this Lincoln and Douglas were slowly emerging into local and national significance.[13] The slavery agitation, lulled into temporary rest by the national compromise of 1850, broke out afresh with the passage in 1854 of the Kansas and Nebraska bill. Here, as elsewhere, the bill nearly marked a revolution. Douglas in the United States Senate felt grave fears for his leadership in the State. The northern half of the State, now grown more influential, wanted no compromise with slavery. Parties went to pieces. Where formerly local interests had been strong, now the attitude of Illinois in the nation was the most important thing to its people.

As a result of these disturbances the Democrats, in 1854, found themselves for the first time since 1841 unable to control the General Assembly of the State on joint ballot. There were Democrats who stood for the Kansas-Nebraska bill, and Democrats who repudiated its doctrine. Opposed or indifferent to them were Whigs, Free-soilers, Know-nothings, and Abolitionists. Out of this strange medley Lyman Trumbull was elected to the United States Senate. Thus was won the fruits of the first anti-slavery battle in Illinois. It was one of the first in the nation, and out of it the Republican party was born. Such is the most significant portion of Illinois' political history, its ideal history.

Following this came the natural but famous convention of 1856, called at the city of Bloomington. Never before had there, nor has there since, been assembled in Illinois the like of this convention. Palmer and Wentworth, Yates and Lovejoy, Oglesby and Browning and Lincoln were its controlling spirits. Men who had been political antagonists for years sat side by side in a common cause. They spoke from the same platform. Palmer from the standpoint of a Democrat, Browning from the view of a Whig, Lovejoy from the sublimer heights of an Abolitionist. And then Lincoln came, inspired, as his friends described him, delivering the unrecorded speech which left his party leadership in Illinois unquestioned. After that the convention adjourned, and there was heralded to the world the birth of the Republican party in Illinois.

Since that time the political and social history of the State has been pleasant enough. Its ways have been the ways of peace. National history records how 135,000 soldiers were given by it to defend the Union in the Civil War, how Grant was drawn from his store at Galena, and the mighty Lincoln sent from his home at Springfield. These are things which are of the history of the United States, and known to every reader in the land.

On its commercial side, however, it has been since those days that Illinois has accomplished the things its poor little legislature of almost fifty years before wrecked itself in trying to accomplish. The seven railroads— they were all present by 1855. One of the old merchant magazines of great fame in that year (Hunt's) published a "statistical view of Illinois," which astounded the rest of the growing country. Chicago had a population of 80,000; the State no less than 851,000. It was eighth in size, ninth in the matter of representation in Congress, tenth in the matter of improved acreage. Nearly every county had from three to thirty thousand population. Coal had been discovered; lead in the northwestern part of the State. The richness of the smooth, unbroken prairie was dotted with hundreds of excellent villages and towns. Already the world was aware that Chicago was destined to be a great city. The wonderful fertility of the soil had made the one-time fear of bankruptcy and the shameless thought of repudiation of the great State debt seem like black shadows. Everything was onward and upward. Then began the era of the later big things.

Marshall Field came in 1856 as a clerk to Coolcy, Farwell & Co.[14] George M. Pullman came in 1859. He was not a car magnate then, but only a house raiser and sewer-building contractor. The first car shop controlled by Pullman was opened in 1863. Philip D. Armour did not arrive, in the sense of a resident, until 1875.[15] The stock yards that were to revolutionize the packing of beef were established there at his direction in 1868.

As a railroad centre and market for cattle and grain, Chicago soon came to be unrivalled in the West. In 1871, however, came that greatest calamity ever suffered by the State, the burning of Chicago, which for dramatic significance is scarcely surpassed by anything in modern times. The city had grown by unparalleled leaps and bounds, until it then had over three hundred thousand inhabitants. There were miles upon miles of wind-swept prairie dotted closely with newly erected homes and manufactories. Hundreds of millions of dollars had been invested in commercial affairs, and the whole country was wide awake to its progress when this thing happened. Suddenly, on the morning of October 8, 1871, a high wind prevailing, the whole city was aroused by an immense conflagration, which had begun, it is said, in a cow-shed on the north side, and was carried irresistibly onward by the power of the wind and the flimsy character of the majority of the structures. Engines were telegraphed for by the major to all neighboring cities, even as far as Detroit, a demand which was very generously responded to; but before assistance could arrive the whole downtown or commercial portion had been very nearly consumed.

To save what little there was of value remaining, dynamite and giant powder were resorted to, and block after block of solid commercial houses in the path of the fire were deliberately blown up. City officials and those who had organized to direct the rescue work were finally driven from the City Hall, and all the prisoners of the community set at large in order that they might save their lives. When the wind died down on the 9th, and the flames were got under control, it was found that over 18,000 commercial buildings and 100,000 dwellings had been destroyed, and that 92,000 people were homeless. Property to the value of $187,927,000 had been consumed, and 250 lives lost. The whole of the burned area was considerably over 2,000 acres, in which nothing but tottering walls and charred skeletons of framework were to be seen.

Congress, however, and the nation came to the rescue, and Chicago recovered. Within a period of a few months hundreds and thousands of better and more imposing structures were erected, and the city began its present career of growth and wealth accumulation which has never been interrupted. In 1873 the first of the modern department stores was organized, and in 1877 the first great railroad strike broke out. This involved complete business prostration for Illinois. Cars loaded with grain, flour, and live stock were side-tracked, and not a wheel was allowed to turn. Railway trains, machine shops, yards, and factories at Chicago, Peoria, Galesburg, Decatur, East St. Louis, and some minor points were given into the hands of furious mobs, as were also the mines at Braidwood and La Salle. Order was only had after the State militia, a body then only recently organized with any effectiveness in the State, was called out, and severe fighting indulged in. It was the first important use of this form of soldiery ever made in Illinois.

Photo by Scharp Bros.
View of the World's Fair buildings, 1893.

Following this came another period of prosperity which has endured with but slight interruption until the present day. Anarchy raised its head in Chicago, a riot resulting from free and long agitation, in which a number of policemen were killed and many persons wounded. This was on May 4, 1886. Great excitement was caused by the details of the outbreak, and in the subsequent trial, which lasted a number of months, the entire nation took a vast interest. All known newspaper records of circulation were broken in Chicago on the day the convicted men were executed, which was November 11, 1887. Spies, Fischer, Engel, and Parsons were their names.

Of a more pleasing national interest was the agitation, in 1889 and 1890, of the need of a great drainage canal from Lake Michigan to the Illinois River, which resulted in 1892 in ground being broken upon a work which has since resulted in the expenditure of $35,000,000, raised in Chicago by taxation, and the reversing of the current in the Chicago River, in a sense the most remarkable stream to be found anywhere in the United States; than which there never was another more useful commercially or more filthy physically.

The revivifying and endowing of the Chicago University, in 1889, under the leadership of Dr. William R. Harper, was another event the interest of which has not yet lost its hold upon the public mind.[16] This aged sectarian college, all but defunct both spiritually and financially, was in the space of a single year thrown into national significance by the efforts of

Dr. Harper, who, strong in the confidence of John D. Rockefeller, the multi-millionaire philanthropist, managed to secure endowments for it aggregating several million.[17] The rapidity with which a plan was elaborated, the magnificence and enthusiasm with which its details were working out, and the material evidence which came rapidly in 1892 in the form of splendid array of buildings, all served to form a chapter of educational adventure unparalleled in the history of the world. Seventeen millions has the Chicago University thus far received in the matter of bequests.

And, lastly, out of Illinois arose the wonder of the World's Fair, that beautiful collection of palaces which ranged along Lake Michigan, under a shining sky, not yet forgotten.[18] It was Illinois, with largely the impetus springing from Chicago, which conceived and executed that. Men may regret now that the wonder of it was not retained, but the smile of tolerance and incredulity has disappeared. In the architectural details which are yet to make this land a land of beauty, the influence of this beautiful White City will not be unapparent. It was one of the royal conceptions with which art has struggled and wrought and triumphed.

It is in the realm of finance and trade, however, that Illinois has achieved most. Through Chicago her record of great deeds in these realms has been made largely what it is. Men such as Levi Z. Leiter, B. H. Hutchinson, George Swift, Nelson Morris, and Philip Armour have sought for, and at times in the past have controlled, the wheat, the corn, and the produce of the world. How these gigantic operations are engineered forms a story scarcely conceivable by the lay mind, but no doubt the purse of the average man feels quickly their influence.

Illinois is essentially a State of new ideas and great enterprises. Among them should be mentioned the wonder of the dressed beef and refrigerator business; the marvel of commercial organization reaching out to every hamlet in the land in the form of the Pullman sleeping-car; the generation and evolution of the idea that it is cheaper to build high than to build wide, and so on. In Chicago—most remarkable of cities—is to be seen the street where cables were first introduced into America, and the only elevator bridge ever erected, put up over its narrow river as an experiment.

But Illinois is young yet. Its ambitions and achievements are those of a boy whose magnificent manhood is yet to come. Great as have been the commercial and social problems encountered and struggled with, the end is not yet. Its greatest city has a third of a century to run before it can celebrate its one hundred years of progress. The State is still a score of years away from centennial, and in that time some of the newer dreams which are now so enthusiastically entertained may yet be fulfilled.

∞

A BIRD'S-EYE VIEW OF ILLINOIS HISTORY.

1634	Lake Michigan discovered by Jean Nicolet, July 4th.
1673	Marquette discovered Mississippi, June 17th.
1673	Kaskaskia or La Vantum Indian village of seven or eight thousand inhabitants discovered, September.
1673	Illinois and Michigan Canal suggested by Louis Joliet.
1673	Marquette visited present site of Chicago, September.
1675	Death of Marquette at mouth of Marquette River, Michigan, May 18th.
1680	La Salle first visits Illinois, January.
1680	Builds the Fort of the Broken Heart, the first thing done on the soil of Illinois with a view to permanent occupation, January 1st to 15th.
1680	Return of his band on foot, Peoria to Montreal, began March 1st.
1680	La Salle's second visit to Illinois, November.
1682	La Salle's third visit and discovery of the mouth of the Mississippi, April 7th.
1682	Mississippi Valley taken possession of for France by La Salle, April 9th.
1682	Tonti made Governor of Illinois by France, December.
1682	Fort called Fort St. Louis, built on Starved Rock, near Utica, December.
1687	La Salle murdered in Texas, March 19th.
1690	Proprietorship of Fort St. Louis granted Tonti for fur-trading purposes.
1700	Cahokia founded.
1702	Fort St. Louis discontinued.
1718	Pierre Duqué de Boisbriant appointed first commandant of Illinois by the French.
1722	First church and first stone residence erected at Kaskaskia.
1725	Chief Chicagou sent to France by French settlers of Illinois.
1754	French and Indian war begun.
1760	Northwestern Territory (including Illinois) ceded to England by France, September 8th.
1765	English take formal possession of Illinois, October 10th.
1768	First English court established at Fort Charles, December 9th.
1777	Clark's conquest of Illinois begins Revolutionary War.
1778	Kaskaskia taken by Americans (Revolutionary War), July 4th.
1781	First permanent Anglo-American settlement.
1783	Illinois formally ceded to United States by England, September 3d.
1790	First settled portion of Illinois organized into a county of Ohio Territory, July.

1800   Illinois becomes a part of Indiana Territory, May 7th.

1803–04   Fort Dearborn built at Chicago.

1805   First legislators sent to represent Illinois in Indiana legislature at Vincennes, July.

1808   Attention of Congress called to idea of Illinois and Michigan Canal by Albert Gallatin, April 4th.

1809   Illinois set off as a separate Territory, February 3d.

1811   The great earthquake severely felt in southern Illinois.

1812   Fort Dearborn burned, garrison massacred, August 9th.

1812   Peoria burnt by Americans.

1816   Tract of land along proposed route of Illinois and Michigan Canal, ceded to United States Commissioners.

1817   American Fur Company establishes the pioneer business house of Chicago.

1818   Illinois admitted to Statehood, December 3d.

1818   State Constitution adopted at Kaskaskia, August 26th.

1820   State Capital removed from Kaskaskia to Vandalia, February.

1820   First Illinois State Bank created, December.

1822   Act authorizing the construction of the Illinois and Michigan Canal, passed by Congress, March 30th.

1822   Slavery defeated at the ballot, August.

1825   Act incorporating the "Illinois and Michigan Canal Association" with a capital of $1,000,000, passed by Illinois legislature, January 17th.

1831   Construction of a railroad in the State first proposed February 15th.

1831   Last Indian war broke out, June 24th.

1832   Black Hawk finally defeated and captured, August 7th.

1833   Chicago incorporated as a city.

1834   McKendree College founded.

1836   Actual work of construction on Illinois and Michigan Canal begun July 4th.

1837   Knox College founded.

1836–37   First railroad built from Naples to Bluffs in Scot County.

1837   Lovejoy riots and his death.

1836–37   Giant improvements voted.

1837   State Capital removed to Springfield.

1838   Monticello Female Seminary, first movement for higher education of women in State, founded at Godfrey.

1840   Mormons settled in Nauvoo.

1840–46   Mormon riots.

1846   Mormons evacuate Nauvoo.

1846   First regiment of Illinois volunteers enrolled for service in Mexican War, May.

1848   First ten miles of Galena and Chicago Union Railway completed.

1848   Illinois and Michigan Canal completed, and first boat, the "General Fry," passed from Lockport to Chicago, April 10th.
1856   Republican party born in Illinois.
1858–59   Lincoln-Douglas debate.
1860   Lincoln nominated for the Presidency, Chicago, May 16th.
1868   Illinois University founded March 11.
1871   Chicago fire, October 8–9th.
1872   Union stock yards incorporated.
1873   First Department Store in the world erected, Chicago.
1877   First railroad riots.

NOTES

"The Story of the States No. III.—Illinois," *Pearson's* 11 (April 1901): 513–43. Edited by William Penn Nixon.

1. Père Jacques Marquette (1637–75), French Jesuit missionary who, with Louis Jolliet (1645–1700), trader and hydrographer, was the first European to explore the Upper Mississippi River.

Hernando De Soto (1500–1542), Spanish conquistador and explorer in the Americas, discovered the Mississippi River in 1541.

Sieur de La Salle (1643–87), French explorer in North America, led the first expedition to trace the Mississippi River to its mouth.

Henri de Tonti or Tonty (1650?–1704), French fur trader and explorer, arrived in Quebec with La Salle in 1678 and helped him build trading posts on the lower Great Lakes and in the Illinois River valley.

2. The Algonquin dialect was spoken by a North American Indian linguistic group that once comprised from forty to fifty separate languages. The group is also known as Algonquian. Before the European arrival in North America, the Algonquian tribes dominated an area larger than any other Indian region in North America. This expanse was divided only by Iroquois enclaves in the eastern Great Lakes area and by the Boethuk tribes in Newfoundland.

3. Jean Louis Hennepin (1640–1705), Flemish Recollet friar, missionary, and author. After going to Quebec in 1675, he served for three years as a circulating curé until he departed westward with La Salle. In his exploration of the Midwest, he discovered and named St. Anthony's Falls (Minneapolis) and spent three months in Central Minnesota as a prisoner of the Sioux Indians.

4. Louis XIV, King of France, had the longest reign in European history (1643–1715). During this time he brought absolute monarchy to its height, established a glittering court at Versailles, and fought most of the other European countries in four wars.

5. James Wolfe (1727–59), English general, son of General Edward Wolfe, played the principal command role in the conquest of Canada from the French.

6. George Rogers Clark (1752–1818), American frontiersman and military leader, won important victories against the British and their Indian allies in the Illinois country during the American Revolution.

7. William Hull (1753–1825), American general, surrendered Detroit to the British in the War of 1812.

8. George M. Pullman (1831–97), American inventor and industrialist, produced the Pullman car. See Drieser's article "The Town of Pullman," republished in this collection.

9. Lyman Trumbull (1813–96), American legislator, was Republican U.S. Senator from Illinois (1855–73) and criticized Lincoln for too little vigor in prosecuting the Civil War.

10. Black Hawk (c. 1767–1838), an American Indian of the Sauk Tribe, led in 1832 a dissident band of his people and their allies, the Fox, in a fight against the loss of their lands in Illinois, Wisconsin, and Missouri.

11. Eliah Parish Lovejoy (1802–37), American newspaperman and abolitionist, became a martyr to the antislavery movement. His fame rests on his valiant defense of the report by a newspaper to advocate unpopular policies.

12. Joseph Smith (1805–44), founder of the Mormon church. His monument is the largest native American church body that in the twentieth century came to be a powerful and widely respected element in religious life.

13. Stephen Arnold Douglas (1813–61), American political leader. A U.S. senator for fourteen years and a contender for the presidency, Douglas was a major force in American politics before the Civil War. However, he often is remembered primarily for his association with Lincoln, whom he defeated for the Senate in 1859.

14. Marshall Field (1834–1906), one of the greatest merchants in American history. See Dreiser's article "Life Stories of Successful Men—No. 12: Marshall Field," reprinted in *Selected Magazine Articles,* 1:130–38.

15. Philip Danforth Armour (1832–1901), American businessman and philanthropist. Dreiser contributed "Life Stories of Successful Men—No. 10: Philip D. Armour," reprinted in *Selected Magazine Articles,* 1:120–29.

16. William Rainey Harper (1856–1906), American educator. He published his writings to promote the teaching of Hebrew. As president of the University of Chicago (1891–1906) he assembled a faculty of leading scholars for the university and promoted advanced study and research: his underlying policy was academic freedom in all areas of learning.

17. John D. Rockefeller (1839–1937), American industrialist and philanthropist.

18. The World's Fair, known as the World's Columbian Exposition, was an international exposition held in Chicago in 1893 to celebrate the four hundredth anniversary of the discovery of America by Christopher Columbus. The exposition covered 666 acres in Jackson Park, converted from swampland as a site for the event. About 150 buildings, designed by leading architects, were constructed of a composition of plaster of paris and jute fibers that resembled marble and gave the exposition the name of the White City.

Part IV
The City

1
The Town of Pullman

THE VISITOR TO CHICAGO SOON LEARNS THAT WHICH THE REST OF THE country hears and thinks concerning Chicago's chief commercial institutions, is to the average citizens of the western metropolis of apparently no interest whatever. Two out of every three men on a Chicago street would tell you nothing at all about the Union Stockyards, scarcely the proper direction. Even less is known concerning Pullman.[1] Yet there is nothing greater, commercially, in Chicago or in the world. Indeed, there is a hotel in Pullman of no mean proportions, whose patronage is largely made up of curious visitors from afar, who come to examine this great manufacturing center.

Pullman is about fourteen miles south of the center of Chicago, but still in the limits and a part of the Thirty-fourth Ward. As a town, it embraces a tract of 3,600 acres on the shores of Lake Calumet, a weedy expanse of harbor. As a manufactory, it consists of a tract of 171 acres, entirely covered with buildings and car tracks, and crowded to the surrounding wall with all sorts of machinery and working paraphernalia. It is a town of some 12,000 inhabitants. The hum and drone of its great energy can be heard all over the section it occupies, and by the wives and children of the men who make up its host of workers.

The view of the town and the shops from the depot is entirely ornamental. A large park occupies the center of the village, from which tree-shaded avenues lead out in several directions. The buildings, diverse and numerous, give a sense of ornate uniformity in architecture, and the great enclosed acreage of shops and mills does not break in upon but rather adds to the beauty of the place. Instead of plain buildings, pleasing architectural designs were indulged in, and one is reminded most pleasantly of the splendid asylums which several States have constructed of late.

One ventures into the immense region of furnaces and machines with a sense of diffidence, so intent is everyone within on things to do. It would have meant little to the writer if there had not been a guide along to "dig up facts" out of the maze of material. In the glare of many a furnace and through the deafening roar of hammers and presses, I was frequently enlightened by the voice of my mentor, who stated that there were 1,100

229

machines of all kinds in the place, and 5,000 men working in conjunction with them, their field of operation extending over 4,600 acres of floor space. The day's work of the entire shops, he explained, consisted of the half of a sleeping car (two days being required to complete one), two passenger cars, three street cars, and fifty freight cars. I marveled at this as being small, until some of the totals, such as 300 freight cars a week, 10 passenger cars, three Pullmans, and so on, were deduced from the daily average, when it grew more imposing. In addition to the sixty-two miles of track in the walls of the company, the train of fifty new cars leaving every evening, and the fact that 100,000,000 feet of lumber (annually used) brought in car loads, which would make a lumber train fifty miles long, helped to superinduce the proper amount of awe.

The facts concerning Pullman are really curious. The Pullman Company was organized in 1867, with a capital of $1,000,000. Its present capital stock is $36,000,000; the number of stockholders, 5,447. The first Pullman car, the "Pioneer," was completed in 1865. The number of cars now owned by the company is 2,408, of which 963 are buffet and dining cars. The company operates its cars under contracts with 84 railroads, covering 124,149 miles of road. The number of miles run by Pullman cars during the year ending July 3, 1897, was 191,862,947, and the number of passengers carried was 5,112,965. The total number of employees of the company in its operating and manufacturing departments for that year was 11,515, and the wages paid during the year $5,669,121.63. The longest unbroken run of any cars in the Pullman service is from Washington to San Francisco, 3,626 miles.

For the 1,100 machines in the Pullman shops the power is furnished by 20 stationary engines, which are rated at 9,600 horse power. The principal one is the Corliss engine, rated at 2,500 horse power, which ran the machinery at the Centennial Exposition at Philadelphia in 1876 and with which is connected 3,000 feet of main shafting and 89,400 feet of belting. In the shops about 50,000 tons of coal are consumed annually, over 100,000 tons of iron, and about 100,000,000 feet of lumber.

The total amount of wages paid by the company to its employees at Pullman from September 1, 1880, to April 1, 1897, was $38,013,992.55, and the value of materials consumed during the same period was $82,740,661.51. The number of employees in all the industries in Pullman at this time, including women and children, is 5,000. Their average length of service is seven years, and their average daily earnings $2.06.

However, Pullman possesses an interest above and beyond that of railroads and wheels. It stands related to the question of how cities should be built in general—how man should live. Young as the village is, it has aroused more interest and created more discussion in its day than any other place of similar size in the world. Whatever one may think of it so-

ciologically, there is no question but that it illustrates the value of thought
and taste in the building of a city or village. It seems also to recognize that
the working people are an important element in the successful operation of
any manufacturing enterprise. The plan to build in close proximity to the
shops, homes for the working men of such character and surroundings that
they would prove attractive to the best class of mechanics and cause them
to seek this place for employment, instead of going elsewhere, was amia-
ble in intention, at least. It was also planned to exclude all baneful influences, such as the saloon, and the result has been a manufacturing village
in which the world has interested itself a great deal more than it ever has in
the immense shop which supports the village. It was Mr. Pullman's idea
that in a manufacturing town, where every home was neat and tasteful, the
workingmen would turn out more work, better work and more profitable
work than in a place where opposite conditions existed.

The purpose of the town of Pullman was to give such employees as
chose to live in it dwellings of varying size and accomodations, well built
and kept in good repair, and with perfect sanitary arrangements; all to be so
arranged and built under the most competent architectural and engineering
skill as to be not only comfortable and healthy, but to have as high a
character for beauty as was practicable. The company, retaining the ownership and control of the place, would be able at all times to present object
lessons in cleanliness and order, which would exert influences for good
upon the people who should be brought into daily contact with them, as
well as upon those who might settle in the immediate vicinity. It was not,
therefore, deemed practicable to sell homes to working men, because if
any lots should be sold in Pullman it would permit the introduction of the
very baneful elements which it was the chief purpose to exclude from the
immediate neighborhood of the shops and from the homes to be erected
about them. It was, however, the intention so to limit the area of the town
that working men in the shops could buy homes at convenient distances
from the works, if they chose to do so, or could avail themselves of the
opportunity to rent homes from other people who should build in the
vicinity.

Accordingly, the present location was selected, and there was gradually
planned and constructed the present town of Pullman. In carrying out the
general purpose every care was taken in making perfect sanitary conditions by a water supply and an extensive and scientific system of sewerage;
paved and well-lighted streets and open places, properly ornamented with
trees and shrubbery, all of which are kept in perfect repair and cleanliness
by the company at its own expense. All the improvements, such as drainage, sewerage, paving, gas and water pipes preceded the population, or
were put in when the houses and shops were built. Brick homes were built
for 1,700 families. They are provided with all modern improvements, and

every house and flat, even the cheapest in rent, is equipped with modern appliances of water, gas and internal sanitation. The sewerage from the houses and shops is taken to a reservoir under the water tower, holding 300,000 gallons, and is pumped as fast as received to a sewerage farm three miles south of the town.

The merchandising of the town is concentrated under the glass roof of a beautiful arcade building. A market-house was erected that is an ornament of one of the handsomest squares of the town.

Churches were built for the various denominations; a schoolhouse was erected in which there are attending over a thousand scholars; a library was founded with more than 8,000 volumes, and which has on its tables more than 100 of the current magazines and periodicals. A theatre was provided, which in design and construction will bear comparison with any building of the same class in our large cities, and a savings bank was established, paying a liberal rate of interest and conforming in its regulations to the greatest convenience of the wage-earner. As a result of these developments, Pullman is a perfectly equipped town of 12,000 inhabitants, built out from one central thought to a harmonious whole, where all that is discordant or demoralizing is eliminated, and where all that inspires to self-respect, thrift and economy and to cleanliness of person and thought is generously provided. The primary object has always been to keep the atmosphere of the place pure and wholesome, morally as well as physically, and filled with incentives to hope and progress, and yet, at the same time, to move in no manner toward anything like an encroachment upon the absolute independence of the individual.

Main gate of the works at noon.

Living under the influence of these conditions, the Pullman workman has a distinct value which is recognized by manufacturers elsewhere. There is, as a matter of fact, hardly a great producing center in this country in the fields covered by the Pullman industries to which Pullman men have not been brought by special inducements of promotion or wages. This fact speaks for itself, as do the further facts that the wage-earners at Pullman have on deposit in the savings bank more than $500,000, and about 600 of them have invested their savings in the purchase of homes in the vicinity.

The company has not now, and never has had, any interest whatever in the business of any of the stores or shops in the town. They are rented to outside parties, free from any control of the company. The people living in the town are entirely free to buy where they choose, and, as a matter of fact, the large disbursements in wages at Pullman, amounting to an average of $2,300,000 a year, have created a great competition for the trade of Pullman in the small surrounding towns as well as in Chicago, the natural result of which would be to bring the prices of all merchandise down to a minimum.

The conditions established and maintained at Pullman, for the health, comfort and well-being of the working men who live there have received official recognition, in the Grand Medal and Diploma of Honor from the International Hygienic and Pharmaceutical Exposition, held in Prague, Austria, in 1896. The town of Pullman was considered in competition with the settlements created by Krupp, the gun manufacturer; Stumm, the great maker of steel, and Baron Ringhofer, and the international jury gave Mr. Pullman the highest award.[2]

Concerning the great industry which this prosperous village indicates, anyone who attempted a detailed description of these shops would need to begin with and trace all raw material to its final abiding place, which, of course, is beyond the scope of any brief account. There are various raw materials used, such as lumber, iron, brass, flax, flat glass, and so on, and the career of each is far removed from the other. The way of lumber is through planing rooms, a trimming department, where as many as sixty different wood-turning and dressing machines are employed, on through paint shops, stencil ornamenting departments, wood carving studios, and finally, for the better class of woods, into the hands of the expert inlayer.

The progress of raw iron is through numerous smelting rooms and foundries, the hammer shop, blacksmith shop and iron machinery shop, where, among the three hundred machines at work, and some which prepare iron for every available use. Car wheels, car axles, car springs, bolts, bars and chains, the fine screws and ornamental wrought-iron trimmings, all are made here in some department from the pig and scrap iron with which a great yard in one portion of the grounds is heaped.

Flax and cotton have a widely different course, the usual machinery of the New England cotton mill being employed. Indeed, the knitting and weaving here is on a scale not often reached by New England manufacturers. All of the 2,408 Pullman cars have to be supplied with linen of various kinds, and rush of work is constant. This also is supplemented by the largest laundry in the world, where not only the new cloth, but all the soiled linen, of the Pullman cars is returned to be cleaned.

No point of interest would be scored by recounting the details of the forty departments where branches of the great task are forwarded. Here and there an incident must suffice, with several special references to the more curious and expensive plants.

One of the most interesting points is the manufacture of paper car wheels, with which the Pullman cars are equipped. This is a branch which occupies a number of buildings. One hundred and fifty thousand of these wheels have been made already and are in use, and at present about 300 men are constantly employed turning out 12,000 wheels a year. Impracticable as the idea sounds from the name, it is yet very feasible. The wheel really consists of a paper core, or center, enclosed between two steel boiler plates one-fourth of an inch thick. These circular boiler plates are given an iron hub, and a steel tire, and look, when completed, very much like the ordinary wheel. The paper used is simply good strawboard, such as forms the basis for book covers, but it is crushed into solid slabs by hydraulic presses of 3,000 pounds pressure to the square inch. The improvement is in soft running and increased durability, the life of one of the wheels being 500,000 miles.

Another interesting section is that devoted to electroplating, the need of which gives employment to several hundred men. Here all metal trimmings used in cars, such as curtain rods, brackets, pumps, cuspidors, locks, hinges, sash trimmings, door knobs and other odds and ends, are plated as required. It is curious to note that all these things are made by the company for its own use in the electroplating laboratory, which is capable of executing every kind of plating known in galvanoplastic art. Excellent curtain rods are made here from good three-quarter-inch gas pipe. The method involves cutting the pipe to the proper length and then smoothing and polishing it on emery wheels. These lengths are then dipped in melted tin and sheets of silver foil are wrapped about them, and made to adhere closely by carefully passing hot soldering irons over it. The silver is then properly burnished. Brass and bronze trimmings, already polished, also come here from the company's foundry, for electroplating.

The art is followed according to the most scientific method known for depositing gold and silver upon less precious metals. The visitor may see beautiful metallic mirror frames bronzed, silvered or gilded. All the metal trappings of a car are rapidly put into good order within the shortest space of time, a day being sufficient to rebronze, silver or gild the trappings of a dozen Pullmans, newly arrived for repair.

The glass industry of Pullman is carried on in the third and fourth stories of the Water Tower, where seventy-five operatives are employed. Here the naked glass of commerce is taken and made into the beautiful forms in which it is found in the palace cars. Of the 600 square feet of glass in every Pullman, 116 square feet is mirror, and 100 more embossed, all of which is prepared in this department. The ordinary glass is received here and prepared by methods common to the best glass manufactories in the country. The work of grinding, bevelling, cutting and silvering is done with machinery similar to that in use everywhere. The silver used is purchased in the form of crystals of the nitrate, which are here dissolved to obtain the liquid. What is known as cut-bevelling is also done in the highest style of the art.

The hammer shop is another point of interest if one does not mind the roar of machinery and the blaze and heat of the incandescent iron, which is beaten into various appropriate forms. This structure is built of iron, and employs 200 men. There are ten steam hammers, ranging from 750 pounds to 5 tons in weight, to the stroke and square inch. There are also twelve heating furnaces. Here 200 car axles are forged a day, and about 25 tons of other iron material, such as equalizing bars, couplers, brakes, and so on. About 100 tons of select wrought scrap iron is used. A feature of the place (more conspicuous here than in other departments of the works, owing to the constant and general need of lifting great weights) is the system of compressed air lifters. No man need lift even an ordinary weight, if he objects, for compressed air lifters are always within his reach, and can be attached and made to do the lifting, by the small labor of attaching the claws and hooks which they carry.

Special mention might thus be given to the iron machine shop, with its 106 machines and 200 men, the knitting mills with six floors of rattling machines and 500 employees, and the lumber and iron yards. Vast as these are, they are of the kind found in dozens of other manufactories, though on a smaller scale.

Of more interest is the marble department, where 25 operatives of the most expert character are employed in preparing the fine stone which the company imports and manufactures to suit his needs. Italian marble, onyx, lapis lazuli and several other forms of precious stone are kept here in great quantity, and by the artisans cut and polished into such forms as the finer needs of the sleeping coaches demand.

One of the most remarkable mechanisms about this place is the great Corliss engine of 2,500 horse-power, which once ran the Centennial Exposition at Philadelphia. It is a simple condensing engine with the Corliss valve gear and cut-off adapted to a vertical engine. It was built in Providence, R. I., by the late Mr. George H. Corliss, in 1876, and required seven months in building. General U. S. Grant started the engine at Philadelphia, the late Dom Pedro, Emperor of Brazil, being also present and deeply interested in the engine. After watching the revolutions of the great fly-wheel for a few moments, Dom Pedro quietly remarked: "This beats our South American revolutions."

At the close of the exposition the engine was taken back to Providence, and was purchased by Mr. Pullman. It required a train of thirty-five cars to bring it to Pullman, where it was set up in its present place during the winter of '80 and '81, and was started here for the first time April 5, 1881, in the presence of a concourse of visitors. Miss Florence Pullman turned the valves which admitted the steam to the cylinders. The engine has been running successfully since that date. Its total weight is 700 tons.

All kinds of cars are built in Pullman—sleepers, parlor cars, passenger, mail and baggage, freight and street cars, the freight car shops being one of the larger branches of the yard. The building where the latter work is done is 1,350 feet long and nearly 200 feet in its widest part. Its floor area embraces 264,155 square feet, or six and one-third acres. It may be truly said of this shop that lumber goes in at one end unplaned and comes out freight cars at the other. Its every onward step is progress, for it is cut, planed, mortised and bored as it passes along, finally reaching the erecting rooms, where car-builders take it and build it into cars upon the trucks which have already been set in place for it. This work is paid for by piece wages. The capacity of this department is easily fifty cars a day, or a finished car for every twelve minutes of working time. To build these, 500 men and a large amount of machinery are employed. One hundred and thirty men control the machines, 270 labor in the erecting shops and 100 in the paint shops. All iron is furnished from the company's forges, and the whole work is expedited by having parallel tracks which furnish standing room for 100 cars, so that while fifty are building on one track, laborers can distribute lumber and iron for fifty more along the vacant track. On the following morning the builders transfer to the new track and erect the cars, the materials for which are all complete at the track side, ready for the setting up into car shape. At present about 15,000 freight cars of the various kinds—flat, box, barrel, poultry, refrigerator, stock, fruit, ore and caboose cars—are turned out annually, representing a cost of nearly $15,000,000.

When an order is received for a given number of passenger cars, it is accompanied by carefully prepared drawings of every detail and by specifications which even enumerate the quantity and quality of screws, nails, bolts, castings, trimmings, to be used. Those unfamiliar with this class of work would be astonished at the elaborate nature of the drawings, many of them full size, with all dimensions marked on them, so that no mistake may occur. Bills for material to fill the order are drawn on each department where they are manufactured. At the same time patterns of the iron and woodwork, to guide the foreman in laying out the work for the departments, are made and distributed. As speedily as possible departments are furnished with the raw and finished material called for in the bills.

As an illustration, the wood machine shop gets out from the rough lumber the exact number of pieces of every kind and form called for, and the blacksmith shop prepares the forgings required; the bolt department makes the exact number of bolts of various kinds and sizes, and the brass foundry fills its order for the necessary trimmings, which are taken in hand by the electroplating department and nickeled, silvered or gilded, as called for. The glass department cuts the glass, etches and silvers it when required, and makes and furnishes all the mirrors. When everything is ready, the prepared materials are delivered as needed at the compartment where the cars are to be erected. First, the bottom material, such as sills, floor joists, flooring, draft timbers and transoms, each arriving in turn, are taken in hand by the bottom builders. At the completion of the bottom of the car it is turned over to a new force of men, the body builders, who put up the framework and complete the body of the car, their work in detail consisting of setting posts, bracing, filling, belt railing, paneling and car-lining. The car is then taken by the roof builders, who apply the ceiling and moulding, and then the tinners put on the metal covering.

After careful inspection, the car is taken by the outside-work painters and is entered at the same time by the inside finishers, who put in and finish the nice inside woodwork, such as oak, ash, cherry and mahogany. The piping for heating and lighting is set in before the seats are placed in position. The inside finish also conceals the electric wires used and such pipes as supply gas.

When the inside woodwork is all in place (and some of this comprises exquisite carvings), the inside painters go over the entire interior woodwork, making the car ready for the trimmers, who place the bronze or plated trimmings upon doors, sash blinds and walls. The upholstering, draperies, seat coverings, carpets, etc., which have all been previously prepared, are now put in, and then the finishing touches are added by the equipment department, and the car is ready for delivery to its purchaser, to whom it is sometimes sent by special messenger. The same detail applies equally to Pullman sleepers, the only difference being that workmen of the first order of ability and trained in the peculiar mechanism of those cars are employed, a special department holding this work in rather exclusive bounds.

A completed Pullman.

As an industrial institution, the works have an interest which comes under the head of problems in social economics. It would have been easier, it would seem, and more in accord with the prevalent business policy, to have set the works down upon the cheapest land in the dreariest spot avarice could suggest and facility permit, and let the community of working-men gather near to the work, and take care of their communal life as best they might. Homestead and Deering and the thousand of poor, bleak mining and milling villages which now disgrace our national domain could as readily have been repeated here. Squalid cottages, unpaved streets, black, tumble-down stores and flaring oil lamps, sties and sloughs, and all the ruck and decay which make up the desolate hamlets in which many of the great industries of America are located, could have been repeated, and with no more complaint than is common at present.

But, from some motive or other, characterize it as you will, the builder of the works saw fit to build also a town to accompany it. He schemed it out that each detail should be in its proper place and proper proportion. The buildings for labor are not joined to the fireside. Home and shop and church and opera house and library and railway station are where each should be, and, instead of making a discord, they verify to the full the definition of him who said that "architecture is frozen music." Here the stores are as numerous as the population demands, the churches pay some regard to the souls which need transportation from sin to goodness; the theatre is adapted to the number of those who need hours of laughter and sentiment; the library fits the community intellectually, and the "saloon" is given all the representation it deserves in a civilized community, and that is none at all.

NOTES

"The Town of Pullman," *Ainslee's* 3 (March 1899): 189–200.

1. The Town of Pullman was named after George Mortimer Pullman (1831–97), American inventor and industrialist. Born in Brocton, New York, he left school at fourteen and learned cabinetmaking. In 1855 he went to Chicago where he became a successful construction contractor. Long interested in the problem of making railway journeys less fatiguing, he remodeled two day coaches into sleeping cars. In 1867 he founded the Pullman Palace Car Company. In 1881 he built the company town of Pullman, Illinois, for his employers. In 1894 the company became embroiled in a historic labor dispute, known as the Pullman Strike.

2. Baron Ringhofer Krupp was the German dynasty of steelmakers famous (or infamous) as the "Canon Kings." The steel-casting plant was established by Friedrich Krupp (1787–1826) in 1811, succeeded by his son Alfred Krupp (1812–87) and his grandson Friedrich Alfred Krupp (1854–1902).

2
An Important Philanthropy:
Prevention of Cruelty to Animals
Fine Work Done by the Society for the Prevention of Cruelty to Animals

INDIFFERENCE TO ANIMAL SUFFERING IS NOT CONFINED TO ANY CLASS OF society. The millionaire's carriage team, tortured by the checkrein drawn back to the last notch for style; the horse of the teamster, worn by a difficult day of toil, turned unclean into a miserable stall for the night, in order that a

Henry Bergh, founder of the Society for the Prevention of Cruelty to Animals.

little labor may be saved; the pack animals of the huckster, left unblanketed in the marketplace through long hours of the wintriest weather, as well as

the overloaded and overdriven equine slaves of the expressman, all empha-
size the truth that no class is free from the sin of indifference to the
sufferings of brute creation.

The cow-dealer, unmindful of the suffering of his stock for want of
being milked, gives them no relief until sold; the poultry-seller, to econo-
mize space, crowds his live stock into crates so closely that many die of
suffocation; the butcher, to enhance the price of veal a few pennies, inflicts
untold agony upon the calf by slowly bleeding the animal to death, to
whiten the flesh; and even the small boy with the bean-shooter, mangles
and breaks the limbs of sparrows and pigeons, while society looks on, quite
unawakened to feeling in the matter—so long has the cruelty continued
unarraigned.

Trapping birds for their plumage, to be used for ornamental purposes;
keeping live turtles, with fins pierced and tied behind the back, in this
unnatural position for many hours until sold; exposing live canaries for
sale in the streets in cold weather; leaving gold fish to suffer in sunlight
which they cannot endure, or to die in stale water; setting dogs to worry
and kill cats—how much of all this wanton cruelty ever strikes the mind of
the average person as cruelty at all? Most people have never given the
matter a thought, and so are guilty of nothing more than intellectual tor-
pidity. When they think at all on the subject it is that every horse is well fed
and well groomed, that every dog has a kindly master, and every cat a
cheery hearth to lie before, and that all lesser forms are similarly provided
for as pets of humanity.

Yet there is another side. What would they think of the fact that thirty-
six thousand dogs are picked up every year homeless and hungry in
Greater New York alone; that fifty-five thousand cats are also gathered in,
all homeless and most of them starving; that ninety-one thousand of such
creatures were humanely destroyed in the year 1898 because there was
truly no shelter for them on earth. Among those patient servants of men,
the horses, nearly four thousand were released by aid of law from service
under pitiless masters because they were sick and disabled, and it was
criminal to work them longer without rest. There were three thousand two
hundred horses, mules and other large animals, not included in the first
number, found by agents of the law to be disabled past recovery, and so
humanely destroyed. Not only was this true, but five hundred and thirteen
men were publicly prosecuted in the courts of the city and state for such a
variety of inhuman actions as precludes the listing of them here—almost
enough to cause unbelief in the charity of humanity.

Men were brought up for starving horses, for driving them when so aged,
lame and decrepit that they could scarcely walk, for beating them mer-
cilessly when they had fallen under burdens too great to be further borne.
There were fines imposed where men cut animals with knives, beat them

**Agents of the society examining suffering
mules used on the canal path.**

with clubs, dragged them over the ground with ropes, left them unsheltered
in bitter cold weather, and burned them, in the case of smaller animals, with
lighted oil. One man (if he deserves the appellation) was fined for cutting a
horse's tongue out; a woman for throwing, in a fit of spleen, an unoffending
dog out of a fourth-story window; a drover for neglecting to water a carload
of cattle for so long that some of them died. The entire five hundred and
thirteen offenses read like the acts of barbarians and had but one grain of
consolation; they were exposed. The age is not so bad in which men are
prosecuted for so offending against animals. Not so many centuries ago
they practiced these cruelties upon one another, and there was no society for
the prevention of cruelty to animals to care or to interfere.

And now, when you come to consider, it is equally a wonderful and
beautiful thing to know that there is such an organization. Yet when one
man entered the field single-handed against all the brutality of a nation he
was laughed at as an enthusiast, ignored as a reformer, scorned as a med-
dler and notoriety seeker, and even jeered at as a fool. Yes, kind-hearted
Henry Bergh suffered all these indignities and did good despite them, and
that is why the Society for the Prevention of Cruelty to Animals exists at
all.[1]

The society is an educational and practical affair, incorporated under the
laws of the State of New York. It is wholly humanitarian in its motives, and
depends entirely upon voluntary subscriptions, donations and bequests.
Five hundred and more members contribute annually to the support of its

work, and it draws from bequests and legacies a modest annual sum, all of which is spent in the prosecution of its object. Last year it spent over $128,000 on behalf of suffering animals.

In the prosecution of its work this society has in constant use three large ambulances for the removal of disabled animals. It has also eight smaller ambulances, especially constructed for the removal of sick, injured and homeless small animals. Besides its permanent quarters at Madison avenue and Twenty-sixth street, it maintains an ambulance house at 111 and 113 East Twenty-second street, and a shelter for animals at One Hundred and Second street and East River, New York; an office at 13 Willoughby street, an ambulance house at 114 Lawrence street, a shelter for animals at the corner of Malbone street and Nostrand avenue, Brooklyn, and a shelter for animals on Wane street, Stapleton, Borough of Richmond. In the Greater City of New York it maintains a uniformed force of twenty salaried special agents, and in other parts of the state it has one hundred and seventy-five volunteer agents. Twenty horses and a large corps of men are employed in the New York ambulance service alone.

This peculiar and voluntary service now grown so powerful that it operates more and more effectually every year to reduce cruelty to animals has not sprung up in a day. During twenty-two years ending in 1888, the late Henry Bergh, was the heart as well as the head of an organized effort for the protection of animals, which had scarcely adequate means of subsistence from year to year.

Mr. Bergh's idea of reform in this field came to him during his stay in Russia, where he had been sent in 1862 as Secretary of Legation at St. Petersburg. While in Russia he found himself, on several occasions, constrained to interfere in cases of atrocious cruelty to animals, and but for his official position he would have been exposed to personal violence. His attention thus once directed to the subject of humanity to the brute creation, he gave the subject much thought. While in London, on his return trip, he chanced to meet the Earl of Harrowby, the President of the Royal Society for the Prevention of Cruelty to Animals. This nobleman gave him much valuable information concerning the operation of that society in England; and not finding any effort in this direction under way in America Mr. Bergh undertook the matter on his return, beginning by delivering a lecture in Clinton Hall in which he pleaded the cause with such force of argument, and such warmth and eloquent conviction that expressions of sympathy and offers of assistance were freely made by persons in attendance.[2] The press then lent its powerful aid, the lecture was published in whole or part in all the great cities of this country, and public sentiment aroused. He then organized the society, and on April 10, 1866, incorporated it.

There is no question but that this man was the whole movement individualized. He framed the first law ever enacted in this country for the protection of animals, by which he provided that "every person who shall, by his act of neglect, maliciously kill, maim, wound, injure, torture, or cruelly beat any horse, mule, cow, cattle, sheep, or other animal, belonging to himself or another, shall upon conviction, be adjudged guilty of a misdemeanor." He then went about the work of practically forcing the issue, and though others aided, he was the spirit of the thing, and his law remained, and still remains, the one force back of the institution. It has been supplemented in a slight degree but never modified.

In Mr. Bergh's plan there were four distinct and clearly marked purposes: First, to educate the people and rouse the public and private conscience; second, to procure efficient legislation; third, to extend the influence of this society throughout the state and, so far as possible, throughout the world, but more particularly on the American continent; fourth, to establish the society itself on a strong and permanent basis. And he accomplished them. He roused the public by personally interfering in cases of brutality. He would rush in where a driver was beating a horse and arrest the offender. It was his aim to attract as much attention to himself as possible. The society had no prestige. It depended on him to give it that, and so he made himself a public character, that the society might draw strength and repute from him. In interfering it was his wont to make as much to-do as possible, and if no newspaper men were about to see it he would accompany the offender to the police station and then hurry back to his office and write a long account of the "vigorous action of Mr. Henry Bergh yesterday," and sent it off post-haste to all the papers. More, he appeared in the courts as chief witness, and never lost an opportunity to wrangle with the judge when such conduct would enliven interest in the case. If a decision were rendered against him he was as apt as not to burst forth in a tirade, declaring the court to be ignorant of the law, partial, indifferent and what not, until he was likely to be incarcerated for contempt. Farther, he would write letters on the subject to the newspapers, complaining of the action of the offending judge and pleading eloquently for public approval of his course.

When he died, in 1888, the society was still what it had been for twenty-two long years—a one-man society. It had grown in prestige under him, had bought and occupied a building, had been the cause of the foundation of sixty-four societies in North America, seventeen of which were branches, but all were in a crude state. The employees of the society, including its clerical staff, and its paid agents in all parts of the state, were only seventeen in number. The material equipment consisted of one single, old-fashioned ambulance which was kept in a shed and when used was drawn by hired horses. There was no shelter at which to receive lost or strayed animals, and there were no appliances for their humane destruction in case of necessity. No library of reference had been collected, though this had been contemplated in the charter of the society, and was earnestly desired by Mr. Bergh. Neither had the society any means of publishing humane literature, and in point of fact published nothing but its annual report. These things were only being contemplated by him as important needs when he fell at his post.

Within four years of his death a removal of headquarters was found necessary; and in 1894 the enormous shelter work which looks after 100,000 animals, small and large, every year, was undertaken. The licensing of dogs was turned over to the society by the state legislature as a perquisite, and an additional force to look after this was employed. Two ambulance houses were built in New York, where these vehicles for the removal of large and small animals are kept. In 1895 one was built in Brooklyn. Fast horses were secured, and a corps of efficient men, trained like firemen, were put in charge. The arrangements for quick harnessing and speedy departure are exactly the same as in fire-houses. The places are equipped with telegraph, telephone and fire-alarm service, and everything is kept in readiness so that an ambulance may quickly be turned to a scene of disaster.

The shelters for animals are quite the most notable features of the great humane work as it stands to-day, and are interestingly equipped. They were made necessary by acts of the legislature, which committed all homeless and strayed animals to the care of the society.

In the shelters now provided, everything for the comfortable maintenance of the animals, as well as apparatus for their painless destruction, is present. There are stalls for horses and cattle, cages for small animals including fowls, excellent equipment for surgical operations, and a destruction oven, into which the animals enter when society no longer provides for their existence.

This oven represents a peculiar idea. It is very much like the oven of a stove, and contains a wire cage set within a sheet-iron pan, both of which are removable. Whenever a number of small animals are to be disposed of, they are placed together, as many as a dozen, in the wire cage, which is then set into the sheet-iron pan. The latter is introduced into the oven and the door locked. All vents are then closed, and ordinary illuminating gas is gradually introduced until the animals become drowsy and fall into sleep, when the full measure is turned on and death made sure.

The use of the wire crate becomes more apparent when the oven is opened and the pan removed, for then it is seen that the crate is intended for a light carrying purpose, the bodies being transferred in it to their final resting place.

In these shelters are stored a wide variety of animal food, each creature being fed upon that which is most suited to it. The sheds and pens are always open for inspection, and many an animal has been saved from an untimely grave by this wise provision. The society is not an insatiable slayer of the helpless, but endeavors by every means to cure the injured and find homes for the homeless. Chance shows itself here in its most unvarnished form, for, if a dog or cat be particularly handsome, it is liable to be picked out by some visitor as a pet, and so have its length of life extended. All are kept for a reasonable period, and if by good fortune any one has the qualities which attract the lover of home pets it will not die.

The manner in which these numerous creatures are gathered in is simple enough. The headquarters of the society contains chambers very much like a police station, where the score of uniformed members of the humane force report. This force is stationed about the city like policemen, and they have equal power of arrest. One is always in evidence at the crowded crossing where Broadway and Twenty-third street meet. Another is to be found at Union Square, a third at Printing House Square, and so on, wherever the danger is greatest. These men patrol the city and are in the truest sense special officers.

They are supplemented, however, by the entire police force of the city, whose duty it is to note cases of brutality to animals, make arrests and prefer charges; and in turn both forces are aided by humane citizens, who frequently call upon officers to make arrests in cases of cruelty. In the absence of an officer, the name and address of the offender, the name, address, and number marked on the vehicle, and a note of the time and place of the occurrence are usually telephoned to the society, which then details an officer to investigate and arrest if necessary.

It is remarkable to note the deep interest taken in the work by children of tender age. Daily, homeless cats and dogs, which have been rescued from vicious youths or picked up from the streets and gutters, are brought to the headquarters of the society by small boys and girls. Parents have frequently informed the society that because of the wish of their little child they desire to invoke its aid for some helpless creature. So evident has this humanity of children become that after years of observation the officers of the society venture the belief that "the civilizing work of animal protection can be safely intrusted to the rising generation of the nineteenth century."

Altogether the service has grown so that now over fifty thousand cases are annually investigated, though the prosecutions have sunk in number to five hundred and thirteen. The comparison between these two figures is the most hopeful showing which the society can make. Since 1895 the cases of prosecution have steadily decreased from nine hundred and fifty-two to five hundred and thirteen.

The wisdom of the courts, together with the general awakening of the people to a sense of the ease with which brutality may be stopped, has brought about a wholesome fear among the ill-dispositioned, and so prosecutions have grown fewer. It is surprising, however, to note the amount and range of cruelty still inflicted. The number of horses which are saved from cruel suffering every year amounts to nearly seven thousand.

From the rat, trapped and inhumanly tortured to death, to the unblanketed horse, shivering in the wintry wind, or the humblest fowl, foot-bound and half smothered in a crate, extends the range of this society's beneficence. The sick horse left all night in an open field exposed to the inclemency of the weather is not always forgotten to-day. A drove of milch cows ill-stalled in an unventilated and filthy stable moved the society to vigorous prosecution. It has fined one man for ruthlessly kicking an inoffensive cat, and another for beating a dog without provocation. An individual who sought amusement in fastening a heavy iron weight about a goat's neck with a cord, and compelling it to run about stumbling, as it often did, came to grief through the society's agency. It has punished more than one official dog-catcher in towns throughout the state for cruelty, and has prosecuted scores of butchers and poultrymen for ignoring the comfort of cattle and poultry when carrying them to market.

Yet the society is not in its powerful individuality a martinet. Discrimination is used, and only sound evidence acted upon.

The officers of the society are beginning to realize that its work must be more and more educative. A reduction in the annual number of prosecutions might mean not so much an improvement as a development of caution. Hence they are setting themselves to the labor of disseminating sentiments of humanity among all classes of the community, so as not only to prevent the commission of specific acts of cruelty, but to make cruelty itself odious. To this end a library has been established, and facilities for printing prepared. It is intended that the library shall be a collection containing all that pertains to knowledge of the animal world, as well as everything related in humanity and law to their care and protection. Already it contains a digest of every law of the United States and of the several states and territories, and also of the decisions of the Supreme Court of the United States, and of the courts of last resort in every state and territory of the Union, bearing upon the protection of animals. By its aid the society has been able to give valuable advice and assistance to other societies and humane persons in every part of the country. The library's collection of medical works, which is equally apropos, is also large.

The society's president, Mr. John P. Haines, who was induced to take charge of the work, upon Mr. Bergh's death in 1888, is a man not only sincerely humane in sentiment, but a trained and active business man in the bargain. To his tact and ability nearly all of the society's rapid progress since 1888 is due. He found its work hampered by a poor system, and proceeded at once to improve it. It might truly be said that, before his arrival, there had been no system. Now, however, the affairs are so well arranged and the work so systematically laid out that delay and mistakes seldom, if ever, occur. By a system of card indexes, ledgers and letter-files he has made it possible to find the past record of any individual who has ever come to the notice of the society because of acts of brutality. This system is as accurate and as ready as the police records of Paris, and an old offender is never allowed to escape without having all his past misdeeds laid before the court.

Mr. Haines has also drawn to his aid everything of value in the way of legislation and the favor of the local metropolitan administration, so that he is aided by the departments of police and fire, and by the courts everywhere. He is not desirous of having the powers of the society arbitrarily extended, preferring rather to work under the law as prepared by his predecessor, which he considers sufficient for all just needs.

At present the society is flourishing because of the interest taken in it by the public. It has a large number of contributors and many influential and charitably disposed friends. Its new building is a handsome structure, not as large as the scope of the work would indicate, but splendidly equipped and capable of being extended with but very little trouble and expense. In course of time it will contain a great library and museum, and otherwise be made more and more public in character. All connected with it are justly proud of its appearance. What it stands for has been well expressed by its president and may here be repeated for the nobility of the intentions involved—that is, "a testimony, a lesson, and a declaration to the people of the land; a testimony to the sacred law of universal justice which forbids the unrighteous torture or abuse of any sentient creature of God; a lesson of God's law of mercy and compassion to all creatures, great and small; and a declaration and advertisement that this society intends, with God's help, to prosecute the work it has undertaken until every habitation of cruelty shall be banished from the land, and the principle of justice and mercy to our humbler fellow creatures shall be as deeply graven on the hearts of the American people as their love of liberty."

Notes

"An Important Philanthropy," *Demorest's* 35 (July 1899): 215–17.

1. Henry Bergh (1811–88), founder of the American Society for the Prevention of Cruelty to Animals. In 1875, with Elbridge T. Gerry and others, he also founded the Society for the Prevention of Cruelty to Children.

2. Clinton Hall, a lecture hall, was named in the memory of De Witt Clinton (1769–1828), mayor of New York City and governor of New York, known for his literary, scientific, and philanthropic contributions.

3

It Pays to Treat Workers Generously

John H. Patterson Says That, Even from a Wholly Selfish Standpoint, It Is Best for an Employer to Devote Money and Effort to the Promotion of the Physical and Intellectual Welfare of His Employees

KINDERGARTENS, COOKING SCHOOLS, MAGIC LANTERN ENTERTAINMENTS, morning glory vines and vegetable gardens are not usually looked upon as necessary adjuncts to a successful factory, and yet John H. Patterson, the wealthy president of the National Cash Register Company, advocates these as the only true means of success. He expressed his views on this subject in answer to the question, by a representative of *Success:*—

"Do you consider existing relations between employers and employed in the United States satisfactory?"

"Those relations," replied Mr. Patterson, "are not only unsatisfactory, but it is impossible that they can continue."

"Why?"

"The money made in manufacturing has been made largely, if not altogether, because conditions were unusually favorable. In the early stages of manufacturing, the demand exceeded the supply, labor was abundant, and wages low, and fortunes were rapidly amassed. Conditions have changed. The supply and demand, in many lines of industry, is more nearly equalized, and the man who would succeed must make the best use of all his resources."

"What are these resources?"

"The resources are the materials which compose his product, the machinery and tools by which they are converted, the men he employs, and the markets of the world. Manufacturers have generally become alert to the importance of developing all these resources, except the men they employ. The manufacturer has expected that this resource would develop itself. Curiously enough, manufacturers have maintained an attitude of antagonism toward this, the important element in the problem of success. They have not seemed to realize that in the men they employ lie unlimited possibilities of profit."

"But, after all, isn't that a rather selfish view to take of the employer's attitude toward his employee?"

"It is a selfish view, as all views are. It is not a question whether we will be selfish or unselfish, but whether in the pursuit of our ends we move along right lines. If we do this, we will find that we cannot better ourselves without bettering those about us. That sounds like a Sunday school precept, but in reality it is one of the first principles of business. The trouble is that employers have sought to secure a profit from their employees, without helping the latter to profit by the arrangement. The manufacturer may be able to do this when not competing with some other manufacturer who has a better way; but, when a system, which is now being developed, has been perfected, by which the employer and the employee work in harmony, progress together, and each thereby receives a continually increasing profit, the old system will be forced out of business."

THE PRESENT RELATIONSHIP

"Now the reason why the present relationship between employer and employee is not satisfactory is because the employee, on the one hand, is not receiving all of the benefits which his labor should produce for him, and because the employer, in failing to provide opportunities for the employed to become better employees, is depriving himself of more efficient labor."

"What do you mean by a better man?"

"As a man's sympathetic knowledge of the world increases; that is, as he knows more of the world, and learns to recognize in it the elements of progress and feels in himself a growing desire to assist, he becomes a better man. As his perception of the beautiful and his love for it grows, he becomes a better man. As his feeling of happiness and content increases day by day, he becomes a better man. Therefore, whatever the employer can do to promote the knowledge of the world, the love of the beautiful, the feeling of content among his employees makes of them better men."

"And better workmen?"

"Everything I have ever done to make a better man has given me a better workman."

"What methods, do you think, can be inaugurated in the average factory which would make better men of the employees?"

"I can answer that best by first pointing out some mistakes that are made. One of the greatest errors in the present system is the operation of a factory through the medium of a superintendent, or single directing head.

However small the business, it can, in my opinion, be best conducted through a system of committees, which act as assistants and consulting boards to the general manager. Every department should have its committee chosen from time to time from among the most efficient workmen in the department. This offers an added incentive to the men to become efficient. All these committees should meet together as often as possible to consult over the best methods of making the departments supplement each other, and to advise with the general manager as to improvement of the whole service. In this way, as these committees are composed at one time and another of the different employees, a general knowledge of the business, its significance and requirements is disseminated throughout the factory. In this way, the men do not work like blind tools fastened to a bench, but knowing to what general end their effort tends, and hence their interest is increased."

"More than that, their mental caliber and general knowledge is increased, and this naturally tends to make them better men."

"Yes."

"Another error is the manner in which the ideas of the employees are repressed. Every intelligent man thinks to some purpose, and his ideas are worth something. Every workman, though he may not be a wise man in other ways, for lack of education and opportunities, may have ideas which, if developed, would work improvement in the particular line of his labor. Yet, if the average workman has an idea and wishes to present it, he is met with a rebuff, because of the peculiar and unnatural air of suspicion that pervades the factory. The 'bosses' seem bent more upon keeping the men in their so-called places, those under them still under them, and by all means preserving their own supremacy and irritable authority, than of using all the forces employed by the factory for its best interest. In reality, every effort should be made to familiarize all the workmen with every detail of the business, to encourage their inventive and executive powers, and to furnish them every opportunity of expressing whatever ideas they may have for improvement along any line. Convenient receptacles should be placed throughout the factory where anybody can deposit signed suggestions, knowing that they will be considered and used, if possible. There should be a system of rewards by which every man will receive a proper recompense for his ideas."

"What do you consider a just system of rewards?"

DON'T CHEAT EMPLOYEES!

"It can only be considered in one way, that is that rewards given shall be just. A man who introduces such a system as this into his factory with the hope of cheating his employees; the man who thinks there may be profit in harmony, proving the men will take the harmony and leave him the profit, would wreck his business in the attempt. Such men must live or die by the present system. It has been built up by them, and is best suited to their peculiar abilities. The man, however, who will exercise justice and pay to the employee who volunteers an idea what he can afford to pay to an inventor, or to any man with ideas to sell, will find that it works to his profit also.

"Another mistake made lies in the employer keeping himself far removed from the life of the employed. It may seem radical to say that the employer should interest himself in and assist in the direction of all the affairs of those who work for him. I do not mean that he should interfere arbitrarily, but that he should be able to offer such suggestions and inaugurate such plans as would be readily received and followed by the people of their own free will, and provide them a life of pleasure and profit. Your average employer holds that he is the employer, and not the employed, solely on account of his superior ability. If that is true, his greater ability should give him the wisdom necessary to so influence the lives of those of less ability about him that they will acquire more ability and receive the benefit of his wisdom. The necessities of the future are going to demand this evidence of the employer's ability. The time will come when a man who is not able to broaden and strengthen the capacities of his employees,

Homes of Mr. Patterson's employees

and lift them a little nearer to his own level, will fail in direct commercial competition with those who can."

"Under any circumstances, Mr. Patterson, don't you think the employees would resent any interference with their private life?"

"I have heard that question before. It is an argument by which many employers seek to justify their indifference or neglect, or it may be their indifference. Let us get away from the theory and see. If a manufacturer builds an auditorium in his factory, or fits up a hall near by, and brings, say on Monday night, explorer Stanley, to speak of his travels; on Tuesday night, Burton Holmes, with his calcium light lecture on foreign lands; Wednesday night, provides some pleasant entertainment from the best local talent of his neighborhood; Thursday night, spreads a dinner for those who wish to come, followed by decent and friendly social intercourse; Friday night, turns the hall over to the young people for a dance; Saturday night, brings some woman exponent of things interesting and improving to women, and on Sunday night, a preacher with ideas,—can he be said to be seriously interfering with the private life of his employees?"[1]

"Not at all if it is wholly optional with them whether they come or not."

"I am willing to allow that shall be as optional as it is with any of us whether we shall be decent. The man who seizes his opportunity and improves in any community or walk of life prospers. The man who doesn't fails. I wouldn't discharge a man who took no part in these entertainments, but show me the man who, lacking the knowledge which these things would give him, and sympathy for the pleasure of others, ignores them, and I will show you the man who can't long work in my factory."

An Undesirable Employee

"I thought you said you wouldn't discharge him."

"Neither would I simply because he failed to attend. But eventually such a man would do poorer work in comparison with those who were interesting themselves in those things and progressing in efficiency. So I have grounds for feeling that he could not work long in my factory, no more than he could survive creditably in any progressive community."

"In what other ways do you think you could influence the lives of employees for the better?"

"One of the best ways, and one which is most completely ignored, is through their families, if they have any. In every factory community, there are hordes of idle and unruly boys. They are not idle because they are inactive, but because there is no way provided for a profitable employment of their energy which is inviting to them. At the same time, in the neighborhood of most factories, there are either vacant lots, or tracts of land which could readily be secured and divided into gardens and offered to the boys free for their cultivation. Give them the profits of their labor, and also offer rewards for those who shall secure the best results. Engage some one to instruct them in gardening, who knows how to get along with boys, and you will materially change the moral atmosphere of your community without violating the private rights of anybody. Can you fancy that the mothers and fathers of these boys will be indifferent, or that it will not touch the inside of the house in a gentle, improving way?"

A KINDERGARTEN

"It does not cost much to establish a kindergarten, and the presence of one in a factory community which offers itself free to all the infants of the neighborhood is not a menace to personal liberty. The workman, however, who would prevent his children from attending, and preferably leave them to hang as a wearisome load upon his wife all day for fear that his rights were being infringed, would not be a good employee in any factory in competition with those taking advantage of such things."

"You take great interest in improving the appearance of the homes and landscape of your community."

"Yes, I do, and it is possible that in that respect I have interfered more than in any other way with the personal rights of the people. We have made it almost impossible for a man to live in this community and neglect his premises. At first I met with a strange and unaccountable opposition in my efforts to get the people in the neighborhood of the factory to beautify their yards, or even to keep them clear of rubbish heaps. Morning-glory seeds are cheap. I bought several hundred packages of these, and induced a few to plant them. I had pictures taken of all the unsightly yards and spots about the neighborhood. These were converted into lantern slides and exhibited with appropriate comments wherever the people congregated. This created a storm of indignation, but in doing this I was exercising the privilege of any citizen. It had its good results."

A VERITABLE GARDEN

"Little by little, the offensive places were cleaned up, and a smoky, disreputable region has become a veritable garden. There are no people about here now who would tear down the vines and litter up their yards. They take a pride in the appearance of the community, and instead of my having to urge further improvement, I am only occasionally called in to assist."

"Do you think all manufacturers should do this?"

"What do you think?" said Mr. Patterson.

Subsequently he said, after viewing all the beautiful gardens about: "I believe it will pay any manufacturer to build a beautiful building which lets in plenty of sunlight, to lay out gardens and grounds about it, and introduce every ornament and device which utility will permit. It is as easy to have chairs with backs as to have stools, and as easy to have footrests for all as to have none. It requires no more time for the employees to eat in a cheerful, airy dining room than at their work-littered tables. Handsome free baths, pleasingly decorated walls, clean floors, growing plants, and fresh laundried aprons and sleeves can be easily furnished free by any manufactory, and are good business investments. They pay in added good will, conserved energy of those that work, and a general activity on the part of those who work under pleasing and satisfying surroundings."

A Paying Investment

"More than this, the manufacturer who adds to the departments of his business a kindergarten, manual training school, cooking school, gymnasium, and a system of educational and social features, makes of his enterprise a well-working and self-improving machine, and will add more to his capital than any system based on retrenchment and cheap labor possibly could."

Notes

"It Pays to Treat Workers Generously: John H. Patterson," *Success* 2 (16 September 1899): 691–92. Reprinted as "The Generous Treatment of Workmen—It Pays: A Practical Demonstration" in *Talks with Great Workers,* 165–73.

1. Sir Henry Stanley (1841–1904) was an Anglo-American explorer of Africa. Born as John Rowlands, in Wales, he at the age of fifteen sailed as a cabin boy on a vessel bound for New Orleans, where he met Henry M. Stanley, who adopted him and gave his name to him. Having completed many successful explorations to Africa, he was knighted in 1899.

4

Delaware's Blue Laws

THE CASUAL VISITOR TO WILMINGTON OR DOVER, IN DELAWARE, OR TO Georgetown, in the southern part of the state, will occasionally encounter a public exhibition of legal punishment which is unparalleled for curiosity and historic interest, and remains unmatched by any other form of punishment now administered within the union. In each of these three places are

Fifteen Stripes for Stealing Five Dollars.

to be seen a pillory and a whipping post, such as were common in England during the eighteenth century, and flourished in the colonies up to the beginning of the present union. It is a form of punishment so interesting in its historic aspect, that every school child is familiar with it. The staples in which the wrists are fastened, when the lash is to be applied; the perforated

256

cross-beam, through which the hands are thrust, when public exposure be ordained—these are here as in the days when old John Winthrop ruled in Massachusetts, and Cotton Mather expounded the virtue of severity in dealing with human error.[1]

When court is holding in either of these three places—a legal process which occurs on an average four times a year—the general public is treated to a sight that seems not only to excite but wholly to satisfy the curiosity of those who love the brutal in the punishment of crime. At New Castle, which is the suburb of Wilmington, in which the northernmost pillory of the state is located, I saw a crowd of at least two hundred gathered to witness the lashing and pillorying of men who had been convicted of offenses covered by these penalties. The spectators gaped with wide-eyed interest, winced unanimously at each separate lash, smiled sometimes at the contortions of the victim, and laughed when his grimaces in torture seemed ludicrous. As each victim was led forth, his face was studied with careful interest. With each detail of fastening him safely to the post his crime was discussed. Usually he was condemned for his action, and many a "serves him right" was exchanged. When it was seen that the criminal was not physically incapacitated by the stripes received he was thought to be well off and deserving of no further care. Of the mental scars, stretching red across the sensibilities and finer feelings, the spectators took no thought. Of the influence which the contemplation of such a spectacle must have upon their own minds—not a thought.

Go into Delaware to-day and you will be invited by the barber, the waiter, and the hotel clerk, to witness this very antiquated form of punishment. By the very first servant that attended me I was so advised.

"They is to be a whipping at New Castle to-day, suh," said this colored citizen.

"A what?"

"A whipping, suh. We has the pillory and whipping post in this state."

"How often do they use it?" I asked.

"Every Friday, suh, when cote's in session."

"Then court's in session now?"

"Yes, suh."

I saw this same servant after witnessing the scene in question and inquired what he thought of it.

"I don't think so very much of it, suh," he replied.

"Don't you think it stops these people from doing the same thing over again?"

"No, suh, not any mo' than jail would. They is men here that has been whipped an' whipped until they is so hard they don't care no more foh it than foh a flea. It juss makes 'em wuss, I think."

Many others of more refined feelings expressed the same opinion, though in different terms. A judge in Dover said that he had his doubts on the subject, and the active head of a charitable institution at Wilmington expressed the belief that this mode of punishment was very far from solving the criminal problem, and added:

"Its strength with the people is due to the fact that it has always been here. Being customary they see virtues in it which do not exist. Increasing liberality will do away with it yet."

There is an opinion that this form of punishment is something new in Delaware, and that it has been revived because of modern moral thought and discussion. This is not true. Delaware is to-day what it always has been, the state of blue laws. It is the only one of the original thirteen, which retains largely intact the original code as formulated by the lawgivers a hundred years ago. Where Connecticut, Massachusetts and Rhode Island have allowed old stringencies of this character to become obsolete, Delaware still preserves them. It punishes as offenses against religion, morality, decency and justice many deeds ignored elsewhere.

We read that: "If any person shall perform any worldly employment, labor or business on the Sabbath day (works of necessity and charity excepted) he shall be fined four dollars; and on failure to pay such fine and costs shall be imprisoned for not exceeding twenty-four hours.

"If any person shall be guilty of fishing, fowling, horse-racing, cock-fighting or hunting game on the Sabbath day, he shall be fined four dollars, and on failure to pay such fine and costs shall be imprisoned as aforesaid.

"If any number of persons shall assemble to game, play or dance on the Sabbath day, and shall engage or assist in such game, play or dance, every such person shall be fined four dollars, and on failure to pay such fine and costs shall be imprisoned as aforesaid."

Under the section relating to offenses against public policy it is enacted that: "If any person shall pretend to exercise the art of witchcraft, conjuration, fortune-telling or dealing with spirits, he shall be fined not exceeding one hundred dollars and shall stand an hour in the pillory," to which is added the power to imprison for not exceeding one year. Such statements must certainly sound antiquated to the residents of every other state; but Delaware is peculiar in its old-fashioned attitude. It was only in 1893, that the law relating to the Badge of Crime was wiped off the books—a law which had its counterpart in the famous Massachusetts act, on which the romance of "The Scarlet Letter" was founded. This badge was none other than a striped jacket which the ex-convict was compelled to wear anywhere from one month to three years after his discharge from prison. Contrast this with the law in England where an ex-convict can recover damages from any person who publishes or otherwise publicly refers to his offense, once he has served his penalty, and you have a measure of the progress of the world in its attitude toward men and offenses—for England once enjoyed the jacket and the pillory—only some time before Delaware adopted it.

It is not strange, however, to find in the code containing these things provision for the pillory and the whipping-post. Burglary, arson, attempted rape and larceny are the crimes punishable by lashes, while forgery, perjury and many smaller offenses call for the public use of the pillory. On the first blush, this seems reasonable enough, seeing that burglary, arson and attempted rape are such heinous offenses; but in the execution of this law a result very different from that naturally suggested is worked out. The cases of large burglary, the cases of house firing or of attempted rape are exceedingly rare. It has been admitted by the Chief of Police of Wilmington, the leading criminal officer of the state, that there has never been but one attempt at bank burglary within the state, and that one proved unsuccessful. The court records, covering the entire state for three years past show not one case of arson or of attempted rape. Hence the burden of the law

New Stocks and Whipping Post at Chester.
Convicts being privately punished
by prison authorities for disobedience.

falls upon creatures committing petty larceny, and this may be readily proved to be true.

At Dover, the capital of the state, as well as the county seat of Kent County, the list of criminals convicted and punished in that county is complete and readily accessible. This discloses that dozens of men have been punished with periods of imprisonment and lashes not exceeding forty-five for stealing or attempting to steal sums of money ranging any-where from two to fifty dollars. Thus, on October 27, 1897, one Albert Gibbs was convicted of stealing two dollars and was sentenced to six months' imprisonment, given fifteen lashes and ordered to restore the stolen money before entering the world again. At the same time George Dennis received exactly the same imprisonment for stealing thirty dollars. A petty burglar, who stole seven dollars from a store at night, received two years in prison, twenty lashes at the whipping post, and one hour in the pillory. Also, he was compelled to return the money and pay all costs.

For the next year a very similar list is seen. Criminals stealing one, five and seven dollars were all whipped with many lashes, and some were exposed in the pillory. For the current year the record is quite the same, and yet the whipping post is kept busy and a certain public is entertained. If an important crime should be committed, no greater punishment could be administered, for the lashes are limited to forty-five and the pillory to a few hours.

There seems to be no public conception of this incongruity, although the stranger is quickly astonished by it. Any one convicted of one of these offenses, in petty or great degree, and either publicly pilloried or whipped is forever disfranchised and can no longer exercise the privileges of a citizen. Thus a youth caught in some early and thoughtless offense is permanently ruined in reputation and practically driven from the state. It is generally declared by those in authority throughout the state that the law is justifiable because it reaches and controls the negro.

"Ninety per cent. of the cases so disposed of," said the sheriff of one county, "are those involving negroes. It is the only way we have of reaching them."

Upon examination, this statement turned out to be only partially true, for negroes form less than seventy per cent. of the total number of cases so punished. There had been several instances in which white men, standing fairly well in the community, have been caught in the toils of the law, and finding themselves doomed to be whipped, have offered all their posses-sions, together with a promise to leave the state, if they could but be saved this wretched indignity. When ignored, they seem to have considered their life blasted and have departed never to return. Such men have paid a thousand times the penalty primarily supposed to exist in fifteen or forty public lashes. The case-hardened negro, or habitual criminal of any color, knows no such torment, and, comparatively, may be said to have received no punishment at all. It is the man with conscience and feeling upon whom this relic of an older order of civilization weighs unjustly. The hardened criminal whom it is supposed to reach does not suffer at all, and is not corrected thereby.

The whole penal system of the state is in a more or less chaotic condition, however, and this, as well as the pillory and whipping post, may be attributed to lack of public thought or study along corrective and charitable lines. The state jails have the qualities of old-time colony prisons. There is no penitentiary. There is no system of prison labor. There is no reform school. For important crimes the county jail at New Castle is selected because it is the largest and much the strongest; for the most trivial offenses the same prison is made to serve. Prisoners with ten-day sentences are mixed with those waiting execution and those who have a life-time to serve. Young and old, boys and gray-haired men, negroes and white, all are jumbled together, and the discrimination made is one which lacks import. It is that the short-term prisoners are allowed to do the small labor, such as cleaning, cooking, coal-carrying, rock-beating and the like in the open court or jail-yard, where stands the pillory, while the long-term convicts are not allowed to do anything at all. This is considered a fairly satisfactory arrangement, although a more modern work-house is sometimes talked of.

There are numerous arguments advanced for the maintenance of the present system, among which may be included that of the Chief of Police of Wilmington, Delaware's largest city, who holds that it reduces crime in the state to a minimum. "In the only bank burglary ever attempted," he says, "the men were punished with ten years' imprisonment, forty lashes, one hour in the pillory and a fine of five thousand dollars each. The term of imprisonment for which these robbers were sentenced did not trouble them in the least; but that portion of the sentence subjecting them to post and pillory struck them with horror, so much so that they offered twenty-five thousand dollars to have it remitted. But they had to submit and take the punishment. Afterwards they made their escape by breaking jail, and have since given the state wide berth.

"Instead of giving a prisoner convicted of larceny two, three or six years' imprisonment, as is done in other states, and keeping him at the public expense, we give him not less than five and no more than forty lashes, grading the punishment. We turn him loose at the expiration of his term, and the occurrence is rare indeed that he comes under the lash the second time. He either gives up his crime or else leaves the state.

"Long terms of imprisonment as punishment do not, to my mind, lessen crime or tend to reform the criminal when corporal punishment is not

included in his sentence. The fear of serving time has no terrors for him, as
the chances for escape are always considered favorable, or, at least, possible. But when he knows that corporal punishment is sure to come immediately after conviction from which there is no escape, he will hesitate
before committing a crime or seek some other locality in which to do his
work.

"As a matter of economy, an important feature of the subject under
consideration, the whipping post and pillory have saved our state large
sums of money by deterring criminals of other states from visiting us.

"Situated as we are between two large cities, Philadelphia and Baltimore, twenty-eight and seventy-two miles distant respectively, and
within three hours of New York City, we would be an easy prey for the
criminal classes of those cities were it not for this particular institution, for
which they all have a most wholesome dread. In fact, thieves passing
through our state, although having committed no crime within our borders,
are in terror until beyond our boundaries, the very atmosphere being unpleasant and uncongenial to them.

"I am well aware that this method of dealing with criminals is not in
good order with the citizens of other states. We are called barbarous,
inhuman, benighted, and are almost ruled out of the pale of civilization on
account of it. Within our own state we have the opposition of a few
sentimentalists who pose as humanitarians, but they have never been able
to have it eliminated from our statutes.

"Sentimentality will never prevent crime, whatever it may do to foster
it; nothing but drastic treatment, such as fits the crime, will have the
desired effect. For the crimes that I have mentioned nothing is better than
that we administer, and which, by long experience, we have learned is the
only means whereby we can protect ourselves from the criminal classes—
that is, the whipping post and the pillory."

To this opinion so honestly given might well be appended another, that
of the jailer at New Castle, whose unwholesome duty it is to inflict the
lashes.

Inspecting his realm one morning, I asked him directly:

"What do you think of whipping as a remedy for crime?"

"I think it is all wrong," he answered.

"Why?"

"Because it degrades the man that does the whipping, and if it degrades
him, I know it must have much the same effect upon those who see it."

"Who does the whipping here?" I inquired.

"I do," he replied, and therewith resolutely stared me into the firm belief
that here was one man, who, unfortunately circumstanced, nevertheless
had convictions and dared to express them.

NOTES

"Delaware's Blue Laws," *Ainslee's* 7 (February 1901): 53–57.

1. John Winthrop (1588–1649), American colonial governor. Born in England, he was the leading figure in Massachusetts for twenty years, serving continuously as governor, deputy governor, or member of the executive council. When governor, Winthrop was lenient in dealing with individuals who committed personal offenses but stern in resisting opponents of the Puritan state. One of his foremost enemies was Anne Hutchinson (1591–1643), leader of Antinomians and perhaps the earliest feminist in the colony.

Cotton Mather (1663–1728), American colonial divine, son of Increase Mather (1639–1723). Cotton Mather's thinking moved somewhat away from the strict Puritan orthodoxy of the seventeenth century toward the rationalistic and deistic religiosity of the eighteenth century.

5

A Touch of Human Brotherhood

A Lonely, Poverty-stricken, but Tender-hearted Man Manages to Assist Others

IN NEW YORK CITY THERE IS A MAN WHOSE LIFE IS A DISTINCT COMMENtary on the social conditions of our day. Short, stocky, thick-necked, and thick-skinned, he is the opposite in appearance of anything that might be considered intellectual or genteel. He is a more or less pathetic and helpless-looking figure,—who, you would say, had been "cheated of feature by dissembling nature," and cut out, in the very body of him, for the slings and arrows of fortune.

This man is a delightful example of sincere dedication of one's life to a social purpose. Not a day goes by but he tramps the streets, visiting the jails, the hospitals, and those numerous institutions which crowd Blackwell's Island. Kindness is his mission,—the spreading of kindness. If you should ask him, "What is the greatest need of the world," he would tell you, "Tenderness." "We must be more tender, more loving, more helpful, man to man,"—that is his doctrine.

Soon after seven o'clock on a winter evening, the captain, as he is called, may be found on Broadway, where it is intersected by Fifth Avenue, fulfilling one of the duties which he considers that of the merciful. It is the hour when Broadway assumes its most interesting evening aspect.

At the approach of the ex-soldier to this particular spot, there is a visible stir among a company of nondescript individuals, who have been waiting. Some, who have been sitting, arise and give evidence of the diffidence which most of us feel when we are in the presence of our superiors.

"Fall in!"

Stepping off the sidewalk, he takes one and then another of the individuals by the arm, and forms them into an orderly company, four abreast. Then he steps aside. After surveying them attentively a moment, he inquires:—

"Who has money?" A dozen hands go up.

"Fall out!" he commands, and they do so.

"Stand over here!" he next says, and is obeyed.

"Those who have ten cents, line up in front."

Possibly two of the dozen take their places at the head. When this arrangement has been completed, the captain takes his place on the sidewalk and gazes about him. Two or three strangers have already stopped. A policeman, passing by, salutes him as "captain." Slowly he begins to walk up and down before this file of men, a significant captain of a significant army. In the ranks are the broken, the aged, the hungry. Here is one with a wooden leg, there another with an armless coat-sleeve. Hats are all drooping, yellow, or cracked with age. Trousers are invariably warped and frayed at the bottom.

As he walks up and down the line, a curious crowd gathers. There are gentlemen and ladies on their way to the theater; a few urchins, clerks, loungers from the hotels across the way, and, occasionally, a being who looks as if he, too, ought to be in the line. Some pause only for a moment, while a few linger to see what will develop.

"Now, gentlemen," says the captain, after walking up and down for a time in silence, a space of ten feet, "these men are without a bed. They have got to have a place to sleep to-night. They can't lie in the street. I need fifteen cents to put one to bed. Who will give it to me?" There is no reply.

"I suppose," he goes on, "that this work needs a little explanation. These men are strangers to me. I don't know one from another. They're old,—a good many of them. Some of them have got where they are to-night through drink and other ways of wearing out the body. Some of them are what a good many of you would call 'bums,—ragged, blue-nosed bums!' That's what I've heard 'em called. A good many of them, if you'd give them a nickel, would carry it to some miserable Bowery gin shop, and buy five cents' worth of whiskey for it. I know it. You know it. There are seven thousand saloons in New York City. But here they are. It's a cold night, and they haven't got a bed."

He pauses, but his audience does nothing.

"Now, I don't promise to get them a bed. I don't do anything except agree to ask for them. If we don't get the money by one o'clock, I put on my hat and say 'good morning.' Then they take the soft side of a park bench or walk the street. I've done all I can. I haven't got any money."

Still the audience stares, and still he talks as if it were the most matter-of-fact thing in the world.

"A good many of you will say that these men don't deserve help, and that they wouldn't take a job if it were offered to 'em. I wish one of you people would offer one of 'em a chance to do something to-night, and see how quick he'd take it. I don't know anything about 'em, but a man must be awfully hard up when he comes and stands here in the cold, from seven in the evening until one o'clock in the morning, for a chance to sleep."

He stops, and walks in silence, the spectators still staring at the band of shifting wanderers lined up in the cold, like soldiers.

"Who'll give me fifteen cents?" No one replies.

"We will have to wait here, boys," he says, "until someone does. Fifteen cents isn't much."

"Here you are!" exclaims a young man who has been peering forward with strained eyes.

"All right," says the captain. "Now I have fifteen; step out of the line,"— and, calling one of the men, he marches him to a place where he stands alone. Going back, the captain waits. Someone else, moved by the dramatic situation, hands him a coin, which he looks at, but returns no thanks.

"I have ten cents here," he remarks, after a time. "These men must be put to bed."

After a few moments, he turns away and counts the company. "One, two, three, four, five, six, seven, eight,"—so he goes on to twenty-five, and still others keep coming. Out of the shadows and the long, cold avenues, they are hurrying in,—no longer willing to continue their fight unaided.

"Twenty-five," he announces. "Five cents more will put the next man to bed; give him a good, comfortable bed for the night, a bath, and a chance to wash out his clothes in the morning,—make him look better and feel better. I look after that. Who will give me five cents?"

A middle-aged man hands in a coin, evidently a five-cent piece for another man is sent forward.

Then the speaker waits again.

"Come, gentlemen," he says, finally, "we are going very slow this evening. You all have good beds. How about these poor fellows?"

"Here you are," says a bystander, putting a coin in his hand.

So it goes,—the slow process of providing the lonely with a lodging. The line of those whose beds are secure grows slowly, while that of the bedless waxes long. Ever and anon, the captain announces the number remaining. Its growth neither dismays nor interests him. His concern is over the next man, and the securing of fifteen cents. Strangers, gazing out of mere curiosity, find their sympathies enlisted, and place in the captain's hands dimes and quarters, as he states, in a short, abrupt, unaffected manner, the predicament of the men.

Standing tells. In the course of time, the earliest arrivals become weary and uneasy. There is a constant shuffling from one foot to the other, a leaning out and looking back to see how many more must be provided for before the company may march away. Comments are made, and crude wishes for the urging forward of things.

A cab stops. A gentleman, in evening dress, hands a bill to the captain, who takes it with simple thanks. There is a craning of necks, as a jewel in the broad, white shirt-front sparkles, and the cab moves away. Even the crowd gapes in awe.

"This fixes up thirteen for the night," says the captain, counting as many from the line near him. "Line up there! Now, then, there are only seven. I need fifteen cents."

Money comes slowly. In the course of time, the curious thin out to a meager handful. Fifth Avenue, save for an occasional cab or foot passenger, is bare. Broadway is thinly peopled with pedestrians. Only now and then a stranger passing notices the small group, hands out a coin, and goes away. The captain is stolid and determined. "Come, I can't stay out here all night. These men are getting tired and cold. Someone give me five cents."

The theaters are closed. Fire-signs disappear. A clock strikes eleven. Another half-hour passes, and he is down to the last two men. A lady, in opera cape and rustling silk skirt, comes down Fifth Avenue, supported by her escort, who glances at the line and comes over. There is a bill in his fingers.

"Here you are," he says.

"Thanks!" replies the captain. "Now we have some for to-morrow night."

The last two are lined up. The captain walks along, studying his line and counting. "One hundred and thirty-seven," he exclaims, when he reaches the head. "Now, boys, line up there. Steady, now. We'll be off in a minute." He places himself at the head of the line, and calls out, "Forward, march!" and away they go.

Across Fifth Avenue, through Madison Square by the winding path, east on Twenty-Third Street, and down Third Avenue trudges the long serpentine line.

Below Tenth Street is a lodging-house, and here the ragamuffin crowd halts, while the captain goes in to arrange. In a few minutes, the men march in, each being given a key, as the captain looks on. When the last one has disappeared up the dingy stairway, the captain comes out, muffles his great coat closer about him, pulls down his slouch brim, and tramps, a solitary figure, into the night.

Such is the captain's idea of his duty to his fellow man.

At the store of one of the leading florists, the captain has been a frequent visitor for two or three years, buying flowers that the florist cannot use, and distributing them personally at hospitals and jails where he thinks they will do the most good. I saw him at this florist's one day, when he had a basket filled with little bouquets of violets. It was some six months later, on a cold, gray day in winter, that I saw him coming down the steps of the Tombs Prison, in Center Street, a picturesque figure in a great army coat, wearing a shovel hat, which gave to his wind-red face, with its small brown eyes, a very grim and determined look. I ventured a few questions, in answering which he told me briefly of his work among the prisoners at the jail and among the poor generally.

He said he preached to them very little, but took them writing paper, frequently helped them to write their letters, and told them the news.

A year passed. I was walking down Broadway, late one cold afternoon, when I saw a group of shabby creatures gathered around the Worth Monument, evidently waiting for something or someone.[1] I learned from one of them, an old man, that they were waiting for the "captain." To my query as to who this captain might be, he replied: "He's the man that puts us to bed."

It gave the old man pleasure to explain to me how this "putting to bed" is accomplished. Having told me that he was friendless, and, when out of work, was obliged to join the company, he paused; but, seeing I was interested, he continued:—

"It's really a good work the captain does, a very good work. He has put forty thousand to bed in the last two or three years. Once a man's down, and out of work, it's hard for him to keep himself looking like anything unless he can get a place to sleep and wash himself.

"Now, if he can go to a lodging-house, it's different. There he gets a good rest. He has a chance to take a bath and to wash his clothes, and, when he comes out in the morning, he looks like somebody. He stands a chance of getting something to do."

The man looked at me, and his quiet, undisturbed manner was something amazing. He was, seemingly, as peaceful in his consideration as if he were discussing some purely philosophical problem. The vast contrasts between his own state and that of the fine "gentlemen at the hotel," who were even then beginning to dine in sumptuous form in the splendid restaurant across the way, seemed not to affect him at all. Everything was at a "dead level" with him. He was out of work, out of food, and would not be able to eat again that night; and yet, there he was explaining the nature of his predicament with an attention to detail that was really wonderful.

"Tell me," I said, trying to shock him into a gleam of feeling, "doesn't it strike you as odd that some of these men don't commit suicide? They've nothing to live for,—they're old,—most of them are useless physically. They have nothing but the meanest drudgery left them to do. Every one of them has to wait out here in the cold for a bed, and the older they get the worse it becomes. Wouldn't you think that they'd see that there is nothing for them, and be willing to die?"

"The man never lived that took his life when he was in his right mind," he returned, most philosophically. "There's no man wants to die as long as he sees anyone else enjoying life."

I was standing near this same place, one day, watching the panorama of life, which is there so entertainingly displayed, when the captain arrived. It was spring, and his rather old frock coat was open, and his worn hat was pushed back from his broad, wet forehead.

"You're the man I want to see," I said.

"What do you want to see me about?"

"Well, I want to know what your attitude toward life is,—why you do what you do? I've seen you among these people now for several years."

"Why I do what I do?" he echoed. "Why do you do as you do?"

"Well, I'm looking after my own mental welfare as best I can. I try to do things that will personally profit me, because I think it essential and necessary if I want to keep alive."

"That's just what I'm doing," he replied.

"Yes, I know," I said, "but mine is self-remembrance, while yours is self-forgetfulness."

"Don't you believe it," he replied. "I get as much fun out of my life as you get out of yours."

"You certainly get it in a different way."

"I get it all the same," he replied, "and I don't have to worry over who is going to hire or discharge me. I have a job, and no one ever tries to take it away from me. They won't try to stop me from giving. It's just the other way."

"But you don't get anything out of it financially, do you?"

I was sorry afterwards that I had asked the question.

Some months later, I sought to study the captain, and, as often as circumstances admitted, to throw a high light upon him, as his actions were shown to be consistent. He had a hall bedroom in one of the poorest sections of Thirty-first Street, where, among negroes, poor whites, and the flotsam and jetsam of the great city, he made his home.

"Just a place to lay my head is all I need," he said to me in explanation; and, when I asked him if he really longed for something better, he replied:—

"Men are queer. They won't believe I'm contented. I am, though. I tell you I have all I need."

"Don't you ever long for fine clothes, a splendid hotel or home, and some of the carriages you see rolling by here?"

We were sitting on the stoop of his lowly tenement, and the rumble of Broadway, throbbing with a spendthrift life, was even then in our ears.

"I'd lie if I said I didn't," he said, almost mournfully. "Those thoughts do come to me at times. I put them down. I face right about, and then I'm just as happy as any man can ever expect to be."

"Yes, I know," I replied.

"After all," he replied, experiencing the change of mood which he had just been discussing, "it's not inside, but outside, that life is beautiful. The hotels and theaters, the carriages and fine homes,—they're all in the eye. If you think of their delights, you have them. It's only for a season,—just for a little while. The lights, the happiness, the gambling, the wine, the high living of whatsoever form you want to think of,—it's only for a season. Besides," he said, more earnestly, "I see them coming down to me,—those that have been up there,—millionaires, college boys, high rollers,—I put them to bed. That's why I'm here. I believe that I should be just where I am,—waiting for them when they get through."

NOTES

"A Touch of Human Brotherhood," *Success* 5 (March 1902): 140–41. Reconstructed, verbatim in some portions, from the story of the Captain in "Curious Shifts of the Poor," *Demorest's* 36 (November 1899): 22–26.

1. The Worth Monument was erected by the city of New York in memory of William Jenkins Worth (1794–1849), American general.

Part V
Other Sites and Scenes

1

Carrier Pigeons in War Time

Their Use on Warships and Capabilities in Carrying Swift Information

EVER SINCE CARRIER PIGEONS WERE SO SUCCESSFULLY USED IN GETTING messages in and out of besieged Paris, during the Franco-Prussian war, there has been a steady increase in the use of these birds as an adjunct of military and naval warfare throughout the world.

With the construction of our present navy the value of carrier pigeons was not forgotten, and an appropriation from the Navy Department, looking to the establishing of a loft of these peculiar birds, was set aside so long ago as 1889. At that time charge of the work was given to the captain of the yard of the Brooklyn Navy Yard, who, in turn, delegated the work to a young pigeon fancier of Brooklyn, Mr. Howard Carter. Authority was given him to construct a loft on the most modern and approved lines, and to buy record birds in whatsoever market they were attainable.

For several years Mr. Carter experimented with birds of various breeds, sending to England and Belgium and buying of foreign fanciers generally. Of these he finally adopted the Belgian breed, and set about increasing his stock. About 1891 the Navy Department decided that the carrier-loft must be located within the official precincts of the navy yard, and also to make the care of them an official duty. To bring this within the rules governing all naval service Mr. Carter was made lieutenant and given a commission.

In the loft, which is located on Cob Dock, close to the receiving ship *Vermont,* at the navy yard, there is, or was before the present war began, some three hundred homing pigeons, all more or less trained for service in the present emergency. Regularly every day, for several years, these birds have been put through practice drill in their special duty, which consists in nothing more than returning straight home from wheresoever released. As the naval preparations for the present hostilities were completed and the fully equipped ships were sent to sea, basket after basket of the feathered recruits were put on board, usually a dozen birds for each vessel, and sent along to battle. Each war vessel, as it came to the navy yard for its final overhauling, was so equipped with these carrier birds. Some of the war-ships in Commodore Schley's fleet, as well as several in Admiral Samp-son's command, did not put into the navy yard at all.[1] To these, baskets of the carriers were sent in care of Government dispatch-boats, and only recently the last of the boats in service along the Atlantic coast was sup-plied, as per the order of the department.

The Government officials regard this homing-pigeon service as of much interest and moment in naval affairs at present. No dispatch boat, even the fastest invented, can approach anywhere near the fleetness of these birds. To patrol-boats on duty off the coast, commissioned to watch and notify the Government of the appearance of any hostile fleet off our shores, the carrier pigeon is a valuable ally. The swiftest dispatch-boat can travel but little over twenty miles an hour, while the most muscular thoroughbred inmates of the navy loft can fly sixty miles in the same time. The average homing pigeon can and does go forty-three miles an hour. It is estimated that if a hostile fleet were sighted two hundred miles off our coast by one of the dispatch-boats and a homing pigeon were instantly released, the of-ficers on shore would have from eight to nine hours in which to prepare to receive it. While the fleet, steaming at the very exaggerated speed of eighteen miles an hour, could not possibly reach the coast in less than twelve hours, the carrier pigeon would reach its loft in the navy yard in less than four hours from the time released. In a situation of that nature eight hours is as good as an equal number of days, where all is in readiness anyhow.

The pigeons are also valuable for carrying news of engagements at sea, when these take place within six hundred miles of land, but beyond that their return is uncertain. The sea offers no water to drink nor food to eat to these lone messengers, and where on land, with opportunity of alighting a few minutes during the day, they can travel 1,500 miles in remarkably short time, on sea it becomes a question whether they can hold out, and very often when released beyond 600 miles from their loft no more is heard of them.

For this reason the birds are specially considered in connection with patrol service. No attempt is made to supply the squadrons intended for service in distant seas. It is an order of the department that vessels going farther than 600 miles from the home loft and intending to remain beyond that distance for more than three months must release the pigeons before reaching the 600-mile limit, and allow them to return home. All boats within near waters, or intending to return in three months, keep their supply of carriers.

Within the last two years this remarkable bird has enjoyed a general revival of public interest. In New York it has been used in bringing messages from visiting warships, such as the *Viscaya,* and from outgoing vessels, when some one desired to send a last good-by. The news of the death sentence of Martin Thorn was rather dramatically brought by a pigeon from Long Island City to one of the daily papers in three minutes— a flight of five miles. The *New York Herald* demonstrated the modern availability of the birds in bringing earliest news of the victor in the international yacht races from the long distance outside the bay. The great Andrée, in his immortal flight into the unknown, carried homing pigeons with him, and the last message, dated July 13, 1897, was found on one of his homing pigeons, shot while flying southward toward Stockholm, from the far northern point where it had been released.[2]

Very few persons, outside the military world, think now of utilizing the pigeons for purposes of daily life. They have the telephone, telegraph and mail, and, of course, so primitive a method of correspondence does not appeal to them. Hence an excuse is devised for relegating the pigeon to the category of the luxuries. Fanciers have sprung up all over the country, men who own lofts and train pigeons for the interest and sport there is in it. Their interest is largely determined by the excitement of gaming, and the discovery of the "better bird" in long flights. Pigeon matches have become a common form of amusement, and there is a "National Federation of Homing Pigeons" which festers the sport, and with which the names and records of all carrier pigeons are recorded. If ever you capture one of these birds, you will be pleased to understand that the little nickel ring on its right foot, engraved with a letter and a number, such as C. 7284, is the registry mark of the American association, and that the date of the birth of the bird, the name of its owner and its life record, can all be learned by sending the mark on the ring to the secretary of the association.

The birds that stock our American pigeon-lofts are of the Belgian breed, which has been developed by centuries of selection from the rock pigeon. This breed differs much from its wild ancestors in habits and instincts. It is not quite so large as the ring pigeon, but has a more expressive head, more elegant form, and a more brilliant and varied plumage.

It is written in books on pigeon culture that the carrier pigeon is hardly ever white. The reason for this is very simple. Pigeons on their journeys are selected by birds of prey, which most readily pick out those of conspicuous colors. Consequently, white birds disappear without ever having an opportunity to found a stock. This observation does not apply to the common pigeon, which, never straying far from habitations, is less frequently struck by the hawk. So, too, pigeons flying near the ground are certain to fall sooner or later under the shot of the fowler, and usually leave very few descendants. These circumstances intervene, independent of the breeder's will, to form the color and character of the bird, as relates to high flying.

Our American bird is the result of breeding the Cumulet to the Smerle and English Dragoon. The Cumulet (a species of Tumbler) is a high-flying pigeon, having great endurance on the wing. In fact, it is known to have flown continuously for fourteen hours on a stretch. There seems to be no question that the Cumulet has been used to induce the habit of high flying, which is a quality absolutely necessary in the homing pigeon. As early as the thirteenth century this pigeon was used extensively for short-distance racing in and around Antwerp.

A considerable part in the make-up of the carrier is the Smerle, a species of owl-pigeon, which for many years was bred in the province of Liége, Belgium. The Smerle is much smaller than either the Cumulet or the Dragoon, very persistent in finding its home, and extremely intelligent.

The Dragoon pigeon, the origin of which seems still to remain unsettled in the minds of many writers, is a large, powerful, and yet compact, hardy and active flyer. Like the Cumulet, this pigeon was also used for short-distance racing in England during the first half of this century. It is claimed by the best authorities that the Dragoon was used in the crossing by which the homing pigeon was formed. From this breed thus obtained only the strongest and swiftest birds were kept and bred from generation to generation, until the present race may be considered the very élite of homing pigeons.

The manner in which the birds are kept and cared for is a subject of real interest, especially to the stranger who looks up the subject for the first time.

A famous flock I recently visited in New York was the means of admitting me into the mysteries of the loft, with the janitor of the building, who was the caretaker, as a subsidized guide. The loft proved to be a solid, handsomely constructed slant-roofed house, some twelve feet long and nine feet high. The room inside was lined on two sides of the walls with shelves or boxes, fitted with small wire doors, in which the pairs of pigeons dwell. Each of these rooms held a cup for seed and a drinking bowl, and slightly more than a handful of clean, new straw. No expense had been spared in making the loft comfortable and complete. Electric light, steam heat, running water for bathing and drinking uses, and a wire aviary were included. The entry window of the birds was explained as being fitted with an electric attachment, which gives notice, on an indicator in the office below, of arrival of the birds. The door and each separate loft of the room was equipped with a burglar alarm, and the whole house was variously barred and padlocked to prevent theft. Estimating the birds cheaply at one hundred dollars each, the fact that there were a hundred of them in the loft made rather valuable property of the place, and hence the precaution.

Here they dwell in company, the young and the old together. At the time I arrived a number were nesting, and several young pigeons looking like the poorest kind of squabs, had just been hatched. The mature birds, tame to the last degree, were not disturbed by the presence of the caretaker. Such of these as he chose to take in his hand to explain the rings on their feet and their pedigree did not seem to mind it, only craning their necks to see what the remainder of the flock might be doing. Most of these birds had records for long flights, in which they had come safely home; others had taken prizes. All seemed a proud lot, strutting and preening themselves about their common chamber with great show.

It is a common delusion with the public that these birds fly to and from different places by direction, and that all one has to do is to catch the bird, tie a letter about its neck; no matter how large or clumsy, and send it off to the required destination from its home. My preceptor explained to me the fallacy of this, and related the anecdote of the good old lady who, witnessing the liberation of a number of these pigeons, asked, "Will you kindly tell me how soon your birds will return to the basket?"

The fact is, that homing pigeons return only to their original home, recognizing as their home that place from whence they first began to fly. Save in rare instances, and after long confinement and much painstaking and careful watching, homing pigeons accustomed to having their liberty have never been settled in strange localities and lofts.

In Europe an experiment has been made looking to the sending of pigeons back and forth between two points, and some success has been attained, although no change of home was attempted. This experiment consisted of taking pigeons whose homes were in Paris and confining them for several days at St. Denis, five miles away, where they were fed at a stated hour every day with some favorite food not given them at their real home. In the course of time they became familiar with their new home and its choice dishes. When set at liberty, they started off at once for Paris, without forgetting, however, the good things they enjoyed at St. Denis. When the time came to send them back to St. Denis, they were made to fast in their Paris home, and were then released at about feeding-time in St.

Denis. Not strangely their hunger caused them to fly to St. Denis, where there was food. It is said that when they had their own way, they timed their going so as to be in St. Denis at the exact moment of feeding. This is the only way birds have been taught to fly to and fro regularly between places. It has never been accomplished for a distance of over five miles.

The flock in charge of the janitor knew only the hut on the top of the high building as their home. To this they had returned time and again from long journeys—one from so distant a point as New Orleans. Each day, for a period of an hour, they are allowed to fly in the open. To show me how indifferently they are turned loose, the loft window was opened and the whole flock trooped out and took wing in the bright sunshine and warm air. While we sat and talked of the training of such birds, I watched the flock wheeling round the summer sky, flying far out over the bay and the East River, and returning past the loft in great circles.

The caretaker informed me that homing pigeons never alight save at their own loft. You never find them in the street with the common barn-yard pigeon. During their hour out they keep steadily on the wing, circling high for pure delight and returning when content to do so. They eat only in their own home, save when flying long distances. Then they must descend to drink and gather such food as they may. It is on these occasions, if ever, that they are shot or captured, since on the wing they fly out of range of gunshot.

The training of the young pigeons begins when they are three or four months old. When they are only a few days old the identifying ring is put on their foot, and in a week, so rapidly do they grow, it cannot be taken off. They are then registered. When strong enough to fly they are let loose at gradually increasing distances from the pigeon house. At six months of age one should be able to return from a distance of 200 miles at a speed of fifty miles an hour. At the end of the second year it should come back from distances of more than 300 miles, and of the third year from 600 miles.

Carrier-pigeon races, or "flys," as they are called, have been made in this country since 1879. No bird made 500 miles in a day, however, until June 14, 1885, when "Ned Damon," owned by T. Fred. Goldman, of Brooklyn, the genial president of the National Federation, accomplished that feat. The birds of other fanciers subsequently forged ahead, and "Ned Damon's" record was beaten the following year by "Queen," a bird belonging to Mr. George Wyatt, of Keyport, N.J. The speed this bird made for the 500 miles was 1,121 yards per minute. Since that time the record for speed for this distance has been successively held by Thomas Brooks, of Germantown, Pa.; Joseph Iverson, of Brooklyn, and T. Fred. Goldman. The present holder of the 500-mile record is Paul Krause, of Philadelphia.

Without question the veteran prize-winner and head of all pigeon flyers in this country is Mr. Conrad A. Mahr, of Newark, N. J. This young man began to breed and fly pigeons in 1888. In ten years he has won no less than thirty-four first premiums, twenty-five seconds, twenty thirds, six fourths, four fifths and two special challenge races. The honors for places after Mr. Mahr are so equally divided among a dozen breeders that it would be difficult to place any of them first.

The best speed made so far in this country, irrespective of length of flight, was made by a bird belonging to Mr. A. Whatten, of Newark. One hundred miles in one hour and twenty-nine minutes was its record, being nearly one and one-eighth miles per minute. The champion long-distance homing pigeon in America is "Sadie Jones," the property of Mr. F. Sullivan, of Philadelphia. This pigeon covered the exceedingly remarkable distance of 1,212 miles, from Lake Charles, La., to Philadelphia, in sixteen days. To the uninitiated this may seem a long time, but it must be remembered that ninety-nine out of every hundred birds are never sent home from beyond the 500-mile limit.

Space will not permit, however, of naming all the fast birds, nor a portion. When it is remembered that eight hundred fanciers, owning anywhere from fifty to a hundred birds each, are constantly contesting for honors and prizes, it will be seen how useless an attempt at such a record would be.

During all the centuries the peculiar instinct which gives the bird its value has been a subject of wonderment, inasmuch as the understanding of it baffles the reason of man. Before its long flights, as from New Orleans to Philadelphia, over a landscape whereon it has never before set eye, the thinker stands, challenged by so peculiar a wonder as to stir him to the most profound speculation. Out of the vainness and futility of the thinking must come the philosophic resignation which Bryant so beautifully expressed in his lines "To a Waterfowl," namely, that:

> "He who, from zone to zone,
> Guides through the boundless sky thy certain flight,
>   In the long way that I must tread alone,
> Will lead my steps aright."[3]

NOTES

"Carrier Pigeons in War Time," *Demorest's* 34 (July 1898): 222–23.

1. Winfield Scott Schley (1839–1911), American naval officer. He led the expedition that in 1884 rescued the survivors of the Greely Arctic Exploring Party.

William Thomas Sampson (1840–1902), American admiral. In 1898, during the Spanish-American War, while Sampson in his flagship headed to Santiago, the Spanish ships tried to escape. Sampson turned and headed west, but when he arrived, the Spaniards had surrendered after a fight to a squadron headed by Commodore Schley. Sampson cabled that the victory had been achieved by the fleet under his command, and a controversy arose between him and Schley.

2. Salomon August Andrée (1854–97), Swedish aeronautical engineer and polar explorer. In 1897 he launched an exploration of the north polar region by balloon. The last

message from him was brought by carrier pigeons to a sealer in the vicinity of Spitsbergen, Norway.

3. William Cullen Bryant (1794–1878), American poet and newspaper editor. Regarded as a romantic poet, he was Dreiser's favorite poet. As a journalist, he supported liberal and democratic causes. Dreiser wrote a magazine article, "The Home of William Cullen Bryant," *Munsey's* 21 (May 1899): 240–46; reprinted in *Selected Magazine Articles,* 1:92–99.

2

Japanese Home Life
Interesting Customs of a Picturesque People

"It takes a Japanese to like a Japanese home," says the very witty J. Charles Arter, famed for his paintings of Japan, who would not acknowledge himself so lacking in originality as to repeat Lincoln's "for people that like that sort of thing, that's just the sort of thing they like."[1] The low, paper-made, screen-ornamented homes, which Lafcadio Hearn says are built in five days, appeal to Americans in summer; but when the winter season sets in and the primitive stone or bronze stoves are set in the middle of the low-ceilinged rooms and the occupants crowd constantly about for comfort, they are inclined to think reverentially of American brick houses, of rugs, carpets, cushioned chairs, and beds.[2] Lightness and beauty are well enough when you are warm, but an American wants something more than those charming qualities in winter.

There is another important fact to be stated about home life in Japan, and that is that foreigners residing there, let alone travelers who come and go, know very little about it. The exterior evidences are plain enough. You can find many volumes detailing costumes and festivals, the character of the architecture, and the beauty of the scenery, and much that is charming about the public ways and ceremonies, but when it comes to the true home life, the average traveler is at a loss. He never had a chance to make friends with a Japanese who had a quiet home, or if he did, the Japanese didn't invite him there. If he was invited he saw little or nothing save of his host, and so he came away uninformed.

The nature of the home life of the Japanese has been, up to the present day, an almost secret thing. Despite much fine-drawn discussion of the subject, Oriental ideas have prevailed, and the social and home life of the nation have been one-sided, because the men were everything and the women nothing. We from the West, used to seeing the streets of America filled with our best of women; used to a frank equality of the sexes, and to clear, straight-forward glances of women, are but poorly equipped to understand or sympathize with the Japanese idea of that modesty and reserve in Japanese women which is the result of enforced ignorance and ancient

281

repressive custom. When it shows itself in the street travelers do not care; they are accustomed to take the outdoor evidences of the life and intelligence of a people with a grain of salt; but when they meet with the effects of repressive, stunting custom in the homes of a nation, find the houses of their native acquaintances secret and the women reserved beyond all understanding, they permit themselves severe private criticism. Naturally they wonder what those mothers and children do with themselves, since they take so little part in the entertainment of guests. They are curious as to what may be the household arrangements back of the reception room in which one is forever so formally entertained; how the mornings and afternoons are passed, the children cared for, the meals prepared, and the whole detail of that inner life managed. It is with interest that the subject is discussed, and the slightest scrap of evidence is always received with pleasure.

To understand the defects and beauties of this home life in the foremost of the Asiatic nations, one should have wandered in Japan and familiarized himself with the condition of the small towns which hold the bulk of the population. He should know of the artistic gardens and parks which they frequent, the schoolhouses which the children attend, the temples wherein the devout regularly worship, and the market-place where they sell and buy. If he could see the host of venders who sell almost everything for the home, the fish dealers, the vegetable sellers, the men who mend utensils and repair wood-work, the coolies who run errands and drag 'rikishas, he would be in a better position to understand the indoor life of this people.

He would find, of course, that no set description applies to all homes there any more than it does here, and that only a certain and large class, the invariable middle, could be described as being in a sense representative. As for the very poor, few have cared to follow the intricate details of their poverty, sufferings, and deprivations; and in the case of the nobles and very rich, still fewer have ever had an opportunity to get in and see how things were conducted by them. One must choose the middle class, and, in that case, those of the middle-sized towns, in order to discover a home life worthy of the name, because in the case of the smaller agricultural villages, they are nearly always so poor, the houses so dilapidated, and the food and clothing of the peasants so insufficient as to make typical home life impossible. In many instances the farm buildings of these places are situated in the midst of the rice fields, or on a hill slope, at some little distance from the road. Even the women and children go out to till the ground from early morning until late in the evening, their labor being sometimes varied by felling trees or cutting brushwood on the hills. In some localities they eke out their means of livelihood by snaring birds, or by fishing in the numerous ponds and rivulets. Those who can afford to do so keep a pack-horse or an ox to be used either as a beast of burden or to draw the plough.

It is to the larger-sized towns then and to the homes of the distinctly middle class that one must resort for some clear impression of what the Japanese idea of living is.

The homes of the townspeople are constructed almost entirely of wooden posts, beams and planks, the roofs being generally tiled. Except in larger towns they are rarely more than two stories high, more frequently but one. The front of the dwelling is either left entirely open, or with the better class of tradespeople, is closed by a kind of wooden grille with slender bars. Those who can afford it, usually shut in the frontage altogether by a fence, through which a low gateway opens upon a small garden, immediately in front of the entrance to the dwelling. At the back there is generally another tiny garden. All around the house runs a narrow wooden veranda of the same height as the floor, over which the roof protrudes. This veranda is completely closed at night, or in stormy weather, by wooden slides known as "rain-doors," moving in grooves like the slides dividing the rooms in the interior.

Within the house the floors are raised to a height of about eighteen inches from the level of the ground, and are covered with large straw mats an inch and a half in thickness. These mats are nearly six feet in length by three in breadth, are covered with a layer of finely plaited straw, and have the edges bound with some dark cloth. The doors of the rooms are formed of sliding screens of wooden framework covered with paper. At one side of the room is generally a recess with a low dais, on which various curiosities and ornaments are arranged, with a painted scroll at the back as a wall decoration. Years ago, before the wearing of swords was prohibited, a large sword-rack, often of fine lacquered wood, usually occupied the place of honor on the dais. The ceilings are of thin boards, with slender crossbeams laid over them at intervals.

These frail, shell-like affairs so remarkable to Americans, contain practically no furniture except a charcoal stove, either of bronze or stone, set into the floor, and a few cushions to sit upon. A cupboard contains the wadded quilt which, spread out at night, forms the only bed.

Every one leaves his clogs or shoes at the entrance on coming in, walking about the room in the conventional cotton socks. Every house has its bath, with furnace, in which the members of the family in succession parboil themselves every evening from five o'clock onward, the maid servants coming last.

Among the well-to-do people the houses have a novelty nowadays in the way of a room furnished "Western style," or supposedly so, though any American would call it about as comfortless a den as could be thought of. Still, the fact that it has chairs, a table, and glass windows, give it a wholly un-Japanese effect—and so it is considered Western.

In the existence of the poorer classes of Japan there are no secrets; but among the upper classes, family life is much less open to observation than in any country of the West. It is a life of which foreigners see little and know almost nothing. Invited into one of these Japanese houses by a friend, you may or may not see the family. It will depend upon circumstances. If you see any of them it will probably be for a moment only, and in that event you will most likely see the wife.

At the entrance you give your card to the servant, who retires to present it, and presently returns to usher you into the *zashiki,* or guest-room—always the largest and finest apartment in a Japanese dwelling—where your kneeling cushion is ready for you, with a smoking box before it. The servant brings you tea and cakes. In a little while the host himself enters, and after the indispensable salutations conversation begins. Should you be pressed to stay for dinner, and accept the invitation, it is probable that the wife will do you the honor, as her husband's friend, to wait upon you during an instant. You may or may not be formally introduced to her; but a glance at her dress and coiffure should be sufficient to inform you at once who she is, and you must greet her with the most profound respect. She will probably impress you (especially if your visit be to a *samurai* home) as a delicately refined and very serious person, by no means a woman of the much-smiling and much-bowing kind. She will say extremely little, but will salute you and will serve you for a moment with a natural grace of which the mere spectacle is a revelation, and glide away again, to remain invisible until the instant of your departure, when she will reappear at the entrance to wish you good-by. During other successive visits you may have similar charming glimpses of her; perhaps, also, some rarer glimpses of the aged father and mother; and if a much-favored visitor, the children may at last come to greet you, with wonderful politeness and sweetness. But the innermost intimate life of that family will never be revealed to you. All that you see to suggest it will be refined, courteous, exquisite; but of the relation of those souls to one another you will know nothing. Behind the beautiful screens which mask the further interiors, all is silent, gentle mystery. There is no reason, to the Japanese mind, why it should be otherwise. Such family life is sacred; the home is a sanctuary, of which it were impious to draw aside the veil.

Should there be grown-up daughters in the family, however, the visitor is less likely to see the wife. More timid, but equally silent and reserved, the young girls will make the guest welcome. In obedience to orders they may even gratify him by a performance upon some musical instrument, by exhibiting some of their own needlework or painting, or by showing to him some precious or curious objects among the family heirlooms. But all-submissive sweetness and courtesy are inseparable from the high-bred reserve belonging to the finest native culture. And the guest must not allow himself to be less reserved. Unless possessing the privilege of great age, which would entitle him to paternal freedom of speech, he must never venture upon personal compliment, or indulge in anything resembling light flattery.

What would be deemed gallantry in the West may be gross rudeness in the East. On no account can the visitor compliment a young girl about her looks, her grace, her toilette, much less dare address such a compliment to the wife. Certain occasions require compliment, after the sense of the word in Japan, but it is only after the humblest apology for making it, that the word of praise is spoken. It will then be accepted with a phrase more graceful than our "Pray don't mention it."

Back of this outer reserve, there is a wholesome family life, used to the peculiar condition, and merry as home life goes. The custom of the country allows but little social intercourse for women in the sense that we understand it, but in the limited home sense they amuse themselves. In the first place there are the children to care for, and this is an important item, for in Japan it is granted by every-one that the child ought to have its own way. Fathers and mothers derive their pleasure from the observance of this accepted idea. Every means of enjoyment for children, every subject of their amusement, becomes a source of personal satisfaction to the parents; they give themselves up to it with all their hearts, and it suits the children admirably. Travelers who have said the Japanese children never cry, have stated with very little exaggeration a perfectly real phenomenon. They have no particular cause.

In the house the children are often left to themselves, without any uneasiness. They have no stairs to fall down, no chairs or tables to bump against, or cover to pull down, with its attendant array of porcelain, and the odds and ends that encumber an American table. Very often there is no stove to burn the unwitting fingers. So there's no cause for alarm. They can roll about among the mats, crawling on all fours, and try to stand upright without danger of bumping their heads upon higher objects. Their companions in play are the domestic animals—little pug-dogs with short legs and tremendously fat bodies, and a particular species of cats with white fur marked with yellow and black stripes, which are exceedingly bad mousers and very idle, but very affectionate.

The child's parents are prodigal of toys and games, and entertainments, as much for their own enjoyment as in the interest of the children's education. They help at the lessons (particularly the mother), which consist in singing in chorus, at the top of the voice, the "Iroha," a sort of historic poem, and drawing with brush and Chinese ink the first letters of the alphabet. There is no compulsion and no precipitation about the lessons, because they are certain things of undeniable utility which can be acquired by long practice. This inner world of play and study, which is so carefully shut off from the world proper and even from the husband's guests, is often

Teacher and pupil.

one of tender beauty. It is narrow and slavish only in the sense that it is so exclusive and shuts out from the women those larger interests common to Americans.

A day with a Japanese family begins early. They rise with the sun, or nearly so, and get about their modest affairs. The noisy opening of the outer shutters at dawn is sure to startle a stranger. House activity begins with the morning meal, of course, for three meals a day in Japan are as common as here. The first of these meals is usually at eight o'clock in the morning, the second at two in the afternoon, and the third at eight in the evening. The women eat by themselves, apart from the men. The diet of the Japanese is composed of a greater variety of articles than that of any other people in the world. Not content with the many kinds of wholesome and nutritive food supplied by the produce of their lands and waters, they contrive to render the less valuable, and even poisonous, vegetable substances useful in the way of harmless sauces and the like. At meals the portion for each person is served up in neat vessels of porcelain or japanned wood. Those coming together to dine salute each other with a bow before they begin to eat. The food is served in courses, and chop-sticks are used, after the manner of the Chinese. After each dish some drink is served, rice beer or tea, while sliced hard-boiled eggs are passed about at all meals, much in the sense that pickles are served here.

Preparing a dinner.

Some of the most common dishes are fish, boiled with onions and a kind of small bean, dressed in oil; fowls, stewed and prepared in various modes, and boiled rice, which supplies the place of bread for all their provisions. Oils, mushrooms, carrots and other vegetables are used in making up dishes, and the whole is rounded off with tobacco, which is served with pipes, and enjoyed by both sexes.

There is a marked similarity in the daily routine of the inmates of the Japanese homes, whether they be the homes of the rich or poor, the official or tradesman. The wife is always the mistress of the home in a reserved and, it must be admitted, slavish sense. Hers is the duty of, in every way possible, rendering the life of her husband happy, and, incidentally, to be happy herself, as far as he knows. The instruction of the daughters of the house in the various domestic duties also devolves upon the mother. The wardrobe of the entire family is the work of her hands, with the assistance, perhaps, of an aunt, a maid, or her growing daughters. The last, by the way, are taught to sew while yet quite little tots, and, as they grow older in years and skill, are initiated into the mysteries of art needlework. Then the daughters are instructed in music, a certain knowledge of the *samisen*, *koto*, or some other musical instrument being regarded as a requisite accomplishment in even the poorer and middle classes.[3] The daughters of the higher classes and nobility are well versed in the art, music and poetry of the country. The other accomplishments deemed desirable in a woman consist principally in the artistic arrangement of flowers and the details of ceremonial tea making and drinking.

Concerning the last two, Americans can have but a faint idea of the importance placed upon them. We are not such sticklers for form and ceremony, but in a country where ceremony is carried to the last degree of minuteness it is not so remarkable. Time and custom have given importance to these two things, so that efficiency, taste and grace in these matters are considered the true and necessary evidences of gentility.

Turning to the common pastimes that make up the pleasure for odd moments in so many homes, these Orientals are well supplied. *Go* and *shogi* are similar to our games of draughts and chess, yet the former is far more scientific than checkers.[4] There are several games of cards, played with playing-cards about as long as those used in this country, but scarcely three-quarters of an inch wide. Another favorite game is that of "One Hundred Poems."[5] It is somewhat similar to our rather childish game of "Authors," with the exception that the Japanese game is by no means childish, and requires an intimate knowledge of at least one hundred poems of well-known merit. Two hundred cards are used in the game, and half a poem is written on each card. The cards being spread before the players, the half-poem on any card is read, and the other half searched for by the contestants. There are typical games also for the different seasons of the year, the most picturesque one being *hagoita,* or "battledore and shuttlecock," which is exclusively a New Year's game.[6] The time of the cherry-blooms brings its games beneath the bloom-laden branches.

Music and song find their way into the homes far more generally than in America, though not in the same intelligent sense as here. The music of either the *koto* or *samisen* is apt to sound strange, and at first, perhaps, almost unintelligible to Western ears, but travelers soon become familiar with the plaintive notes of the *koto* or the sonorous vibration of the *samisen,* and learn to both recognize and appreciate the quaint minor harmonies.

The recitation or reading of historical poems is a favorite study, especially if some romance is interwoven into the story. Usually the dramatic poems are ceremoniously read or sung by the young maidens, while an elder sister or teacher will thrum a minor accentuated accompaniment on the *samisen.* Sometimes the story of a historical poem is told in prose to the eager group of children gathered around the glowing brazier in the middle of the room. The latter, it must be confessed, in spite of its cheery appearance, radiates but a scant amount of heat in comparison with the open grate of the Occident. Such a family group may be seen in thousands of homes in Tokyo alone on a winter's afternoon; the boys, if back from school, resting contentedly on the white *tatami,* or studying the morrow's lessons in some quiet nook; the little maidens demurely grouped about the *hibachi,* busily plying their needles, while listening to some story told by the old aunt or nurse that may be acting as instructress.[7] The contented hum of the quaint old iron kettle, resting over the glowing coals, supported by an iron tripod thrust into the ashes of the stove, suggests its entire readiness to assist in the preparation of tiny cups of fragrant tea for any chance guest that arrives or any member of the family.

Stories are told best at this time. The deeds of the heroes, the romances of ancient dynasties, mystical lore, stories of ghosts and ghouls, and of the wicked and revengeful deeds of fox and badger sprites, all are recounted from time to time. Indeed, this fable lore has become so blended with the home life of the people that one cannot well be disassociated from the other.

Of course, this indoor life is varied. Guests call; the wife and daughters walk or ride in the popular 'rikishas; there are shopping and theatre-going, also picnicking, in the sense of outdoor country parties. The men have business, more and more patterned after the Western idea of late years, and to this they attend Western fashion. They leave in the morning, return for dinner, and again for supper, and in many instances now dress like Americans, although it is customary to exchange the European dress at evening for the Japanese *kimono* and girdle. As for the women, they have never, except in rare instances, abandoned the native costume, which so well becomes them, but look after their personal appearance with the same care and enthusiasm that characterize the feminine native the world over.

Much has been said in favor of the beauty and the charm of these Japanese daughters and mothers; but by some, who are not so favorably impressed with Japan, this praise is considered the result of a tendency to overpraise, and we now hear from more than one critic that the Japanese woman, married, single, or sold into bondage, has no individuality; she is a slave—a slave to her parents, a slave to her husband.

Yet these women are extolled and their grace and beauty are often set above those of European women, and even above those of our own ideal American. The home life here set forth is pictured as something most artistic and charming, and we are even told by one so able as Lafcadio Hearn that the Japanese ideal is bound to affect and improve that of Europe and the West. Strange and deficient as it looks to Americans, the women repressed in mind and body, the men left lords of the country and the home, we are told that it will not change. They will accept our telegraph and our telephones, will build railroads and establish newspapers, will introduce Western ideas of mental training for men, but this ideal of home life will not be changed. The women will remain uneducated, save in the so-called graces. They will continue to learn music and a little painting, to understand pretty games and how to prepare flowers and serve tea. All this is going to go right along, and yet the men are going to grasp all that is worthy and important in Western civilization.

Americans who know the influence of intelligent motherhood won't believe it. There isn't anything that can convince even this day and generation of the possibility of any such harmony and results. Japanese women will either not continue to be mere toys and ornaments, graceful adjuncts of their husbands' estate and dignity, or they will remain as they are, and train their children according to their light and prejudice. If it is to be the latter, there will be no grasping of Western ideals by the Japanese, and if it be the former, this curious form of Oriental home life will pass away.

NOTES

"Japanese Home Life," *Demorest's* 35 (April 1899): 123–25.

1. J. Charles Arter was born in Hanoverton, Ohio, and studied in Cincinati and Paris. He had studios in Venice, London, and New York, and died in Alliance, Ohio, in 1923.

2. Lafcadio Hearn (1850–1904), Greek-born American writer, became a Japanese subject. See a note on him to Dreiser's "A Notable Colony," included in this volume.

3. *Samisen* (or *shamisen*) is a three-string Japanese musical instrument derived from China, which resembles a banjo. *Koto* is a long Japanese zither having silk strings.

4. *Go* is a Japanese game that is played with black and white stones on a wooden board marked by 19 vertical lines and 19 horizontal lines to make 361 intersections and that has as its object the possession of the largest part of the board and the capturing of the opponent's stones. *Shogi* also is a Japanese game resembling chess, which is played on a board of 81 squares with 40 pieces to the set.

5. "One Hundred Poems" is a literary card game in Japan that was originally played in the court. The game is played on the contestant's memory of the one hundred famous classic Japanese *tanka* (a five-line verse of 5–7–5–7–7 syllabic measures) by one hundred poets. On each of the one hundred cards spread out before the contestants is written the last two lines of a poem. The referee recites the first three lines of a poem and the players compete in capturing the card.

6. *Hagoita* is a traditional game often played by young women on New Year's Day. Feathered balls resembling badminton balls are hit back and forth among players by wooden boards.

7. *Tatami* is a straw mat with a fitting, in a rectangular size of about 3 by 6 feet, used like a carpet to cover floors in a Japanese house. *Hibachi* is a small charcoal brazier used in a Japanese house in winter months to warm hands and upper body.

3

Human Documents from Old Rome

Being the Story of the Common People
told in Drawings

W HEN ROME WAS AT HER ZENITH, PATRIOTIC HISTORIANS WROTE DOWN her wealth and power and fame in a manner which is cherished for the charm and the exactness with which the facts involved have been recorded. Of the common people and of common things of that day there is a

**The Roman Forum, where the first crude inscriptions
of the early Christians were discovered.**

lack of evidence. These historians wrote more in the spirit of the aristocrat and the æsthete, and so had a two-fold contempt for the crowd. Most references to the masses, found in the literature of that and subsequent periods, are made in the spirit in which Petronius thought of them: "Men with the odor of roast beans, which they carried in their bosoms, and who, besides, were eternally hoarse and sweating from playing *mora* on the street corners and peri-styles."[1] They made up simply the mob, and as the

291

intelligence which centered at Rome got its idea of the common people from the unruly, sycophantic crowd which it saw daily idling in the forum, it felt that the people were worth little consideration.

This attitude on the part of the intelligent Romans, and our consequent ignorance, is the very spur to our interest in every scrap of evidence illustrative of the life of the common people. We know only that they arose with each new sun, millions in number, and went about their affairs. They clothed themselves humbly, ate humbly, worshiped humbly, and passed into the unknown unheeded. Not a genuine, human touch of them remains save in scraps and bits—here a leaf of papyrus, there a rude scratching on a wall.

In recent years two Italians have thought considerably on this subject and yearned to know more of the one-time people who made up the population of the Roman Empire. The first was John Baptist de Rossi, a member of the executive staff of the Vatican, and the other, Professor Orazio Marucchi, director of the Egyptian and Ethiopian Museum at the Vatican, who is a pupil of the former. Both were engaged in historical research among the ruins of the capital, and so were in constant contemplation of the marks of the hands of these countless thousands so little accounted for in history. Naturally their senses were sharpened for the discovery of any trace. When here and there they discovered the rude scratching of an object, or a sentence made unquestionably when the Cæsars ruled, and the Forum was still the centre of the world, they were not unlikely to set great store by it, and to consider it comparatively with all others which they had come across, indicative of the hands and hearts of the common men. They found these scratchings to be numerous and unquestionably of ancient date. Therefore they took them as a class and made them a separate study, giving them a name and accounting the prosecution of their study a science, the science of graffitology.

The first occasion on which the public was made acquainted with the word graffitology was when Professor Marucchi discovered the rude scratching, which he took to be a first-century representation of the Crucifixion. It was an uncouth piece of workmanship, but to the professor it was of the utmost importance, and his theory about its origin interested the entire world. He had an Italian word ready to describe it, the word, *graffito.* Now *graffito,* with its plural *graffiti,* is a common term in the vocabulary of the archæologist, especially since the excavations made at Pompeii. The word means a rough drawing. It is what we find penciled on our street walls to-day. We are more likely to call them defacements, and to post signs, threatening to prosecute anyone who dares to scratch or pencil a name, a sentence or a picture upon public monuments or buildings. Yet these are *graffiti*—the very things which the Italian students are looking for, and with which they expect to build up this science, which is to

**The Famous Blasphemous Graffito
from the House of Geloziano.**

[This was drawn by a Pagan soldier, and represents a
Christian brother-in-arms, worshipping God. The inscription reads: "Alexander adores God."]

contribute so much to our knowledge of that unknown world. To speak of
graffiti as compassing an exact science may strike some as an overestimate, and yet the statement is not without justification. Its chief defense
has been made by another student of the subject, Howard M. Breen. He
says:

"Suppose these rough scratchings are found on the tombs of the Pha-
raohs and are known to have been made centuries before our Saviour was
born; or that they represent or allude to persons or events contemporaneous
with Alexander the Great, Julius Cæsar, or Boadicea, then their evidence
becomes of importance for the study of history.[2] Suppose that rules are laid
down and principles formulated, according to which these scratchings on
the walls may be methodically studied and passed into the service of
history or of art or of philology, then the investigation of them assumes
nothing less than the garb and character of a veritable science. That science

may well be termed graffitology. *Graffiti* are old, graffitology is new. It is not the thing but the scientific use of it that is recent."

As a science graffitology rests on the work of the gentlemen named and upon that of Rev. Bonaventure F. Broderick, D. D., of the Roman Catholic Seminary of Hartford, who during a period of years spent in Italy conducted investigations of the subject. Thus far no work has been done outside of Italy, and all that has been discovered there forms but the mere beginnings of a science. It includes *graffiti* or sketches of lions and crosses, deities and emblems, monograms and sentences, and a number of gambling squares or tables scratched deeply in those secluded parts of houses and public places, where gaming went on among servants and soldiers. Some of these *graffiti* served most important ends, particularly those of the dove with branch, the palm branch, the fish, and the bark. They were used when Christianity was under the bane of the Cæsars, and when it meant death either to declare yourself a believer in the Man of Galilee, or to make any expression of the doctrines of the new and abhorred faith.[3]

The investigators who come at this late date, find other justification for the use of these *graffiti* by the common people of that time, and what they have discovered gives excellent credit to the science. The practice of drawing *graffiti* was larger than it is to-day, because in a sense such drawing was justifiable and serviceable. In the halcyon days of the republic and later, general sentiment commended the display of wit. The law did not forbid defacements of this kind even on the most sumptuous and most recently constructed public buildings. Crowds lounged in places which to-day would be preserved from any such untoward intrusion. The forum with its forest of columns, its array of shops and temples with ample stairways, was the resort of crowds of idle people, assembled to stroll among the pillars to tell and hear the news, to see noted people borne past in litters, and finally to look in at the jewelry shops, the book shops, the arches where coin was exchanged and all those fine stalls with which the buildings covering that part of the market opposite the capitol were filled. Crowds passed under the arches of the *basilica* of Julius Cæsar, crowds sat daily on the steps of the temple of Castor and Pollux, or walked around the temple of Vesta.[4] From above, down immense steps from the sides of the temple dedicated to Jupiter Optimus Maximus, came other waves. At the rostra people listened to chance orators, in other places they collected to hear the arguments of cheats who offered marvelous medicines, soothsayers who guessed for hidden treasures, and interpreters who explained the mysteries of dreams.

Here were the soldiers lounging in groups or advancing with measured tread among the unordered throngs, pushing all authoritatively aside and preserving order. Here, too, gathered all those people without any occupation, who appeared every week at the storehouses on the Tiber for grain, who fought for lottery tickets to the circus, who spent their nights in rickety houses in districts beyond the river, their sunny, warm days under covered porticos, and in foul eating-houses of the Suburra, on the Milvian bridge, or before the "insulæ" of the great, where from time to time remnants from the tables of slaves were thrown out to them. Last of all, portions of these always took advantage of that custom of the Roman nobles, who desired to shine as patrons of the public, to make themselves hangers-on. It must be remembered that in those days a patron's nobility was measured by the number of clients who mustered in the morning and saluted him at his first appearance on the balcony of his house. Thereafter they lounged for the remainder of the day in the temples and porticos of the forum. They whiled away the lagging hours which separated them from the hoped-for invitation to dine with their patron by scratching rude verses and coarse jests on the walls or pillars against which they leaned, or by tracing on the pavements gaming tables whereon to play dice.

Here, then, and in places partaking of a similar atmosphere, were scratched those *graffiti* which come under the first or pagan subdivision of the new science. Did the crowd open from time to time before the litter of some famous senator or some renowned beauty, an idler might trace the features of the occupant or write some ribald remarks for his own sarcastic beguilement. Did a few soldiers or loungers agree to gamble, they would trace on the stone pavement their square, marking on each side their gains or losses. Sometimes, as in the illustration of the gambling *graffiti,* the victor would heap sarcasm upon the departing loser by writing as was done in this one, "Vanquished; get thee gone; thou knowest not how to play; give thy place to one who does." In another place, some lounger dangling his legs comfortably over the side of a temple portico, no doubt would idly sketch things which he had seen. What these might have been is well illustrated by the *graffiti* found on the temple of Antoninus and Faustina. One such, as shown by the sketch, was a military bust, possibly intended to represent some dignitary of the time known to the artist. Another was a rude drawing of a gladiator fighting with a lion, which the artist had probably seen at the amphitheatre. A third was a conception of Hercules and his club. Perhaps the two concentric circles were drawn to show some one a point in an argument concerning the Coliseum. Others from the same place afford food for speculation as to thoughts of the individual who scratched them there—for instance "the *graffito* of Victory" and that of the individual with the horn of plenty.

Messrs. Rossi, Marucchi and Broderick, wandering among these Roman ruins of all that was once magnificent, encountered the first ancient scribblings. In the Domus Geloziana on the Palatine Hill, Prof. Marucchi discovered so far back as 1857 the now famous *graffito* known by its accompanying phrase, "Alexander adores God."[5] On the steps of the temple of Castor and Pollux the first *graffiti* scenes inspired by surrounding objects or passing events were noted. About the temple of Antoninus and Faustina were found all but obliterated, more than a score of objects, including a sketch of the Coliseum and a seated Byzantine figure of the Saviour with nimbus. On some stones belonging to the crumbled temple of Jupiter Optimus Maximus a number of sketches of heads, possibly celebrities, and more inscriptions, epigrams and parts of ribald songs.

When the import of these drawings became apparent, the investigations were extended to other cities including Pompeii, Herculaneum and Baiæ.[6] Here similar pagan *graffiti* were discovered, and now and again something pertaining to the early Christians. The latter were eventually classified and studied separately, and so came to be made up that second division of graffitology known as *sacred*. In it were included not only all those crude sketches which were made during the first century of the Christian era, but everything with any religious reference made previous to the twelfth century. The majority of the *sacred graffiti* discovered, belongs to the period of the Cæsars and covers a chapter of persecution and sorrow all too insufficiently indicated heretofore by any positive evidence.

To appreciate rightly the historical value of the discoveries in this branch, it is important first to consider the state of the times in which they were made. In the first centuries of our era the Christian religion was periodically under the ban of persecution. The new theology was but ill-reported and scoffed at. Its followers were made the scapegoats of every political scheme and intrigue. Did a conspirator high at court wish to escape the penalty of the discovery of his crime it was most easy to implicate the despised Christians. Did a Nero fear the ire of the mob he could readily charge that the mysterious unfortunates burned Rome, and be believed.[7] Their meetings were outlawed, their places of worship sought out and destroyed. Naturally they felt constrained to resort to the so-called rite of secrecy. In order to save their holy places from desecration by the pagan and yet to indicate them to the observation of the initiated they "used signs." What more natural than that these signs should be chosen out of the phraseology and simile of the Master. The bark, the branch of palm, the vine, the sprig of olive, loaves and fishes, a shepherd with his crook, or a lamb on his shoulder, the monogram of Christ and other rough drawings of objects, which in the Bible are taken for doctrinal symbols, were gradually employed to indicate their places of assembly, their altars and their tombs.

These symbols were only occasionally noticed at first. Unlike the pagan *graffiti,* they were found in secret and out of the way places, and it was long after the extent and import of the first division of the science had become clear that the second was formulated and was found to be of even greater interest. A proper classification of them was made, covering three main subdivisions. The first comprises prayers of pilgrims visiting sacred shrines and tombs. Thus "Eutycian Vivas," the full meaning being "Eutycias, mayest thou have eternal life." The second covers the names of pilgrims and records of their visits to the tombs of the Apostles, to the Catacombs and the like. The third includes the symbols spoken: the fish, the bark, the dove, and so on.

The Christian *graffiti* of all kinds thus far discovered, number hundreds. That excellent example "Eutycian Vivas" comes from a crypt in the Catacombs where the body of Eutycian was no doubt secretly laid. Another, a kind of hieroglyphic combination of P and F standing for "Palma Felicitas" was a common Christian *graffito* and signified "victory happily won." It was inscribed in places which, no doubt, witnessed scenes of martyrdom, though no direct evidence proved this. The best preserved *graffito* of this kind is to be seen in the pavement of the Julian Bascilica, where it was discovered by Professor de Rossi. On a rock some distance outside of the former confines of Rome, in one of those bare hollows which were used in the early days by the Christians as a meeting place, was discovered a fine example of the bark *graffito*, signifying the refuge of the Christian church. In another such space was found a crude scratching of a dove with a palm branch in its mouth, symbolizing the soul in heaven. Both of these possibly were scrawled by the leaders of some little Christian circle, to indicate to approaching worshipers the exact spot of some early meeting. In the stadium of the palace of the Cæsars the investigators found a *graffito* of two palm branches which was a common symbol signifying victory through martyrdom. In various parts of the forum *graffiti* have been found, some scrawled there so late as the seventh century and some so early as the first. The best preserved of these are a *graffito* of St. Peter; another of a Lombard cross, drawn in the seventh century; a monogram, P X, the letters written separately and transposed, and another monogram of the same letters, joined, and the initials of Alpha and Omega transposed and encircled, both thought to be the work of a Hebrew convert. A sentence "M Asclepias Vivas" (Long Life to Asclepias) also found there, is thought to be a farewell to some departing brother of the faith.

What is chiefly to be observed of the drawings is their simple humanity. In them we find a natural and spontaneous expression of faith and purpose. All graffitology is appallingly human, and manifests, more plainly than anything else yet discovered, the state of reason and the methods of the common mind. Through them we see, however dimly, the ancients in their places of idleness or of secret assembly—their habits and manners, and the naiveté of their opinions. This is very important to the historian who would gain a true knowledge of them. They are better than the inscriptions on monuments and tombs, because the latter are merely the show pieces of a nation and represent nothing but its intellectual pride in philosophy and distinguished phraseology. They show the people prim and garnished for posterity's inspection, while the spontaneous scribblings of the common mind are of all things unaffected and natural.

We must attach no more importance to the subject than is given to it by its sponsors, however. Dr. Broderick believes that when studied with method, graffitology becomes one of the most interesting of the large group of historical sciences. He is not willing to give any great credit to the work thus far, but submits that many of the principles which guide and have guided the investigators of the subject are deduced from a study of human nature, of man in his natural state. He claims that *graffiti* are found in all inhabited regions, and, if carefully noted and compared, may yet furnish us with many clues to what has constituted the natural progress of civilization from the earliest ages down to our own.

Professor Orazio Marucchi, who of all the investigators of the subject has been most diligent, is equally conservative. He claims not even originality of discovery for his master, John Baptist de Rossi, whom he sincerely credits with nearly all that has been accomplished. Graffitology, he suggests, had followers in the past. Many Italian and German scholars having noted the *graffiti* discovered on the excavations of Pompeii. They made some effort to utilize their discoveries, but could do so only in a small measure. Drawings and writings there were, together with symbols and suggestions, common enough in pagan life, but they were of such a character as the more refined morality of the Gospel has made obsolete.

Concerning the *graffiti* and inscriptions which he himself has discovered he has said: "They resemble those found in the ruins of Pompeii. These rude scratchings on the coatings of the walls, of, for instance, the palace of the Cæsars, were, I believe, made chiefly by soldiers and slaves. They are the most difficult form of inscription to decipher, as their letters are formed quite differently from those which we find in the current hand of the papyri and parchments, and as in many cases earlier inscriptions are covered by later ones.

"Inscriptions of this class have been found in the Catacombs and have been made the special study by my illustrious master, the late John Baptist de Rossi. One particular inscription written on the wall opposite the crypt of the Popes in the cemetery of St. Calixtus, involved him in long years of patient investigation.

"The chief spots on the Palatine Hill where *graffiti* inscriptions are found, are the House of Tiberius, the neighborhood of the Stadium, and the so-called Pedagogium.[8] This last was a military school for the youths destined to become members of the emperor's body-guard. Here in 1857 was made the discovery of the caricature of Christian worship. It represented a figure in the traditional act of worship, before a man with an ass' head attached to a cross. These words formed a part of it—*Alexamanos sebete Theon*—'Alexander adores his god.' It was immediately recognized that this was a satire by a pagan soldier on a Christian comrade named Alexander.

"It is an established fact, though the precise motive is not clear, that the pagans were in the habit of calling the Christians, adorers of an ass' head. This *graffito* has all the internal evidence of dating from the beginning of the third century, probably from the days of Septimius Severus.[9] It was detached from the wall where it was found, and is now in the museum of the Roman College. Near this spot several *graffiti* names are found, and I myself, examining the locality, came upon one inscription, with what appears to be a phrase of Christian origin. It seems to be a pious ejaculation to the effect that trust is to be placed in the protection of God. If this interpretation is correct the phrase might be regarded as a reply by Alexander or by another Christian soldier in his name, to the preceding insult. The matter, however, still requires study.

"Continuing my examination, I came some time since upon a little drawing, fifteen inches by eight. It was on the wall of a room in the soldiers' quarters in the House of Tiberius. The lines in it were almost completely obliterated. Nevertheless, by the aid of powerful glasses I thought I discerned a pictorial reproduction of some striking event. There seemed to be two crosses with ladders leaning against them. On one of these a soldier was mounting, carrying something like a tablet. Above the transverse bar of this same cross was another soldier with a hammer. Beneath was a figure dragging another toward the cross. Yet another figure was raising a ladder to the second cross, and on a third ladder a solder was mounting. Two ropes hang from the cross beams which unite the crosses. Names are written near the figures. One is Pilatus, or Piletus (written *Piletus*). High above the drawing is a word resembling *Crestus,* and near it is a hammer, which, as is known, was the emblem of the Crucifixion.

"All the circumstances brought me to imagine for a moment, that I might be in the presence of a picture of the Crucifixion of our Saviour, and possibly even drawn by soldiers who had assisted at the event. Many others were of the same opinion, though there were competent authorities who read in it a different signification. They suggested, for instance, the launching of a ship, or the representation of an acrobatic performance. One thing is now clear, the large inscription over the drawing can be no part of the idea therein represented. It is the work of many hands, written at various periods, and composed almost exclusively of libertine expressions."

Signor Marucchi continues: "I myself have recently had an opportunity of settling a rather important dispute by means of some *graffiti* which I discovered. On that part of the Palatine Hill which stretches over in the direction of the Baths of Caracalla, is an important series of ruins which Libby had declared were a stadium built by the Emperor Septimius Severus.[10] Latterly some German archeologists had contested this and gave out points arguing the theory that it was not a stadium, and endeavoring to show that it was merely a commonplace portion of the Imperial gardens. Having recently had some time at my disposal, I made investigations among these ruins, and unearthed a number of important *graffiti*. Every single one of these had allusions to horse racing, chariot racing, discus-throwing and gladiatorial combats. These were exactly such as were discovered among the ruins of the Coliseum, the Flaminian ampitheatre and other places that had been dedicated to sports and combats.[11] The commonest of all were *graffiti* of gladiators' helmets and the word "palma" which was frequently repeated by the pagans as an augury of victory during the games. With the aid of these documents, I once more laid forth the arguments in favor of the stadium theory and the German scientists, who had formerly attacked the theory, were now the first to admit the value and the convincing nature of the arguments."

NOTES

"Human Documents from Old Rome," *Ainslee's* 3 (June 1899): 586–96.

1. Petronius, Roman author of the first century, who is credited with writing the *Satyricon,* one of the first examples of the novel in Western literature. *Mora,* in Roman and civil law, means culpable delay in the performance of an obligation.

2. Alexander the Great (356–323 B.C.), King of Macedon, is considered the greatest general in ancient times. Julius Caesar (100–44 B.C.). Boadicea, Queen of the Iceni, a British tribe that rebelled against the Romans in A.D. 60.

3. Galilee is revered by Christians as that part of the Holy Land where Jesus of Nazareth spent most of his life and carried on much of his ministry.

4. The temple of Castor and Pollux is noted in classical mythology for its brotherly love. It exemplifies manly strength, skill, courage, and inseparability. Castor, the mortal, was famed as a horse tamer and charioteer; Pollux, the immortal, was a champion boxer. Vesta, in the Roman religion, is a virgin goddess of the hearth and its fire. The illegitimate daughter of Jennie Gerhardt in Dreiser's novel is named Vesta.

5. The Palatine Hill was one of the ancient seven hills of Rome.

6. Herculaneum was a city of ancient Italy, buried in the great eruption of Mt. Vesuvius in A.D. 79. Baiæ was a favorite bathing resort of the ancient Romans.

7. Nero (A.D. 37–68), Roman emperor.

8. Tiberius (42 B.C.–A.D. 37) was the second Roman emperor.

9. Septimus Lucius Severus (A.D. 146–211), Roman emperor.

10. The Baths of Caracalla were the famous baths built by Marcus Aurelius Antonius (originally Bassianus) Caracalla (A.D.188–217), Roman emperor.

11. The Flaminian amphitheater was one of the projects on which Gaius Flaminius (died 217 B.C.), Roman soldier, statesman, and reformer of the republic, left his name.

4

Why the Indian Paints His Face

WHEN THE JESUP NORTH PACIFIC EXPEDITION SET OUT TO BRITISH CO-
lumbia in 1897 to discover the origin of the Indian in America, and to study
all matters concerning past and living tribes, it went about a task of which
the end is still many years distant.[1] Only one little side issue of the great
investigation has so far been brought to a conclusion; and that is the answer
to the question—Why do the Indians paint their faces?

Those who are interested in the study of mankind are well aware that the
savage is prompted by a definite motive for every deed that he does. This
custom of the Red Indian to daub his face with colour has long been a
puzzle to scientific men, though possibly the average layman has never
thought that there might be any significance in this common aboriginal
practice. It might be supposed that the Indians use paint for the same
reason that prompted the ancient inhabitants of Britain to cover their
bodies with woad—to protect themselves, that is, from the cold. This,
however, is far from being the case.

The fact of the matter is that every paint mark on an Indian's face is a
sign with a definite meaning which other Indians may read. When an
Indian puts on his full war paint, he decks himself not only with his own
individual honours and distinctions won by his own bravery, but also with
the special honours of his family or tribe. He may possess one mark of
distinction only, or many; in fact, he may be so well off in this respect that,
like some English noblemen, he is able to don a new distinction for every
occasion.

Sometimes he will wear all his honours at one time. The Jesup Expedition investigators met, at notable Indian functions, chiefs who bore upon
their persons as many as twenty distinctions—feathers, skins, strings of
beads and teeth, but above and beyond all in importance, face marks, eight
or nine in all.

To interpret the true meaning of the various paintings, it is now only
necessary to look among the records in the American Natural History
Museum, thanks to the patient work of the scientists connected with the
anthropological department. These gentlemen have spent several years
living with the Indians, and moving from tribe to tribe, in a region where

301

white men are exceedingly rare, and where the wildest and most primitive sort of life must be endured for the sake of science. In all, the Museum authorities now possess one hundred drawings of Indian heads, fully decorated with the symbols, which were designed by Edensa, chief of the Haida Indians in British Columbia, a great picture-maker among his people.[2]

To be quite certain that the drawings were absolutely accurate, they were submitted to other Indians, who were asked what they represented. With one or two exceptions, no mistake was made.

It is fascinating work to translate the symbols with the help of the key, and to follow out the Indians' thoughts that prompted the various designs. One of the drawings, for instance, represents an Indian with his lips painted copper red. This, we learn, shows that his tribe was the possessor of large copper deposits. Another Indian is adorned with a halibut drawn across his forehead—his tribe made a living by halibut fishing, and was famous for its great catches. In addition to the halibut symbol, he sometimes, on great occasions, wore another distinction, in the shape of round disks of mother-of-pearl pasted to his cheeks. The moon, it is clear, was one of his ancestors, for the pearl shows her faint light.

The art of the Indian shows a most remarkable and peculiar development. While most primitive people use only straight lines, the Indians of Northern British Columbia have advanced so far that they have mastered the idea of curves, and use animal designs almost entirely. They have, however, no idea of perspective, and so they represent any form in a highly conventional manner: they dissect it, and distort it, and show only the most characteristic part! The cleverer an artist is in dividing his animals into their chief parts, and showing all the parts on the surface at his command—arranged in any order irrespective of Nature!—the greater will be his success.

Parts of the face are often used as parts of the design which the Indian paints upon it. When the head of an animal is to be drawn on a man's face, his eyes are allowed to stand for the eyes of the animal, and so with his teeth and nose. In the case, for instance, of the Indians who use the beaver as a symbol, no attempt is made to design the whole form of this animal. Only the beaver's typical, and peculiar, scaly tail is painted with criss-cross lines, extending from the chin up to the nose, as though standing upright. No trouble is taken to paint the beaver's body—that is represented by the man's chin.

Indian artists invariably represent an animal's ears as above the eyes, and the ears of the beaver are painted above the eyebrows. The paws are shown on the cheeks, as though they were raised to the mouth, in the manner in which the beaver is usually represented in Indian carvings. Any Indian would recognise the sign of the beaver, but to the white man the marks would convey no meaning, except that the Indian was possessed with a love of colour.

The Indian considers heavy, regular eyebrows a sign of beauty. His eyebrows are naturally very wide, covering a part of the upper eyelid, and ascending on to the temple. They are largely used in facial decoration. One tribe, for instance, employs the killer whale as an emblem, adapting its form to the form of the brow, and by a little judicious colouring making the eyebrow represent the whole whale. The hair is sometimes plucked away from the eyelids—especially by the women—to produce a sharp line, to show off the whale design, painted black, to the better advantage.

Among the Indian tribes is one designated by the symbol of the dog-fish, painted in red on the face. The various parts of the fish are scattered heterogeneously on the surface of the face; the peculiarly long snout is painted on the forehead, the gills are represented by two curved lines below the eyes, while the tail is shown as cut in two, and hanging from either nostril. When only one or two parts of an animal are painted on a man's face, it is an indication of inferiority; when the whole animal appears, even though in many oddly assorted parts, the sign is one of great value, and indicates a high rank.

Very peculiar are some of the honourable symbols painted on the Indians' faces. There are fish, flesh and fowl of all kinds—dog-salmon, devil-fish, star-fish, woodpeckers, eagles, ravens, wolfs, bears, sea lions and sea monsters, mosquitoes, frogs, mountain goats, and all manner of foot, claw, or beak marks—each with a special meaning of its own.

One of the most interesting phases of the face-painting art relates to material forms other than animal—fishing nets, for instance, to indicate the chief industry of a tribe, or a representation of timber logs on a mountain timber slide, showing that the Indians who wear this symbol are engaged in timber cutting.

One family paints red across the upper part of the forehead and hair to indicate the evening sky. Another daubs small semi-circles of red about the outer edges of the face to indicate cirrus clouds on the horizon of the ocean; still another draws lines across the face, red, blue, and green, crossing from the right ear to the left side of the lower jaw. A red sun with black rays is adopted by one family, painted between the eyes, sometimes covering the nose and mouth, and sometimes made with wood instead of paint, and worn on the forehead, when the rim of a red wooden disk is inlaid with pieces of abalone shell.

This aboriginal art takes an equally peculiar turn when it comes to the treatment of other surfaces than the face. If a bracelet is to be decorated with an animal, for instance, it is shown as though it were cut from head to tail, and the arm were pushed through the opening, the whole animal thus surrounding the wrist. This strange method is also followed in the decoration of dishes. On the sides of the dish the sides of the animal are shown, the opening of the dish is supposed to represent the back of the animal, and its bottom the lower side. If a lid were used it would be the back, and the animal's form would be complete. Another eccentricity of Indian art is seen when an animal is drawn on a flat surface. It is then shown as though split in two, so that both sides may be seen.

[Note.—We are indebted to the Canadian section of the Imperial Institute, London, for permission to use the photographs which illustrate this article. The actual face-markings have been added in accordance with the report of the Jesup North Pacific Expedition.—Ed. P. M.]

NOTES

"Why the Indian Paints His Face," *Pearson's* 11 (January 1901): 19–23.

1. The Jesup North Pacific Expedition was an American organization for archaeological research, supported by Morris Ketchum Jesup (1830–1908), American banker and philanthropist. He was president of the American Museum of Natural History (1881–1907). He gave liberal sums as well as much time and thought to the establishment of schools for the African American population of the South.

2. Edensa was chief of the Haida Indians, a North American tribe, that lived on the Queen Charlotte Islands, British Columbia, and on the Southern end of Prince of Wales Island, Alaska.

5

Rural Free Mail Delivery

A great reform in the postal service of the country is being perfected. Before long there will be no home so isolated that letters are not delivered at its door and outgoing mail collected there. This article describes the development of this social revolution and the wonderful system by which it is accomplished.

RURAL FREE DELIVERY HAS COME AT LAST, AND IT HAS COME TO STAY. Year by year the appropriations for this service have been increased by Congress, from $50,000 to $150,000, then to $450,000, and lastly for last fiscal year, to $1,750,000. All this has been brought about in response to the irresistible demands of the plain people, who, having once tasted the service, demanded more. One year ago only Idaho, Montana, Mississippi, Utah, and Wyoming were without practical examples of the new service. Each of these States, Mississippi and Montana excepted, has since been supplied with rural free delivery. Two hundred and fifty new services, each averaging 25 miles in length, and serving about 1,000 persons, are being started every month. It is confidently expected that the appropriation for the rural delivery of mails will not be less than $5,000,000 for the present year, and nearly every cent of this expenditure will come back into the Treasury in the shape of increased postal receipt or reduced cost of collateral postal service. Yet, strange to say, there is still much public ignorance regarding this innovation in United States postal methods. It has been deemed such a far-off thing, and so wholly impossible with our present poor roads, that when heard of, it has been taken for granted that it was merely an experiment, not to be considered as permanent, and never to be extended over the whole country within the lifetime of any living American.

That rural free delivery should be such a novelty as to excite a general feeling of distrust concerning its primary application, is all the more remarkable when it is taken into consideration that the United States is the only country among all those comprising the International Postal Union that fails to deliver the mails to rural addresses. England has had an approximately perfect system for years, and so have Belgium, France, and Switzerland. Yet when the Hon. Perry S. Heath first asked for an appropriation of $150,000, with which to further experiment in the matter of delivering mail daily to farmers, an Eastern senator said to him:

"You have acted unwisely in this recommendation. You will have these farmers demanding a rural delivery of mail and causing no end of trouble."

Mr. Heath replied that if the farmers did so demand, they would be strictly within their rights, and pointed out that during the past year the farmers, after supplying home demands, sent abroad $856,000,000 worth of farm products, and that they bear a burden of taxation sufficient to justify the Government in giving them every facility which can be rendered to a citizen.

As recently as 1893 the Postmaster-General reported to Congress that the introduction of any system of rural free delivery of letters and papers would be impracticable, as involving an expenditure of $20,000,000 a year without any commensurate revenue. In his annual report for 1894 Postmaster-General Bissell declined to spend the appropriation of $10,000 made by Congress to test the feasibility of rural free delivery.[1] When Congress increased the appropriation for a test to $20,000 in 1895, Postmaster-General Wilson adopted the opinion of his predecessor and of the House Committee on the Post-Office and Post Roads, that the plan of establishing rural free delivery was wholly impracticable.[2] He added that he had assumed control of the department too late in the fiscal year to take any action under the appropriation, but should Congress see fit to make it available for the current year, he would carry out the experiment ordered by the best methods he could devise.

Congress made $50,000 available for the purpose, and in 1896 Post-master-General Wilson put the idea to its first test. Forty-four places were selected, and the business of organizing the new system was placed in the hands of the Division of Post-Office Inspection and Mail Depredations. Inspectors were detached from other pressing duties to perform this, which they understood was not really wanted by the department. They were hampered by orders which left them no discretion, and compelled to start tests in specially selected localities, whether the conditions seemed favorable or not. It was very evident that the whole idea was one of killing the proposed scheme, and only its superlative merit ever saved it from destruction.

For instance, the inspector who started service over three routes from Cairo, Mo., reported officially that he had "labored under serious disadvantages," arising from the instructions of the department and the slowness of appreciation on the part of the patrons, who, he said, "have only just begun to realize that it is unnecessary to wait until it is convenient to visit the post-office before replying to their correspondents." The three routes which he started accommodated barely 400 patrons.

At Allensville, Todd County, Ky., the service started by a post-office inspector had three carriers in a country without turnpike roads, township divisions, or a county map. Nobody wanted it. Many of the leading farmers on the routes had business which took them daily into the town of Allensville, on the Louisville and Nashville Railway, where they received their mail at the post-office, and some of them were connected with the town by telephone. The rest of the population consisted chiefly of colored people, many of whom were unable to read or write. The service was an unwelcome gift, and an embarrassment to those upon whom it was imposed without their solicitation. It cost the first year within a fraction of 4 cents for every piece of mail handled, and was finally ordered discontinued, the whole idea suffering thereby.

Another inspector who, under instructions from the department, laid out a route from Hartsville, Bartholomew County, Ind., reported, in regard to the character of the people living on the line of the prescribed delivery:

"I find that they are not demanding free delivery of their mail; their correspondence is largely social in its nature, and a question of a day or two in the delivery is of no importance to them. While the majority of the farmers take weekly papers, and some take magazines, but few take daily papers, and most of those reside near post-offices. It will, therefore, be seen that the quantity, nature, and importance of the average farmer's mail is not such as to make rural free delivery an essential."

In the matter of the Cairo route nothing was done until a new administration came in, when a reorganization of the territory was ordered. Two routes were made out of the original three, and all portions which led by impassable roads were discontinued. New territory, where the roads were good, was added, and thus more patrons were served. The whole thing was seen to be wrongly handled, and that with the intention to discredit it. Two carrier routes thus revised served more patrons than three did formerly, and the system thus reorganized paid from the time of the change.

In the case of the Hartsville service it was temporarily discontinued because everything seemed to go wrong. After it had been in existence a month the postmaster, in reply to questions addressed to him by First Assistant Postmaster-General Jones, replied that only one person had changed his address to Hartsville to get the benefit of the service, and that the amount of mail handled had not increased. A month later he again reported that the carrier was travelling 24 miles a day to serve 38 persons. At the end of the fiscal year 1897 the cost of rural free delivery from Hartsville was found to average more than 6 1/3 cents for every piece of mail handled.

Some time after it had been stopped leading citizens visited Washington and prayed for its restoration. They said it had never been given a fair chance. Accordingly a special agent, in sympathy with the service, was sent out there to find some route which would pay. One was observantly laid out, and the very first month 2,538 pieces of mail were handled, thus reducing the percentage of cost from 6.34 cents to 1.28.

This is the story of the service right straight through, but its principal success remains yet to be detailed. This is concerning the service in Carroll County, Md. The working of the new system there is of such special interest that it cannot be ignored, because there the fact was finally settled that rural free delivery is the greatest thing for the improvement of the condition of the rural citizen that has yet been devised. To begin with, the conditions of the test were most severe. The country was selected because it was mountainous and difficult to traverse. The most unfavorable season of the year—namely, December, 1899—saw the inauguration of this experiment. Then the weather was extremely cold, the roads in poor condition, and the mails choked with holiday packages.

"Now," said the government agents, "if rural free delivery succeeds here, it will succeed anywhere."

The plan inaugurated called for the discontinuance of 63 of the 94 fourth-class post-offices in the county, as well as 33 star routes and 2 messenger services, and the substitution therefor of 4 postal wagons or travelling post-offices, and 26 rural carriers.

The postal wagons introduced there and still running are fully equipped post-offices on wheels. The clerk in charge sells postage stamps and stamped paper, issues and pays money orders, registers letters, postmarks and back-stamps all mail, and supplies the rural carriers on outlying routes with mail for dispatch. In fact, these wagons do all the work now done by a Presidential post-office of the first class.

On the morning of December 19, 1899, all the clerks and carriers who were to carry on the new system assembled at Westminster, the chief town of the county, and received their supplies and final instructions. Each carrier was given a cancelling stamp bearing the number of his route, and he was authorized to cancel stamps on letters collected by him for delivery on his own route.

The perplexing difficulties and annoyances usually attending an innovation or radical change were, in this case, greatly added to by the concerted action of 60 ex-postmasters, who attempted to convince the people that the killing of their small post-offices meant the destruction of all postal facilities. Their word, however, was not of much weight in the face of the actual service rendered. A complete map of his route was furnished each carrier, showing the location of every residence, and to the front doors of these he now betook himself. From the very first day each carrier served an average of 408 families; the postal wagons 858 each. They travelled an aggregated of 834 miles every day, and reached considerably over 19,100 people. Where formerly every farmer had been obliged to travel to the nearest country post-office, his mail was now brought within 176 yards of his door, at the worst, and, in many instances, actually to the door. This created a great stir. During the first month the new service handled 15,000 odd pieces, a substantial increase over all the business done by the combined post-offices which had been discontinued. During the second month the same service handled over 195,000 pieces, and the third month saw this increased to over 220,000. Letters were registered as never before. Where, by the old system, 451 money orders were issued in three months, now 633 were issued, an increase of 40 per cent. The general revenues rose from $6,429.21 for three months under the old system, to $7,930.36 or $1,501.15 more.

It was said, however, in the beginning, that the service might do very well in fair weather, but that storms and bad roads would put an end to the daily service. The opponents of the new system waited for this catastrophe in order to set up a hue and cry. The determination, as well as the ability, of the government to maintain a daily rural service, under any conditions, was demonstrated early in March, 1900, when a severe blizzard swept over the country. The roads were blocked by impassable snowdrifts—in many places from fence to fence. Traffic was practically suspended throughout the country. The contractors who hauled the postal wagons, however, were instructed to hitch four horses to each wagon, and gangs of shovellers were sent out several hours in advance to cut the drift. Amid storm and sleet the service was performed, without interruption and with but little delay, much to the surprise, of course, of those who had waited cheerfully to see the government confounded.

After this experience there was not one among all the farmers who was not enthusiastic about the new service, and the few who complained were compelled to admit that they had not fully realized the great importance of the service, nor the real convenience it afforded. The men who, every winter previously, had been cut off for weeks by snow and the impassable condition of the roads, now received their correspondence and daily papers the same as if they were in the heart of the most populous community. Since then there has been no doubt in the minds of the postal authorities as to the greatness and importance of the new service.

One more example may be cited, however, as illustrating what really can be done under difficult conditions. It is from a report made by one of the special agents employed by the government to inaugurate the system.

"When, before my assignment to the Eastern Division," he writes, "I was called upon to inspect the rural region adjacent to Murphysboro, Ill., it seemed to me that if rural free delivery could exist there it would thrive anywhere. The mud in the roads appeared to be bottomless, the population was sparse, the farms were large, and there was much waste land. I selected the most available localities, and service was established. Very soon there was demand for additional service. Under orders, I again visited Murphysboro, and found to my surprise that the service was successful beyond the highest anticipations of its most ardent friends. The gross receipts of the post-office had increased 50 per cent., and there was not one complaint, except from those who felt they had been slighted. I recommended an extension with three additional carriers, covering the entire region within 6 to 8 miles of the office. There was but one fourth-class post-office within the Murphysboro district. The postmaster resigned immediately after the establishment of the rural service, and the office was discontinued, thus affording an opportunity to demonstrate the practicability of rural free delivery on an elaborate scale in a region devoid of stone roads and traversed by numerous streams. That which has been accomplished at Murphysboro can be duplicated anywhere without cost to the department, as the growth of receipts at the post-offices from which the service originated is more than sufficient to defray the cost of the service."

In the matter of the details of the actual service the tendency is to make it as perfect and well-appearing as that now in operation in the large cities. Thus at Lafayette, Ind., the postmaster and carriers seem to have vied with one another in their efforts to establish a model service.

The rural carriers are governed by the same rules as the carriers of the city delivery service; they wear the same uniform, provided at their own cost, and each has furnished himself with a special-delivery wagon with "Postal Wagon—U. S. Mail" painted on the front and sides. Each wagon

Model letter boxes for a colony of country homes.

has a sliding door at the sides, with a glass front, and is fitted up with pigeonholes, in which the carrier sorts his mail as he goes along. There is also a contrivance for heating the wagon in cold weather. All the boxes along the routes are of galvanized iron, of uniform size, painted, and closely resembling in appearance the regulation boxes used in cities, and are nailed on posts of such height as to bring them to a level with the postal wagon. As he drives up alongside the box the carrier opens his sliding door and drops the mail in the box, at the same time raising a zinc signal which is riveted to the box. If there is any mail for him to collect he finds this signal raised; if he has none to deliver in return he turns the signal down. If the signal is not raised, and he has no mail to deliver at the box, he drives by without stopping. Each carrier has a whistle with which he signals the owners of the boxes in case they live some distance away, so as to let them know he is coming with the mail.

There are many quaint features about the rural free delivery service. One of the most diligent of carriers in Massachusetts is the charming little lady whose picture is reproduced on page 237, Miss Susie E. Gifford, of South Westport. Her father is the regular carrier, but she is the bonded substitute, and does most of the work, driving twenty miles a day in all kinds of weather and never missing a trip. "Miss Susie," as she is called by all the people on her route, is a splendid equestrienne, and, in fact, is a born horse tamer. The most vicious and refractory steed will yield to her persuasions and become docile after a few minutes' private interview and whispering.

One of the most faithful and efficient of local unpaid rural carriers is a thoroughbred Newfoundland dog. "Dom Pedro" by name, whose owner lives a quarter of a mile off the route of the Carroll County, Md., wagon service. "Dom" accompanied his master to meet the wagon the first day the rural delivery was started, and proudly received and carried home the mail then delivered to him. He learned to recognize the peculiar rumble of the mail wagon, and every morning, unbidden, meets it at the corner of the road and demands and receives his master's mail, never failing to deliver it safely at the house a quarter of a mile away. If there happen to be no letters the postal clerks have to make up a dummy package with a note to that effect and hand it to "Dom" for delivery, or he would follow them all the rest of their twenty-five-mile trip.

Wayside gatherings of children and others sent to meet the rural postmen are the constant accompaniment of rural delivery, which is brightening the home of the farmer, and bringing him into closer touch with the great outside world than he ever dreamed possible a few years ago. The sentiment in favor of the service is so strong wherever it has been tried that it would cost the seat in Congress of any representative (no matter what his politics) who attempted now to check the development of this great social revolution.

NOTES

"Rural Free Mail Delivery," *Pearson's* 11 (February 1901): 233–40.

1. Wilson Shannon Bissell (1847–1903), American lawyer and public official, was U.S. Postmaster-General (1893–95) under President Grover Cleveland.

2. William Lyne Wilson (1843–1900), American legislator and educator. Following his defeat for reelection to the Congress in 1894, he was appointed Postmaster-General by President Cleveland. Wilson served in this position from 1895 to 1897, during which time he inaugurated rural free mail delivery and made other improvements in the postal system.

Appendix:
Dreiser's Magazine Articles, 1897–1902

THE FOLLOWING IS A COMPLETE LIST OF FREELANCE MAGAZINE ARTICLES
Dreiser had written before *Sister Carrie* was published in November 1900.
All articles are signed by Dreiser unless otherwise noted. A great majority
of them appeared in 1898 and 1899. Since several articles published in
1901 and 1902 seem to have been prepared during, if not before, the
writing of *Sister Carrie* (1899–1900), they are included in this list. Excluded are all his poems and short stories, and two reviews that appeared in
the period.

The articles preceded by an asterisk (*) are included in Theodore
Dreiser, *Art, Music, and Literature, 1897–1902,* ed. Yoshinobu Hakutani
(Urbana: University of Illinois Press, 2001). The articles preceded by a
plus (+) are included in Theodore Dreiser, *Selected Magazine Articles
of Theodore Dreiser: Life and Art in the American 1890s,* 2 vols., ed.
Yoshinobu Hakutani (Rutherford, NJ: Fairleigh Dickinson University
Press, 1985, 1987).

The unmarked articles are collected in this edition. Republication of the
articles in the collection is indicated in the footnotes for the specific items.

1. "On the Field of Brandywine," *Truth* 16 (6 November 1897): 7–10.
2. "New York's Art Colony," *Metropolitan* 6 (November 1897): 321–26.
   Signed "Theodore Dresser."
*3. "Our Women Violinists," *Puritan* 2 (November 1897): 34–35.
+4. "The Haunts of Bayard Taylor," *Munsey's* 18 (January 1898): 594–601.
*5. "A High Priestess of Art: Alice B. Stephens," *Success* 1 (January 1898):
   55; signed "Edward Al."
6. "A Talk with America's Leading Lawyer: Joseph H. Choate," *Success* 1
   (January 1898): 40–41.
+7. "The Art of MacMonnies and Morgan," *Metropolitan* 7 (February 1898):
   143–51.
+8. "Henry Mosler, a Painter for the People," *Demorest's* 34 (February
   1898): 67–69.
+9. "A Photographic Talk with Edison," *Success* 1 (February 1898): 8–9.

*10. "Anthony Hope Tells a Secret," *Success* 1 (March 1898): 12–13. Reprinted as "A Secret Told by Anthony Hope" in *How They Succeeded: Life Stories of Successful Men Told by Themselves,* ed. Orison Swett Marden (Boston: Lothrop, 1901), 300–305.

*+11. "Historic Tarrytown," *Ainslee's* 1 (March 1898): 25–31.

12. "A Vision of Fairy Lamps: H. Barrington Cox," *Success* 1 (March 1898): 23; signed "Edward Al."

*13. "Work of Mrs. Kenyon Cox," *Cosmopolitan* 24 (March 1898): 477–80.

*14. "Art Work of Irving R. Wiles," *Metropolitan* 7 (April 1898): 357–61.

+15. "Benjamin Eggleston, Painter," *Ainslee's* 1 (April 1898): 41–47.

+16. "The Harp," *Cosmopolitan* 24 (April 1898): 637–44.

*17. "How He Climbed Fame's Ladder: William Dean Howells," *Success* 1 (April 1898): 5–6. Reprinted as "How He Worked to Secure a Foothold" in *How They Succeeded: Life Stories of Successful Men Told by Themselves,* ed. Orison Swett Marden (Boston: Lothrop, 1901), 171–84. Reprinted as "A Printer's Boy, Self-Taught, Becomes the Dean of American Letters—William Dean Howells" in *Little Visits with Great Americans,* ed. Orison Swett Marden (New York: Success Company, 1903), 283–95, and in *American Literary Realism* 6 (Fall 1973): 339–44.

18. "A Prophet, but Not without Honor," *Ainslee's* 1 (April 1898): 73–79. Signed "Edward Al."

*19. "The American Water-Color Society," *Metropolitan* 7 (May 1898): 489–93.

+20. "A Great American Caricaturist," *Ainslee's* 1 (May 1898): 336–41. On Homer Davenport.

*21. "Artists' Studios: Hints Concerning the Aim of All Decoration," *Demorest's* 34 (June 1898): 196–98.

*22. "A Painter of Travels," *Ainslee's* 1 (June 1898): 391–98. On Gilbert Gaul.

23. "Where Battleships Are Built," *Ainslee's* 1 (June 1898): 433–39. Signed "Edward Al."

24. "Carrier Pigeons in War Time," *Demorest's* 34 (July 1898): 222–23.

25. "The Making of Small Arms," *Ainslee's* 1 (July 1898): 540–49.

26. "Scenes in a Cartridge Factory," *Cosmopolitan* 25 (July 1898): 321–24.

+27. "The Harlem River Speedway," *Ainslee's* 2 (August 1898): 49–56.

*+28. "Haunts of Nathaniel Hawthorne," *Truth* 17 (21 September 1898): 7–9; (28 September 1898), 11–13. Published as one article in two separate issues.

*29. "America's Sculptors," *New York Times Illustrated Magazine* (25 September 1898): 6–7.

+30. "Brandywine, the Picturesque, after One Hundred and Twenty Years," *Demorest's* 34 (September 1898): 274–75.

+31. "Fame Found in Quiet Nooks: John Burroughs," *Success* 1 (September 1898): 5–6.

+32. "The Sculpture of Fernando Miranda," *Ainslee's* 2 (September 1898): 113–18.

+33. "Great Problems of Organization III: The Chicago Packing Industry," *Cosmopolitan* 25 (October 1898): 615–26.
+34. "Life Stories of Successful Men—No. 10: Philip D. Armour," *Success* 1 (October 1898): 3–4.
+35. "The Smallest and Busiest River in the World," *Metropolitan* 7 (October 1898): 355–63.
*+36. "Birth and Growth of a Popular Song," *Metropolitan* 8 (November 1898): 497–502.
  37. "Life Stories of Successful Men—No. 11: Chauncey M. Depew," *Success* 1 (November 1898): 3–4.
+38. "The Real Zangwill," *Ainslee's* 2 (November 1898): 351–57.
+39. "Life Stories of Successful Men—No. 12: Marshall Field," *Success* 2 (8 December 1898): 7–8.
  40. "A Leader of Young Manhood: Frank W. Gunsaulus," *Success* 2 (15 December 1898): 23–24.
+41. "The Treasure House of Natural History," *Metropolitan* 8 (December 1898): 595–601.
+42. "When the Sails Are Furled: Sailor's Snug Harbor," *Ainslee's* 2 (December 1898): 593–601.
+43. "He Became Famous in a Day: Paul Weyland Bartlett," *Success* 2 (28 January 1899): 143–44.
+44. "Electricity in the Household," *Demorest's* 35 (January 1899): 38–39.
+45. "The Making of Stained-Glass Windows," *Cosmopolitan* 26 (January 1899): 243–52.
*+46. "His Life Given Up to Music: Theodore Thomas," *Success* 2 (4 February 1899): 167–68. Reprinted as "How Theodore Thomas Brought People Nearer to Music" in *How They Succeeded: Life Stories of Successful Men Told by Themselves,* ed. Orison Swett Marden (Boston: Lothrop, 1901), 314–26.
*47. "America's Greatest Portrait Painters," *Success* 2 (11 February 1899): 183–84.
+48. "The Career of a Modern Portia: Clara S. Foltz," *Success* 2 (18 February 1899): 205–6.
*49. "Literary Lions I Have Met: James Burton Pond," *Success* 2 (25 February 1899): 223–24.
+50. "The Chicago Drainage Canal," *Ainslee's* 3 (February 1899): 53–61.
*51. "E. Percy Moran and His Work," *Truth* 18 (February 1899): 31–35.
*52. "Karl Bitter, Sculptor," *Metropolitan* 9 (February 1899): 147–52.
*53. "A Painter of Cats and Dogs: J. N. Dolph," *Demorest's* 35 (February 1899): 68–69.
*+54. "Amelia E. Barr and Her Home Life," *Demorest's* 35 (March 1899): 103–4.
+55. "Edmund Clarence Stedman at Home," *Munsey's* 20 (March 1899): 931–38.
  56. "The Town of Pullman," *Ainslee's* 3 (March 1899): 189–200.

+57. "Women Who Have Won Distinction in Music," *Success* 2 (8 April 1899): 325–26.

 58. "Japanese Home Life," *Demorest's* 35 (April 1899): 123–25.

+59. "The Real Choate," *Ainslee's* 3 (April 1899): 324–33.

*+60. "The Home of William Cullen Bryant," *Munsey's* 21 (May 1899): 240–46.

+61. "The Horseless Age," *Demorest's* 35 (May 1899): 153–55.

+62. "A Monarch of Metal Workers: Andrew Carnegie," *Success* 2 (3 June 1899): 453–54.

+63. "A Master of Photography: Alfred Stieglitz," *Success* 2 (10 June 1899): 471.

*64. "American Women as Successful Playwrights," *Success* 2 (17 June 1899): 485–86.

+65. "The Foremost of American Sculptors: J. Q. A. Ward," *New Voice* 16 (17 June 1899): 4–5, 13.

*66. "American Women Who Play the Harp," *Success* 2 (24 June 1899): 501–2.

*67. "Concerning Bruce Crane," *Truth* 18 (June 1899): 143–47.

 68. "Human Documents from Old Rome," *Ainslee's* 3 (June 1899): 586–96.

 69. "An Important Philanthropy," *Demorest's* 35 (July 1899): 215–17.

+70. "The Log of an Ocean Pilot," *Ainslee's* 3 (July 1899): 683–92.

*71. "John Burroughs in His Mountain Hut," *New Voice* 16 (19 August 1899): 7, 13. Reconstructed, verbatim in some portions, from "Fame Found in Quiet Nooks," *Success* 1 (September 1898): 5–6.

+72. "Christ Church, Shrewsbury," *New York Times Illustrated Magazine* (27 August 1899): 12–13.

+73. "From New York to Boston by Trolley," *Ainslee's* 4 (August 1899): 74–84. Signed "Herman D. White."

 74. "A Notable Colony," *Demorest's* 35 (August 1899): 240–41. Reconstructed with substantial changes in content from "New York's Art Colony," *Metropolitan* 6 (November 1897): 321–26.

 75. "It Pays to Treat Workers Generously: Joseph H. Patterson," *Success* 2 (16 September 1899): 691–92.

*76. "American Women Violinists," *Success* 2 (30 September 1899): 731–32.

+77. "C. C. Curran," *Truth* 18 (September 1899): 227–31.

*78. "The Camera Club of New York," *Ainslee's* 4 (October 1899): 324–35.

*79. "American Women Who Are Winning Fame as Pianists," *Success* 2 (4 November 1899): 815.

+80. "Curious Shifts of the Poor," *Demorest's* 36 (November 1899): 22–26. Each of the scenes in the article was incorporated into chapter 45, "Curious Shifts of the Poor," and chapter 47, "The Way of the Beaten: A Harp in the Wind," of *Sister Carrie* (New York: Doubleday, Page, 1900). Reprinted in *Sister Carrie,* ed. Donald Pizer (New York: Norton, 1970) 403–12; Donald Pizer, ed., *American Thought and Writing: The 1890's* (Boston: Houghton Mifflin, 1972), 288–97; and *Theodore Dreiser: A Selection of Uncollected Prose,* ed. Donald Pizer (Detroit: Wayne State

University Press, 1977), 131–40. The second scene was republished as "The Men in the Storm" in *The Color of a Great City* (New York: Boni and Liveright, 1923).

81. "Our Government and Our Food," *Demorest's* 36 (December 1899): 68–70.

82. "Atkinson on National Food Reform," *Success* 3 (January 1900): 4. Signed "Edward Al."

*+83. "The Story of a Song-Queen's Triumph: Lillian Nordica," *Success* 3 (January 1900): 6–8. Reprinted as "Nordica: What It Costs to Become a Queen" in *How They Succeeded: Life Stories of Successful Men Told by Themselves,* ed. Orison Swett Marden, (Boston: Lothrop, 1901), 149–70. Reprinted as "A Great Vocalist Shows That Only Years of Labor Can Win the Heights of Song—Lillian Nordica" in *Little visits with Great Americans,* ed. Orison Swett Marden (New York: Success Company, 1903), 541–57.

+84. "The Trade of the Mississippi," *Ainslee's* 4 (January 1900): 735–43.

+85. "Little Clubmen of the Tenements," *Puritan* 7 (February 1900): 665–72.

+86. "The Railroad and the People," *Harper's Monthly* 100 (February 1900): 479–84.

+87. "The Real Howells," *Ainslee's* 5 (March 1900): 137–42. Reprinted in *Americana* 37 (April 1943): 274–82; *American Thought and Writing: The 1890's,* ed. Donald Pizer (Boston: Houghton Mifflin, 1972), 62–68; *American Literary Realism* 6 (Fall 1973): 347–51; and *Theodore Dreiser: A Selection of Uncollected Prose,* ed. Donald Pizer (Detroit: Wayne State University Press, 1977), 141–46.

88. "New York's Underground Railroad," *Pearson's* 9 (April 1900): 375–84.

89. "Good Roads for Bad," *Pearson's* 9 (May 1900): 387–95.

90. "Champ Clark, the Man and His District," *Ainslee's* 5 (June 1900): 425–34.

91. "The Descent of the Horse," *Everybody's* 2 (June 1900): 543–47.

92. "Thomas Brackett Reed: The Story of a Great Career," *Success* 3 (June 1900): 215–16.

+93. "The Transmigration of the Sweat Shop," *Puritan* 8 (July 1900): 498–502.

94. "Apples," *Pearson's* 10 (October 1900): 336–40.

95. "Fruit Growing in America," *Harper's Monthly* 101 (November 1900): 859–68.

*+96. "Whence the Song," *Harper's Weekly* 44 (8 December 1900): 1165–66a. Illustrated by William J. Glackens. Reprinted, with minor stylistic alterations, in Dreiser's *The Color of a Great City* (New York: Boni and Liveright, 1923), 242–59.

97. "Why the Indian Paints His Face," *Pearson's* 11 (January 1901): 19–23.

98. "Delaware's Blue Laws," *Ainslee's* 7 (February 1901): 53–57.

*99. "Lawrence E. Earle," *Truth* 20 (February 1901): 27–30.

100. "Rural Free Mail Delivery," *Pearson's* 11 (February 1901): 233–40.

101. "The Story of the State No. III.—Illinois," *Pearson's* 11 (April 1901): 513–43. Edited by William Penn Nixon.

+102. "Plant Life Underground," *Pearson's* 11 (June 1901): 860–64.

*+103. "The Color of To-Day: William Louis Sonntag, Jr.," *Harper's Weekly* 45 (14 December 1901): 1272–73. Reprinted, with many stylistic revisions, as "W. L. S." in Dreiser's *Twelve Men* (New York: Boni and Liveright, 1919), 344–60.

+104. "A True Patriarch: A Study from Life," *McClure's* 18 (December 1901): 136–44.

105. "The New Knowledge of Weeds," *Ainslee's* 8 (January 1902): 533–38.

+106. "A Cripple Whose Energy Gives Inspiration," *Success* 5 (February 1902): 72–73.

107. "A Touch of Human Brotherhood," *Success* 5 (March 1902): 140–41. Reconstructed, verbatim in some portions, from the story of the Captain in "Curious Shifts of the Poor," *Demorest's* 36 (November 1899): 22–26.

+108. "The Tenement Toilers," *Success* 5 (April 1902): 213–14, 232.

*109. "A Remarkable Art: Alfred Stieglitz," *Great Round World* 19 (3 May 1902): 430–34. Unsigned. Reconstructed from "A Master of Photography," *Success* 2 (10 June 1899): 471.

110. "A Doer of the Word," *Ainslee's* 9 (June 1902): 453–59. Reprinted in Dreiser's *Twelve Men,* 53–75.

+111. "Christmas in the Tenements," *Harper's Weekly* 46 (6 December 1902): 52–53.

Index